FROM GREED TO WELLBEING

Joel Magnuson

"Magnuson presents an ethical critique of conventional economics based in Buddhist principles, offering a hopeful and creative path to system stability, personal satisfaction, and liberating transformation."
Stephanie Kaza, Professor Emerita, University of Vermont, USA

"This is an insightful critique of our dysfunctional economic system, informed by Buddhist principles. Magnuson shows that the reforms usually proposed cannot alleviate the basic problem: a system that is self-destructive because it institutionalizes greed. And he offers a way forward implied by Buddhist teachings."
David Loy, author of The Great Awakening: A Buddhist Social Theory

"Restructuring individual consciousness and restructuring society are complementary activities, and both are desperately needed. This new book from Joel Magnuson shows us how to do this."
Sulak Sivaraksa, author and founder/chair of the International Network of Engaged Buddhists

FROM GREED TO WELLBEING

Joel Magnuson

First published in Great Britain in 2017 by

Policy Press
University of Bristol
1-9 Old Park Hill
Bristol BS2 8BB
UK
t: +44 (0)117 954 5940
e: pp-info@bristol.ac.uk
www.policypress.co.uk

North American office:
Policy Press
c/o The University of Chicago Press
1427 East 60th Street
Chicago, IL 60637, USA
t: +1 773 702 7700
f: +1 773-702-9756
e:sales@press.uchicago.edu
www.press.uchicago.edu

© Policy Press 2017

British Library Cataloguing in Publication Data
A catalogue record for this book is available from the British Library.

Library of Congress Cataloging-in-Publication Data
A catalog record for this book has been requested.

ISBN 978-1-4473-1894-1 paperback
ISBN 978-1-4473-1895-8 ePub
ISBN 978-1-4473-1896-5 Mobi
ISBN 978-1-4473-1898-9 ePdf

Cover design by Soapbox Design, London
Printed and bound in Great Britain by CPI Group (UK) Ltd, Croydon, CR0 4YY
Policy Press uses environmentally responsible print partners

Contents

Introduction

Economic globalization was once a topic of much interest and political debate. Now its existence appears as a foregone conclusion. The global economy is a complete entity comprised of a web of corporate and market institutions that wrap around the planet like an electronic sheet. When this entity roils and shudders or starts to burn, the effects are felt everywhere simultaneously as profound crises, the most pernicious of which are the acute waves of recurring financial system instabilities and the steadily intensifying slow cook of global warming. Both are undoubtedly the most extreme dangers we face as we tread our way through the twenty-first century, and both are indifferent to national boundaries.

For those who look closely, it is not difficult to see how we are allowing these dangers to continue. The conditions for another dramatic banking and financial meltdown remain intact. Carbon is spewing into the atmosphere at high volume as people everywhere burn cheap fossil fuels faster than ever. Yet we seem very reluctant to change what we are doing even though the consequences of economic and climate instability are clear to see. Government efforts aimed at stabilizing the financial system and attenuating climate change remain elusive and symbolic. Populations stay largely complacent, like so many of the mythological boiling frogs, as long as they are not being personally and acutely traumatized. Nothing really changes except that our economic and environmental conditions are becoming more unstable.

But to change course is hard. As a case in point, look at the story of global warming and our perennial inability to address it. Some time ago, a group of scientists prepared a report for the President of the United States titled "Restoring the Quality of

1

Our Environment." The panel explained that as we humans have been powering our economies with fossil fuels, we are releasing massive amounts of carbon that has been locked in sediment for over five hundred million years into the atmosphere. "In a few short centuries," the report says, "we are returning to the air a significant part of the carbon that was slowly extracted by plants and buried in the sediment during half a billion years." The report goes on to say that the consequence would be significant changes in climate and those changes could be, "deleterious from the point of view of human life on the planet."[1] That report was submitted in November, 1965 to American President Lyndon B. Johnson. We were warned about the dangers of global warming over 50 years ago, yet widespread public skepticism and denial about the reality of global warming persists among the consumer populations, and any kind of comprehensive attempt to deal with it seems woefully out of reach.

The kinds of changes we would have to make are hard because it would mean working for something that is at odds with the priorities forged by the most powerful economic institutions in the global economy. Gigantic banks and investment companies are endlessly contriving ways to rush money around the world as they look for opportunities to turn a quick profit, creating rollercoasters of instability. Along with them are central banks that are providing assurances that financial markets will boom forever and that speculation—a kind of legalized gambling— will always have a place in world. Big business carries on with its agenda of maximizing profits by producing more and more stuff, enticing consumers to buy all that stuff, and most of this producing and consuming is still powered by oil, coal, and natural gas. Large banks, hedge funds, corporations, and central banks like the Federal Reserve or the Bank of England are the institutions that dominate this global economy. In fact, they dominate virtually everything including our political processes, the content of our media, and our cultures.

Indeed, to change course would be to swim against a powerful current. It would require that we develop entirely new and different types of economic institutions that are cultivated from a completely different set of values. This makes change even more challenging because it would also require that we take a hard at ourselves, our own lives, and our expectations about what business should prioritize. For most people see big businesses and financial institutions doing what they expect of them—compounding and accumulating financial wealth.

Accumulating financial wealth is something of an obsession in our societies. In a word, such an obsession is greed, or a kind of softcore greed. To say this not to place judgment about what is virtuous or bad economic behavior. Rather, it is an observation of how our economic systems work and why. Greed is a human emotion that we all potentially experience, but it is also a pervasive force in the economy where it has become normalized and even expected. It keeps us obsessively running for more and more like hamsters on a wheel. And all this running, even if it does not lead to anything truly meaningful or authentic, is regarded in our economic society as success. The mad scramble to spend and accumulate is what causes gross domestic product (GDP) to rise, and rising GDP is the supreme priority of the global economy. In this sense, greed is institutionalized as a normative fixture in the rules and social structures that govern our economic life.[2] In other words, greed is seen as a good thing for the economy, and economics is always about making money.

Capitalistic institutions such as the publicly traded corporation were created as vehicles for endless accumulation of wealth. To that end, most corporate enterprises have a single mandate to maximize steady returns to investors' wealth portfolios. This mandate has evolved into a system of contractual obligations in which managers of corporations are locked into a fiduciary responsibility to their shareholders to make sure robust investor profits are realized. Pensioners, fund managers, and the general population have come to expect our economic institutions to live up to this mandate. To do this, businesses must continually find ways to produce and sell more and more quantities of products to the consumer population. Financial growth is the taskmaster that drives growth in GDP. Social and environmental concerns are marginalized in this system, which, for the world's population that is captured by the obsession to accumulate, makes perfect sense.

The historical record shows that human and environmental protections have generally run counter to profit making and businesses have fought tooth and claw against them. Strip mining and clear-cut logging reap more short-term profits than environmentally sustainable methods. Sweatshops exist because they are profitable. Price gouging and manipulative advertising are practices that bring in more profits. Shareholders and others who get returns from all this should rejoice, yet most of us see these practices as unseemly. Occasionally people demand action against them, yet genuine accountability remains ephemeral. Corporate managers or directors are generally not responsible for any social or environmental destructiveness that might result from their business actions as they are merely following the legal covenant they have with their shareholders. The shareholders also cannot be held accountable for they have limited liability status, are not directly involved in the operations of the business, and most of them pay no attention to anything but the returns measured in their portfolios. In such a system, profitability runs without accountability and everyone is off the hook. Institutionalized greed gets a free pass, at least until it causes another massive financial meltdown.

One of the central points I develop in this book is that institutionalized greed underlies much of the financial instability we experience. Economists and government officials have thoroughly examined the causes of the last major crisis that began in 2008 and they concluded that it happened because of things like inadequate government regulations, lack of good financial reporting, or misunderstood risk factors. These conclusions are undeniably well considered and indicate steps that can be taken to help deal with the complexity of these problems. But they sidestep the most important thing of all. Underlying every boom and bust cycle of financial instability in modern history is a dangerous undertow of greed. In its current form, it is global, electronic, and it rushes massive amounts of cash through markets at the speed of light heaving up tsunami waves of misfortune.

Financial crises come and go and people forget about them just as they forget about the last airline crash. As long as enough feel some measure of gain from all of this, they are likely to hold on to the idea that such greed-inspired systems are benign. But if this changes and it becomes clear that the damage from instability outweighs the benefits, a crisis of perception will emerge. In fact, this crisis of perception is already emerging as we see everywhere that events of instability are becoming increasingly violent and staggering in magnitude. As it becomes more severe, economic turbulence highlights the cruel discord between the way our economic systems work and our need for stable livelihoods. We have become trapped in our own systems and their popular mindset; we struggle against traps that are of our own making, our troubles multiply, and we suffer.

Buddhist philosophy and practice can help us find a way out of these traps. The core aspects of all Buddhist traditions are straightforward: to recognize that suffering exists; to identify the root causes of this suffering; and to work toward liberating ourselves from these causes. The Buddha talked about some of these root causes in one of his first lectures about the *three fires*: greed, aggression, and delusion, which he saw as the source of a whole galaxy of human misery. The Buddha's way is simply to see that misery exists, see that misery can be caused by these three fires, and see that to relieve ourselves from misery we must pull ourselves out of the fire.

The three fires are fairly identifiable in our contemporary economic society. As we live and work in this system, we are all expected to pit ourselves against everyone else in a mad grab for market share and profits. Our businesses are compelled to become manipulative, remorseless, and aggressive in their practices. This is to say that institutionalized greed is inseparable from institutionalized aggression. And in the popular imagination all of this is accepted as business as usual, and it is somehow believed that it will lead us toward happiness and wellbeing, even though it tears at our social fabric and fosters a belief that infinite economic growth is somehow possible on a finite planet. This is further to say that institutionalized greed and institutionalized aggression are inseparable from institutionalized delusion. With all of this, markets undulate as wild ocean waves, causing endless cycles of instability, fear, anger, and genuine ruin.

The central theme of this book is to explore how we can work both inwardly work on ourselves and outwardly work on our social institutions to liberate ourselves from the three fires. In the Buddhist way, this would begin with seeing things clearly. It would begin with recognizing that economic trouble and angst exist; that institutionalized greed, aggression, and delusion underlie these troubles; and that the path toward genuine wellbeing is to liberate ourselves from all this with active work toward building new institutions that no longer keep us in a dungeon of pathology. That is, to begin the process of developing a new approach to economics that I call *socially engaged Buddhist economics*.

The chapters that follow provide suggestions for how people can coordinate efforts in direct and practical ways to make economic change. In socially engaged Buddhist economics, the idea is to free our minds, and from this place of clarity set to work on crafting new economic institutions shaped from entirely new and different models of business. The hope is that by taking the initiative to change both our minds and our institutions we can begin the process of evolving our economic system and culture from greed to wellbeing.

The Buddha conveyed to his followers practical ways to help people transform greed into spontaneous joy and wellbeing, hatred into compassion for others, and delusion into wisdom. At the core of his teachings is the transformative experience of Buddhist mindfulness. As we will see, with the inner work of mindfulness, people can unshackle themselves from greed, aggression, and delusion, and become empowered to do the outer work of social change. There are already many people from socially engaged Buddhist movements who are creating new models ranging from local bakeries to new global development paradigms at the United Nations with the hope of making change for the better in local communities and internationally.

We will further see that there is a body of ideas that is being created by Buddhists and non-Buddhists that are important in this movement—scholars, economists, philosophers, and activists—who are helping us gain a deeper understanding of our problems and providing guidelines for developing new ways of thinking and acting in the economic world. This exploration includes a sampling of the ideas of legendary economist E.F. Schumacher as well as other less well known economists who sought to build a values based economic framework which placed human wellbeing over the priorities of business as usual. Not least of which were the intrepid economists from Columbia University—the founders of gross domestic product—who sought to develop a measurement of national economic wellbeing for a broad spectrum of the population (national income) only to have their work eventually swallowed up by corporate interests as a yardstick of capitalist growth (GDP). Similarly, the government of Bhutan developed its own and profoundly original metric, gross national happiness (GNH), and sought to share this with the rest of the world at the United Nations. Though it seems the world is not yet ready to embrace something like GNH unless it can be made into a commodity to be sold at a profit.

As part of this story, we will also see how large and powerful institutions, mostly based in the US, pushed a neoliberal agenda of international finance into the global economy as a stunt in post-Cold War politics. The agenda was to create an environment such that speculative money could dash seamlessly from one country to another following the magnet of greed. Key figures in this agenda are the Federal Reserve System and other central banking authorities that contrived a model of economic policy based on the notion that greed is what keeps everything from collapsing and keeps us all running madly on the hamster wheel. The presumption was that greed-inspired financial market bubbles—such as soaring real estate markets or stock markets—create an illusion of wellbeing in the popular imagination. The illusion keeps people spending, and as long as enough people are in their spending mode, GDP ramps up and there will be cheers all around. In other words, our central banks have built a new global economy on a foundation of hot air and greed. This works as along as the bubbles are inflating, but it quickly turns to catastrophe when they burst, and bubbles always burst. We have already seen how dangerous this is with the last global crisis and the damage wrought from it which is still being calculated.

Another crucial message here is that we are institutional beings as much as we are flesh and blood. We need to change our institutions as much as we need to change our habits of mind and personal behavior. The things that defile us personally also plague our social institutions, which in turn defile us even more, in a vicious circle. In socially engaged Buddhist economics, there is no distinction between the personal and the social. We suffer individually and on vast social scales. A way toward wellbeing, therefore, is mindful change of ourselves and our social surroundings. When we say mindfulness in this context we mean something very specific.

Mindfulness meditation has always been an integral part of a Buddhist practice. It is by no means a quick fix, but is a rigorously cultivated skill, and like any other skill, it requires care and patience.

It was discovered that mindfulness meditation is also an effective way to deal with stress and can help people cope with the problems at work and in life that seem overwhelming. Corporations are finding that with this meditation practice, people are more productive, spend less time away from work, and the end result is improved bottom-line profits. But once again, business as usual rears its head. The danger in this process of coopting is that mindfulness, part of a 2,500-year-old spiritual tradition, loses its most important aspect—transformation. Transformation does not mean getting better or more efficient, it means becoming something else. The original power of mindfulness is being diluted as true mindfulness becomes untethered from it Buddhist roots and becomes a pop culture commodity, or what Buddhist critics call McMindfulness. The socially engaged Buddhist economics movement is not merely about alleviating stress at the workplace, it is about fundamentally transforming the conditions of economic life everywhere, which means changing ourselves and our institutions.

Once again, this is hard work. When we talk about changing our institutions, we are talking about changing deeply rooted social structures. But to say that this is hard is not to say that it is impossible. People can and do create institutional changes that have deep and lasting impact on their economic lives. In June 2016, for example, voters in the UK decided in a referendum to untie their commonwealth from the European Union (EU), which, measured in GDP, is the largest economy in the world. The vote, commonly referred to as "Brexit," a linguistic blend of "Britain" and "exit," determined that the UK will no longer be institutionally tied to the other 27 members of the EU.

It is unclear whether the voters completely understood the implications of the vote and it will be years before they are known, but what is important is that it proves that people can and do mobilize for institutional change in their economies and on a large scale.

In this book, we will demonstrate that the socially engaged Buddhist movement encourages citizens everywhere to work toward such institutional change in a way that is skillful and based on mindfulness and wisdom. It exhorts people to free themselves from the tyranny of institutionalized greed, aggression and delusion and to work proactively for things like developing right livelihood banks (RLBs) that are chartered to promote community development and wellbeing, or to push reforms of the charters of their central banks to make them socially responsible and democratically accountable.

In the socially engaged Buddhist economics movement, we embrace the fact that all things are changing and acknowledge that impermanence is the fate of every entity in the world, including the global corporate system that stands astride the planet like a leviathan. We celebrate the flux of change because we can make into a healing force that will allow us to evolve into what we were meant to be—spontaneous, joyful, creative beings.

ONE

Buddhist economics and the three fires

Shortly after the 2008 banking crisis exploded across the planet, former Goldman Sachs executive Greg Smith publicly announced his resignation in a *New York Times* editorial. Smith had worked for Goldman Sachs in New York for about a decade before transferring to its operations in London, where he managed equity derivatives, and then soon after resigned in protest. The reason he gave for his departure was that he felt the elite investment bank had become "toxic and destructive" and increasingly focused on its own profits at the expense of its clients. According to Smith, greed rather than client trust was Goldman Sachs' primary operating principle. In a blog response to Smith's letter, American economist and former labor secretary Robert Reich posted, "The problem isn't excessive greed. If you took the greed out of Wall Street all you'd have left is pavement." Reich was making light, of course, but he went on to argue that the problem with banking establishments in New York and London is rampant abuse of power and trust, and his solution for better and more responsible banking would be better government regulation.[1]

It is not surprising that a former government official would advocate for better regulation, but it is remarkable that he should claim that excessive greed is not a problem. His assertion is even more notable when weighed against the recent greed-inspired banking calamity that had spread economic ruin like a pandemic. The global crisis was indeed toxic and destructive, and was unprecedented in scale. Looking at Reich's assertion through a different prism, however, we can make a very different story. The problem is not a lack of government regulation; the problem is greed. If you took the greed out of Wall Street and Lombard Street and everywhere else, this would be a fabulous and liberating step forward in human evolution, and in doing so you would eliminate the need for so much government regulation in the first place.

Reich was not the first economist to see greed as a benign condition. Standard economics considers greed—an obsession with accumulating more and more as if there could never be enough—as the primary source of human industriousness and economic development. This view holds that craving and self interest are necessary because they are the only really motivating forces that lead to economic action.

To be fair, there is some truth in this view. It is not difficult to see how motivation is unleashed by financial incentives. As the records show, throughout the history of capitalism, entrepreneurs and industrialists, driven by an aggressive passion for money, have set out to build their corporate empires. Empire building, whether in steamships, railroads, or consumer electronics, is a basis for economic development, investment, and growth. It is undeniable that the promise of individual financial gain can be a powerful motivator—and it can equally be a demotivator when that promise is taken away. Therefore, one could draw a superficial conclusion that greed and self interest are unavoidable yet necessary aspects of human nature, without which economies could not develop and societies would remain materially backward and stunted.

But an important part of this story is being ignored here. Greed and self interest are aspects of human nature, but they exist alongside a multitude of other aspects, including compassion, creativity, and cooperation. The human potential for greed-inspired behavior is like a seed, lying among many other seeds in a garden bed. Depending on social context and institutional priorities, some receive the water and nutrients they need to thrive, while others remain dormant. It is not a coincidence that the "greed is good" belief is largely accepted in societies that are dominated by corporate capitalism. The rise of capitalistic institutions and the shrugged-shoulder acceptance of greed are one—an economic force cloaked in ideological apparel. This is particularly true in the West, where in the last two centuries capitalist ideology has become so deeply woven into the cultural fabric that it is nearly invisible—invisible that is, to those without mindful awareness.

Capitalistic institutions such as publicly traded corporations, organized securities exchanges, and the market system all rose to prominence in the eighteenth and nineteenth centuries. Nearly a hundred years ago, economic historian and critic Richard Tawney observed the coming corporate domination of attitudes in Western society and the ascent of greed. Tawney writes: "the quality in modern societies ... consists in the assumption, accepted by most reformers with hardly less naïveté than by the defenders of the established order, that the attainment of material riches is the supreme object of human endeavor."[2] All notions of progress came to be measured purely in terms of monetary gain, and virtually everything under the sun became commodified and financialized. With its emphasis on aggregating financial capital, buying and selling, taking profits wherever they can be found, the corporation rose to prominence with a singularity of purpose: to ceaselessly maximize and compound shareholder returns. Financial wealth accumulation became an economic priority, and along with this came an addiction to economic growth and consumerism. Zen teacher and scholar David Loy has often pointed out that greed is not just a human emotion; it is an institutionalized force within the capitalist world: "our economic system institutionalizes greed in at least two ways: corporations are never profitable enough and people never consume enough."[3]

In this sense, corporations are not just businesses; they are structures of power built on a foundation of greed. On this, Canadian attorney and author Joel Bakan writes, "Over the last 150 years, the corporation has risen from relative obscurity to become the world's dominant economic institution. Today, corporations govern our lives. They determine what we eat, what we watch, what we wear, where we work, and what we do."[4] As corporations control markets, banks, employment, and the media, people everywhere are inundated with corporate culture.

Bakan further notes that, "like the church and the monarchy in other times, they posture as infallible and omnipotent, glorifying themselves in imposing buildings and elaborate displays. Increasingly, corporations dictate the decisions of their supposed overseers in government and control domains of society once [they are] firmly embedded within the public sphere."[5] By virtue of sheer economic power, the corporate agenda has become society's agenda, and the imperative to generate investor returns has become translated into national priorities for market expansion and growth. The endless accumulation of financial wealth, endless economic growth, and the idolatry of money have all become societal norms, unassailable, and virtually all other questions of purpose have been drowned out and forgotten.[6] Bakan concludes, "We are inescapably surrounded by their culture, iconography, and ideology."[7] Accordingly, economics poses as a hard objective science, while formulating ways to convince us that greed is not a problem.

"Greed is good" economics

The economics profession spins elaborate theories about how greed is a kind of vice that renders benefits for societies overall. Among the first to argue this was the eighteenth-century Anglo-Dutch philosopher Bernard Mandeville. Mandeville published a famous poem on political economy, titled *The Fable of the Bees*, and writes,

> Thus vice nurs'd Ingenuity,
>   Which joined with Time and Industry,
>   Had carry'd Life's Conveniences,
>   Its real Pleasures, Comforts, Ease,
>   To such a Height, the very Poor
>   Liv'd better than the Rich before,
>   And nothing could be added more.[8]

Adam Smith, writing in the latter half of the eighteenth century, argued that there are multiple ways that humans can find economic motivation, including benevolence. But it was his passage on "self-love" that resonated with the entrepreneurial classes: "It is not from the benevolence of the butcher, the brewer, or the baker, that we expect our dinner, but from their regard to their own interest." Expecting people to be motivated by anything but their self interest, according to Smith, will ultimately be in vain: "We address ourselves, not to their humanity but of their self-love, and never to them of our own necessities but of their advantages."[9]

This idea was further developed by nineteenth-century utilitarian economics,[10] in which consumers' choice-making behavior is based on utility theory—a pleasure/pain principle in which people rationally calculate what things to buy so as to maximize the pleasure of consumption and minimize the pain of sacrifice. Similarly, businesses strive for more profit because ever more profit translates into ever more pleasure.[11] This view of economics, which can be found in virtually any modern textbook, holds it to be self-evident that having more goods and more money is always better than having less. Greed is a good thing as long as it keeps everyone running, like rodents on a hamster wheel, in a continuous chase after stuff, riches, and financial gain. More is always better. Always.

Twentieth-century author and intellectual Ayn Rand celebrated these so-called virtues of greed and selfishness. Although Rand is not considered a major contributor to economic theory, her ideas were nonetheless influential. Her belief system, which she called "objectivism," is centered on an assertion that societies do not actually exist, only individual people and their desires. Therefore, any attempt to pursue values or ethical codes that place the social good above that of the individual is mere whimsy.[12] Former British Prime Minister Margaret Thatcher echoed Rand in a 1987 interview in which she declared, "There is no such thing as society. There is a living tapestry of men and women and people and the beauty of that tapestry and the quality of our lives will depend upon how much each of us is prepared to take responsibility for ourselves."[13] For Rand, there is only one code of human conduct: the hedonistic and individualistic pursuit of pleasure and avoidance of pain. Grasping, selfish, egoistic behavior, for Rand, is a natural inclination for our species and therefore is correct behavior as long as it results in physical sensations of pleasure. Rand's objectivism helped to shape the thinking of legendary US Federal Reserve chairman Alan Greenspan, who, along with Thatcher, former American president Ronald Reagan, and others, forged the way toward a massive economic deregulation movement based on economic individualism and free market ideology. In this movement, naked self interest was unleashed like never before—most notably in the banking industry.

Even the eloquent liberal economist John Maynard Keynes was captured by the alluring notion that greed is a good thing. Keynes writes, "The love of money as a possession ... will be recognised for what it is, a somewhat disgusting morbidity, one of those semi-criminal, semi-pathological propensities which one hands over with a shudder to the specialists in mental disease." Although Keynes sounds moralizing, he nonetheless held on to the idea that societies need to embrace greed for another century in order to be set free from economic depressions and insecurity. "For at least another hundred years," he writes, "we must pretend to ourselves and to everyone that fair is foul and foul is fair; for foul is useful and fair is not. Avarice and usury and precaution must be our gods for a little longer still. For only they can lead us out of the tunnel of economic necessity into daylight."[14] Thus it should not come as a surprise that, elevated to god-like status, greed and self interest have become idealized in Western culture and mindsets. Reflecting on this, economic historian Dirk Philipsen writes, "If greed is culturally dominant, and ... it leads people to what our culture considers success, we are likely to emulate it as a model for ourselves."[15] When something becomes culturally dominant in this way, it typically escapes critical examination and it becomes easy for all of us to fall under its control.

In cultures captured by greed, running pointlessly on the hamster wheel of economics is considered to be a behavioral norm, not an exception. It is as if everyone has an internal voice in their head that keeps repeating, "more, not enough, faster, newer, better, more." The chase is never ending, and leaves us with a deepening sense of dissatisfaction which eventually becomes a barrier between us and genuine wellbeing. As Zen Buddhist and author Thich Nhat Hanh reminds us, "you probably have a notion that there's some as yet unrealized condition that has to be attained before you can be happy … a promotion or income level. But that notion may be the very thing that prevents you from being happy." For Nhat Hanh, the first step to be taken toward wellbeing is fostering mindful awareness: "To release that notion and make space for true happiness to manifest, you first have to experience the truth that entertaining your current ideas is making you suffer."[16] This kind of suffering, which arises from being trapped by habits of thought and behavior, is depicted in Buddhist literature as the Realm of Hungry Ghosts.

The Realm of Hungry Ghosts

In some interpretations of the myth, the Realm of Hungry Ghosts is a place where people languish in a kind of hellish world of discontent. Each person is trapped in a body with an enormous stomach, a very narrow throat, and an unquenchable thirst. As people try to drink, the liquid instantly turns to fire and their thirst intensifies. Hungry ghosts are also overwhelmed with appetite, but the narrowness of their throats prevents them from swallowing food, leaving them to suffer from escalating cravings that will never be satisfied. People everywhere seem to be captured by compulsions to chase after what seems to be an illusory good life, only to experience fleeting moments of joy that are soon overshadowed by the heavy feeling that things are never good enough. Physician and author Gabor Maté calls this the domain of addiction, "where we constantly seek something outside ourselves to curb an insatiable yearning for relief or fulfillment." Maté sees contemporary Western culture as awash with addictions: to chemicals, phones, computers, sex, and, not the least of them, to work, shopping, and gambling.[17]

Greed, aggression, and delusion

As we will see in the chapters that follow, work, shopping, and gambling addictions are part of the regular economic scene.

And, like any other addiction, if left unchanged, they will always have ill-fated results. But it is important to keep in mind, so as to not pass judgment, that these are cultural and institutional problems, just as much as personal experience. Maté asserts that those who are suffering from addictions "have much in common with the society that ostracizes them," and he poses the important question: "how do we approach the healing of the many behavior addictions fostered by our culture?"[18]

To put it in another, more specific way, greed, craving, and addictions are fostered by the powerful corporate institutions that dominate our society. Saddled with the imperative to sell more and more so as to generate more and more profits, corporate institutions cannot survive in a culture that is free from people's addictive and compulsive behavior. This is precisely why they spend hundreds of billions in media advertising. Corporate media is an enormously powerful institution. It instills vain and capricious values into large numbers of people who perhaps otherwise would not have a propensity for self-indulgence. It compels people to consume less intelligently and to gravitate toward flashy and ostentatious products rather than to things that are wholesome, genuinely beneficial, or reliable. Corporate advertising exploits prejudices and yearnings for no other reason than to sell and expand market share, and has little or no ethical consideration or concern for public wellbeing. Ads imbue the public with unrealistic ideals of what is considered a standard of living, or the so-called "American dream," and condition all who come under their spell that the perfect consumer is a person who is indifferent to the environmental damage consumerism does and has no higher purpose in life than to consume ever-growing quantities of stuff. Although so many of us feel overwhelmed by all this consumerism, we still prefer not to think of ourselves as being slavishly pushed around and controlled by corporations. Yet most of us do not know what genuine liberation feels like. So we keep running on the hamster wheel.

A general state of endless craving and dissatisfaction inevitably spills over into other destructive conditions of aggression and delusion. The image of spinning hamster wheels starts to look like a full-blown rat race in an economic system that is comprised of self-seeking individuals pitting themselves against every other individual in a competitive struggle over scarce resources. Greed comes to be expressed as aggression. Capitalism is ultimately a system that rewards greed and acquisitiveness, and that legitimizes the harshness and violence associated with gross disparities in wealth and income distribution with mantras such as "look out for number one" or "devil gets the hindmost." Economic aggression manifests as the ruthlessness that comes from striving to "make a killing," and a lack of compassion or concern for the wellbeing of others. And when we add to this the fact that the endless growth of wealth on a finite planet defies even the most basic concept of sustainability, greed and aggression give way to delusion.

Delusion is a state of ignorance and witless attachment to mental fiction. In an economic sense, it encompasses a general belief that more is always better, and that economic growth will continue for all time, despite the physical reality that it cannot. Greed, aggression, and delusion are thus human conditions that have been part of our social structures and consciousness for a very long time, and nowhere is this more evident than in our financial institutions. Financial institutions were originally created for the purposes of fostering economic development, but now have largely abandoned that function and become massive gambling casinos that create recurring avalanches of instability.

The social institutions and technologies that comprise the business world, according to Buddhist economist Sulak Sivaraksa, "pressure us to adopt desired dogma, establishing what is then regarded as normative." They create the boundaries of what is considered acceptable and what is not, what is thinkable and unthinkable. "These boundaries define 'the truth'."[19] As we strive to liberate ourselves from greed, aggression, and delusion, it is imperative that we see the two facets to our circumstances. One is our personal conditioning and experiences, along with our struggle to overcome them. The other facet is that greed, aggression, and delusion are institutionalized as priorities in our corporate dominated society.

Buddhist philosophy and practice can help us here. To be clear, this is not about puffing up with religious self-righteousness, or finger pointing aimed at stigmatizing the afflicted, or climbing to some moral high ground. Rather, it is a way of seeing clearly and deeply into what is happening to ourselves and our society, and from this clarity to chart a path toward change. According to legend, one of the first things the Buddha spoke about, some 2,600 years ago, was how greed, aggression, and delusion lie just beneath the surface of a whole spectrum of human suffering. The Buddha said, "All is burning ... burning with the fire of greed, with the fire of hate [aggression], with the fire of delusion."[20] In this spirit, the inner work of personal transformation and the outer work of social change constitute the way of socially engaged Buddhist economics.

As with any Buddhist practice, socially engaged Buddhist economics is a long journey toward change. It seeks to transform the personal and institutional affliction of greed into spontaneous joy and societal wellbeing; hatred into compassion for others; and delusion into wisdom. We will see that many of the Buddha's original talks contain practical insights into daily life, illuminated by a broader vision of how these activities of daily economic life impact everyone and everything around us. These insights establish the foundation for engaged social change, as well as a framework for a system of living ethics. We will explore a convergence of ideas, in particular, ideas that challenge conventional assumptions about what economic wellbeing is. The hope is to create a better understanding of how our economic systems are becoming increasingly problematic and unstable, how the instabilities are growing in magnitude, and how this is impacting our lives. To this end, the first leg of our journey will be to follow along the path set down by E.F. Schumacher, who introduced the idea that a Buddhist approach to economics could be enormously beneficial for Western cultures.

E.F. Schumacher

E.F. Schumacher was one of the most prominent intellectuals of the post-Great Depression era. As Chief Economic Advisor to Britain's National Coal Board between 1950 and 1970, he had an inside view of the troubling prospects of ongoing economic growth powered by a limited resource base. He anticipated that economic expansion would eventually ebb as a result of energy scarcities and high prices. Schumacher openly challenged the typical economist's infatuation with technology and their notion that technology will solve every problem of scarcity. In doing so, he became something of an economic heretic.[21]

Schumacher was also a protégé of John M. Keynes, whose ideas glow with orthodox economics. But, unlike Keynes, he made no pretense about the virtues of greed. Schumacher assailed Keynes' contention that "foul is fair," and argued that if people accept this notion, economic society will be fashioned into a culture of plunder based on "greed and envy, which destroy intelligence, happiness, serenity, and thereby the peacefulness of man." Foul cannot be fair, as it leads to a general collapse of intelligence and a loss of wisdom, people become blinded by their own rapacity, and it eventually strips bare all that has meaning. Schumacher lamented that greed is nonetheless deftly rationalized by economists with the simple stroke of pen—vice leads to virtue. He writes, "If whole societies become infected by these vices, they may indeed achieve astonishing things, but they become increasingly incapable of solving the most elementary problems of everyday existence"—the problems being frustration, alienation, and chronic dissatisfaction. People in these societies become hungry ghosts.[22]

Schumacher was not alone in challenging the assumptions of conventional economics. The Nobel prize-winning economist William Vickrey confessed that his own research was of "minor significance in terms of human welfare."[23] According to notable scholar and critic E.K. Hunt, "From the 1870s until today, many economists have abandoned any real concerns with existing economic institutions and problems. Instead, many of them have retired to the rarefied stratosphere of mathematical model building, constructing endless variations on esoteric trivia."[24] In his well known classic, *When Corporations Rule the World*, David Korten claims that standard economic theory functions as "an ideological shield against intelligent introspection and civic responsibility."[25] When it is closely examined, it becomes clear that conventional economics struggles to make useful contributions to real-world understanding, which was never really the point. The point, rather, has always been to legitimize greed and self interest and provide banal, unreflective justifications for the economics of plunder. But Schumacher saw a much deeper problem: the miserable state of conventional economics is a symptom of a spiritual crisis stemming from the defilement of society's shared beliefs and innermost convictions—a defilement of what he calls the "eye of the heart."[26]

Schumacher's eye of the heart is that which informs the mind and liberates the soul. It is the true wisdom that can be found in all the great spiritual traditions of Christianity, Judaism, Islam, and Buddhism. In true spiritual practice, wisdom, love, compassion, reverence for beauty and nature are elevated above the world of scientific facts. For Schumacher these spiritually informed qualities are what allow us to live peacefully with each other and within our natural environment. Schumacher was concerned that such qualities have been purged from serious inquiry and dismissed as authoritarian megalomania or preachy dogma. The eye of the heart has been replaced with what he calls "materialistic scientism," in which spiritual traditions have been largely destroyed in the West by a mechanistic worldview. That is, we have been reduced to mere moving parts.[27]

Economics, in particular, is filled with mechanical representations of human behavior. People are seen as nothing more than billiard balls in motion, mindlessly rolling in one direction or another. For Schumacher, such a hollow view blinds the eye of the heart and ignores the most profound qualities of human life. We remain adrift without insight and are increasingly incapable of knowing our true natures. In this condition, it becomes easier to accept a cynical view of ourselves as empty beasts spinning mindlessly on the hamster wheel, and nothing more should be expected from us except naked self interest, which further rationalizes predatory competition and aggression in the marketplace. We erase our capacity for spiritually informed wisdom to the extent that nothing really matters; we become indifferent. And when nothing matters, we develop vicious attitudes toward our natural habitat, which becomes a mere quarry for exploitation, and as such becomes a transgression against the wellbeing of future generations. Schumacher concludes: "The idea that a civilisation could sustain itself on the basis of such a transgression is an ethical, spiritual, and metaphysical monstrosity. It means conducting economic affairs of man as if people really did not matter at all."[28] By regarding ourselves in a paradigm that consists of moving, mechanical parts, we are mirroring ourselves as inanimate. We ignore the spiritual and intuitive aspects of our natures, which for Schumacher are not tangential but, rather, are what constitute the most significant and elevating aspects of our species. In the bulk of his writing, Schumacher reached far beyond criticism of conventional economics and explored what the discipline might look like if we disregarded the egoistic and materialistic interpretation of economic life and, in its place, restored the eye of the heart.

To that end, Schumacher began exploring Buddhism while living in Burma as an economic advisor and spending time with Buddhist monks. Of course, one does not need to become a Buddhist in order to restore a spiritual core, and Schumacher noted that "the teachings of Christianity, Islam, or Judaism could have been used just as well as those of any other of the great Eastern traditions."[29] But he was inspired by the way Burmese Buddhists saw economics and technology and how their views stood in such contrast to standard economics. He wrote a short essay titled "Buddhist Economics," which was published in 1973 as part of his enormously influential book, *Small Is Beautiful*. In this essay, Schumacher emphasizes that, "'Right Livelihood' is one of the requirements of the Buddha's Noble Eightfold Path. It is clear, therefore, that there must be such a thing as Buddhist economics."[30] By no means did Schumacher's essay convey a comprehensive picture of Buddhist economics. It simply explored a sampling of the differences between the Buddhist's view and the views of Western economics. More importantly, it opened the door for the development of a new and lively subdiscipline of economics based on interpretations of the dharma—the teachings of the Buddha and the notion of spiritual liberation.[31]

As there are many different interpretations of the teachings of the Buddha, the implications for economics are as broad as the ocean. Much of what we understand about the original teachings of the Buddha is the stuff of legends passed down over two and half millennia in literature, including the Pali Canon and a multitude of sutras. It would be beyond the scope of this project to summarize the entire body of this work, and for our purposes here, which is an exploration of economics and not religion, we will focus on the very basic and central ideas of Buddhism. As Buddhist philosophy and practice deals particularly with the suffering that arises from the three fires of greed, aggression, and delusion, it can help us find a way clear of the flames and toward peace. Buddhist teachings can provide insight into our motivations, sharpen our abilities to see into them deeply, and, perhaps most importantly, change them. Through a gradual process of dissolving the confusion between what is harmful economic activity and what is truly beneficial, our insights can eventually lead to a profound sense of liberation and self-awareness. Such insights provide a foundation both for a living model of ethics and for social change. We will begin by looking briefly at how the Buddha—a man and not a god or messenger from a god—came to see the world in a profoundly liberating way.

Siddartha's journey

According to the legend, about two and half millennia ago a man named Siddhartha Gautama set out on a remarkable journey of discovery and became a Buddha. *Buddha* is a Sanskrit word meaning "awakened one." Siddhartha was not trying to find some solution to the endless conflagration between good and evil, or immortality, or some otherworldly experience that would establish him as an immortal among flesh-and-blood human beings. He sought meaning and truth in the deepest possible sense, as he was motivated by compassion for the multitudes who seemed to be caught in an endless vortex of human suffering. He experienced a profound awakening in a flash of insight into the true nature of things, including the causes of and liberation from suffering. His was a deep, existential experience after a long and painful quest for an end to human misery. His experience was so powerful and transformative that it compelled him to spend the rest of his life teaching others about its implications. His teaching became the foundation of Buddhism.[32]

Siddhartha was the son chosen to succeed his father as head of the Shakya dynasty, which was sovereign over a vast territory in a border region between India and Nepal. By the time Siddhartha had reached adulthood, he had everything that a young man could possibly desire: considerable wealth, social status, dynastic privilege, and his own family. He was nonetheless discontent. Siddhartha felt intuitively that although wealth brings certain comforts, the wealthy and poor were alike in that none is immune from what appears to be a universal human condition of suffering. He ventured restlessly outside the gilded confines of his home to nearby villages and witnessed what must have seemed a mass of human population sinking into a sea of disease, famine, humiliation, and poverty. Yet, within his own home he witnessed the wealthy and powerful suffering from worries, uncertainty, jealousy, and fear. Siddhartha became convinced that there had to be some deeper truths that would provide solutions to all this suffering and became determined to discover them, but he knew that he could not do so while basking in privilege. Siddhartha pondered,

> The thought came to me. The household life, this place of impurity, is narrow ... It is not easy for a householder to lead the perfected, utterly pure and perfect holy life. What if I were now to cut off my hair and beards, don yellow robes, and go forth from the household into homelessness?[33]

He steeled himself with determination and did just that. He left the comforts of his family and wealth and set out on an arduous quest to find these deeper truths and to discover the way to transform suffering into wellbeing.[34] He renounced his wealth and position in Indian society and became a mendicant wanderer. He survived largely by begging, and drifted from one place to another seeking instruction from various masters on yoga, meditation techniques, asceticism, and every form of spiritual practice that he could find in ancient India. But Siddhartha remained frustrated, as none of the practices provided him with the kind of deep insights he was intuitively seeking. However, these practices did help him to achieve states of consciousness that helped him to endure great hardship, particularly during a phase in which he committed to self-mortification.

Siddhartha joined a group of ascetics who took him under their wing. These ascetics were committed to a spiritual practice that is based primarily on self-denial and extended periods of fasting. They believed that this practice would purify the spirit from the corruption of sensual pleasures. For some time, perhaps years, Siddhartha routinely subjected himself to starvation and dehydration, hoping that such physical stress would bring him closer to some kind of pure realization of a certain truth lying beneath the surface of consciousness. He eventually came to realize that asceticism was literally self-defeating, as it brought him to the very precipice of death, as he told his followers:

> Because I ate so little, my buttocks became like a camel's hoof, my backbone protruded like a line of spindles, my ribs corroded and collapsed like the rafters of an old and rotten shed, the gleams of the pupils in my eye sockets appeared deeply sunken, my scalp became wrinkled and shrunken ... Though I have undergone severe ascetic practice, I cannot reach the special and wonderful knowledge and insight transcending the affairs of human beings. Could there be another way of enlightenment?[35]

Siddhartha avowed that such practice leads only to the deterioration of one's health, loneliness, and emaciation, which can only make steeper the path away from suffering. He left the ascetic community and, after a time of regaining his strength, set out once again to wander alone. He eventually settled in Bodhgaya, still in the northeastern part of India. It was at Bodhgaya that he experienced a turning point. He realized that he was not going to find what he was seeking outwardly in the world and redirected his journey inwardly, to the inherent potential of the mind.

This turning point is exemplified in a familiar Buddhist story called *The Door*. The story is about a man with a recurring and troubling dream in which he is trapped inside a room with no windows or light and from which the only exit is a door. He finds the door and pushes on it repeatedly, trying to escape. In desperation he slams his body against the door with all his strength, trying to force it open, but it doesn't budge. He eventually tells a friend about his dream and, after listening, the friend tells him that when his dream returns he should try imagining pulling the door inward, rather than pushing. The next time the dream comes to him, the man does as his friend has instructed, the door opens with ease and he is set free.[36] Siddhartha's experience was like pushing relentlessly on that door until he realized that he could not find what he was seeking outside himself. He resolved instead to search within. Siddhartha sat in deep inward meditation under a pipal tree (a kind of large fig with heavy branches that spread out to provide shade like an elm), resolved to remain in meditation until he experienced true wisdom or enlightenment, a state that he knew he was coming close to.[37]

As Siddartha meditated, he was reminded of a pleasant childhood memory of sitting in the shade of a large tree in one of his father's fields. He had let his mind wander freely, without attachments, until it had become quite still, and for a moment he had experienced a kind of perfect serenity and equanimity. He remained for some time, completely unattached to his thoughts or feelings, with the pure calm that he had once known in his childhood, and finally a breakthrough came in a deep and sudden flash. In that moment Siddhartha realized that the truth he had been searching for all this time was something that he had known all along, but it had become clouded over by a deluded state of mind. This was his enlightenment, his nirvana, and he was momentously liberated from what had seemed until then to be an inescapable state of suffering and despair.[38]

His discovery was simple but profound: the end of human suffering is to liberate ourselves from the defilements of our minds. From that point forward, Siddhartha was known as Shakyamuni Buddha, meaning "the enlightened one from the Shakya dynasty," or simply the Buddha. The Buddha devoted the rest of his life to teaching—like Socrates—by way of oral tradition the things he had learned and understood about the way of enlightenment—the dharma. The Buddha summarizes,

Dear friends ... I tell you that if I have not experienced directly all that I have told you, I would not proclaim that I am an enlightened person, free from suffering. Because I myself have identified suffering, understood suffering, identified the causes of suffering, removed the causes of suffering, confirmed the existence of well-being, obtained well-being, identified the path to well-being, gone to the end of the path, and realized total liberation, I now proclaim to you that I am a free person.[39]

With this proclamation of freedom, the wheels of the dharma began to turn. What the Buddha taught was not conventional religious doctrine as understood in the West, nor was it a metaphysical discourse on divinity, heaven and hell, or the wrath of deities. His teachings were reflections on the mind—a kind of spiritual psychology for living a liberated life. The Buddha also taught that every person has an inherent ability to be liberated from their own mind, but this cannot be taught, it has to be experienced. The Buddha's awakening was his own, and he taught his followers that their awakening, too, must be their own. In this view, each of us has the capacity to eliminate their own suffering caused by the dark clouds of confusion over what is beneficial and what is harmful. Much of what constitutes the substance of these dark clouds is deep psychic attachments and the three fires of greed, aggression, and delusion.

The middle way

Some of the very first lectures given by the Buddha were based on practical matters of living. Among these was his talk on a mode of living as a middle way between the deprivation he had experienced as an ascetic and the feverish clamor for wealth that he had known as the spoiled progeny of the powerful Shakya clan. He had experienced both and rejected both. The Buddha taught that "There are these two extremes ... giving oneself up to indulgence in sensual pleasures; this is base, common, vulgar, unholy, unprofitable ... [or] giving oneself up to self-torment; this is painful, unholy (and also) unprofitable."[40]

To be clear, unholy and unprofitable in this sense implies suffering. Poverty, disease, wretchedness, and humiliation obviously make it hard to be free from suffering. During his time of asceticism and self-emaciation the Buddha learned that the suffering caused by such deprivation should not be underestimated. For him, the experience was profound, and his body of thinking could not have developed without it. It brought him near to death, and so it was not difficult for him to draw the conclusion that real poverty is a tremendous source of suffering. But he also noted that suffering is not brought to an end by chasing after great wealth; the chasing itself only leads to suffering of a different kind.[41]

The Buddha saw that the suffering caused by grinding poverty is palpable, and no less real than the suffering of those in the opulent classes. In his young life he was well fed, adorned with fine clothing, sheltered from the harshness of the world, and protected from the harshness of the sun by parasols held for him by servants. As he matured, he became increasingly disaffected with this sheltered life and the splendor of extreme affluence, and sensed it to be false kind of existence. He observed that neither lifestyle—the walking skeleton nor the bloated hungry ghost—could lead to wellbeing and concluded that there had to be another way.

The Buddha's notion of the middle way is not a compromise between the extremes of delusion and pain, for a positive cannot be found between two negatives. Rather, it is a departure from two opposing pathways that lead to the same result of suffering. The Buddha taught that to be liberated is to subject neither ourselves nor those in our community to damaging poverty, nor should we become blindly enslaved by dreams of power, possessions, and money—addictions from which no amount of material wealth can provide freedom.

Perhaps the first challenge for socially engaged Buddhist economics is to foster a creative vision and awareness of what middle way economics could be. The so-called material good life in the West is much coveted, and our covetousness is so common as to be a behavioral standard or norm. Possession by materialistic desires and cravings, and forming attachments to money and materialistic lifestyles are not only normal, they are structured into the governance of the powerful institutions that control our lives. On the other hand, being unemployed, homeless, sick, and hungry is obviously miserable. The overall aim of socially engaged Buddhist economics is liberation from both—to be free from the compulsions or obsessions that are consuming us and our planet like a raging wildfire, and to be free from grinding poverty. As we will see, such liberation comes through the skillful means by which we work for institutional change and economic transformation. Buddhist philosophy and practice is uniquely suited to illuminating the dark and opaque forces that motivate people to produce and consume in an addictive way. It provides a framework for understanding what keeps the hamster wheel turning and what drive everyone on it over the edge, toward crisis and self-destruction. It also provides insights and practical methods for developing economic activity that can be carried on in ways that are healthful and a means to joyful living. At the very heart of this philosophy and practice are what have come to be known as the four noble truths and the noble eightfold path.

The four noble truths and the noble eightfold path

Socially engaged Buddhist economics (SEBE) is a convergence of socially engaged Buddhism with a specific approach to economics that centers on institutional change. It is an approach to economics that springs from Buddhist philosophy and practice, but emphasizes active engagement for institutional change—specifically the transformation of economic institutions. As we will see, the way of a Buddhist practice, particularly mindfulness, can help people to skillfully break away from their habituated ways of living in the world economically that are resulting in so much social and environmental destructiveness, instability, and despair. Liberating ourselves individually from greed, aggression, or delusion, however, is not enough to achieve genuine wellbeing. We are social beings. If our institutions and cultures are saturated with these poisons, we cannot be truly liberated. SEBE focuses not on religion or metaphysics, but on practical ways to have a positive effect on social change. It emphasizes the transformation of economic institutions in ways that can help societies, particularly in the West, begin evolving from destructiveness and instability to wellbeing and stability. This work of social change can be highly effective if the agents of change first do the hard work of letting go of destructive habits of mind and action. The four noble truths and the noble eightfold path can give us guidance and inspiration in this effort.

After his arduous journey, during which he probed deeply into the nature and causes of human suffering, the Buddha conveyed what have come to be known as the "four noble truths." The first is simply to know that suffering exists, the second is to know the causes of this suffering, the third is to know that changes need to be made to free ourselves from this suffering, and the fourth is to know a pathway that charts a course for this change toward a more healthful living that puts an end to suffering. Although many variations of Buddhist philosophy and practice have evolved over the last two and half millennia, virtually all schools of Buddhist thought hold these basic elements as their foundation.[42]

As we explore these concepts, it is important to keep in mind that the central aim of socially engaged Buddhist economics is to come to terms with the spectrum of disagreeable conditions that we find ourselves in, both personally and societally. In this sense it might be easier to see Buddhism as a healing practice rather than as a religious one, although many Buddhists would not see the distinction. All healing practices start by identifying pathologies—sickness, unhealthy conditions, and disorders—and then finding out what causes the pathology and discovering a treatment or process for achieving greater wellbeing. The four noble truths are simply the realities the Buddha identified about our suffering and about taking steps that lead out of suffering and toward wellbeing.

As noted above, the *first noble truth* is to avoid denial and simply acknowledge that suffering exists. This is not to say that living out a human life is nothing but suffering from beginning to end as some have interpreted.[43] Rather, it is just to acknowledge that aspects of life can be hard and painful. Sometimes the troubles we encounter are relatively mild, such as a winter cold, a bee sting, a flat tire, or a scratch on the arm while gardening. Or we might experience suffering more severely as we are pulled down by physical trauma, incurable disease, hunger, or the death of a loved one. Somewhere on that spectrum are the specific experiences of suffering that arise from our economic lives: stress at work, job or financial insecurity, unemployment, bankruptcy, foreclosure, or poverty. This is the suffering that needs to be acknowledged in socially engaged Buddhist economics. And while we are acknowledging this, it is equally important to recognize that there are also joys in economic life. The Buddha taught that there is not only the truth of suffering, but also the truth that the potential for true joyful living exists in us all. To be critical of dominant economic institutions and theories is not to say that economic life is nothing but dismal. We can, and many of us often do, experience great joy in being part of a vibrant and wholesome economic system. Nonetheless, we must first develop an awareness that certain disagreeable conditions do exist so that we can take the next steps to transform those conditions into authentic wellbeing. Genuine awareness takes work, because it requires us to liberate our minds from the fog of confusion that exists both within and all around us.

The *second noble truth* is more challenging, as it requires that we see through the fog. It is to know the root causes and origins of our suffering. There are perhaps as many root causes as there are varieties of dislikable conditions of life, but for the project of developing socially engaged Buddhist economics our focus must be on the kinds suffering that are of our own creation—specifically, the troubling individual and societal conditions that are traceable to the fires of greed, aggression, and delusion.

The Buddhist view of the root causes of suffering is holistic. Everything is connected to everything else, and the existence of suffering is connected to deeper existential defilements, which are connected both to our own sense of self and to societal conditioning. To find the root causes of suffering in economic society, we have to look both inwardly and deeply into ourselves as well as outwardly to the conditions of our surroundings. Much suffering originates from the troubled conditions wrapped up in our individual sense of self, the ego, and from the same defiled conditions that are embodied in our social structures.

In this view, the human ego is something that is constructed, sometimes monumentally so, out of fear. It is as if we fear not to have a prominent self, even if it is a fantasy, because without it is simply nothing. Perhaps we instinctively fear nothingness or emptiness in the same way we fear death. For Buddhists, such self-attachment is where so many of our troubles originate. As we become self-attached, we are grasping on to a figment of our imagination like identifying with a character in a movie. A deep sense of dissatisfaction looms as we try to constantly affirm a fabricated "self." It is like trying to fill a void that cannot be filled, yet feeling eternally frustrated because the more we try to fill the imagined hole, the more we realize it is a bottomless pit.

Paradoxically, as we try to feel more alive we go out of our way to mask who we really are. We cling and grasp on to impermanent, illusory things, feelings, and sensations that we believe will affirm our ego. We become figment-attached, which can serve only to make us feel even more vulnerable and thus strengthen a resolve to reject anything that seems to pose a threat. All of this begins to take on a life of its own, and a sense of vulnerability builds; we cling, grasp, and covet out of worry that if we stop, everything will fall to pieces. It is almost as if the clinging itself is what makes us feel alive. On this Ken Jones notes that "Liberation from our sense of lack is impossible as long as we evade accepting its ultimately ego-created nature and instead go on trying to fill the imagined hole by top-loading our lives and the world with ego-affirming behavior that is needless, ineffective, and destructive."[44] Our need for security is insatiable; that is, until we come to understand the fact that it is the grasping neediness itself that is the problem.

Nowhere is this more evident than in the relationships people have with money and material wealth. This is the existential origin of greed. Jungian psychologist and financial analyst Deborah Gregory looks at this from the point of view of modern psychology and draws the same conclusions: "when examined on the unconscious level from a psychoanalytic perspective ... [greed] is being driven by an inner need to accumulate money

... the compulsion to amass wealth is akin to an empty hole that will need continual filling."[45] Compulsions lead to craving and hoarding and chronic dissatisfaction, which leads to jealousy, prejudiced hostility toward others, and aggression. We make ourselves and those around us miserable.

Suffering arises from an inability to experience a broader sense of goodness or wholesomeness, and holding on to things that are serviceable only to immediate ego-gratification. In a very fundamental and existential way, we slide into a vicious circle of pathology and deeper into a state of delusion that is formed by a desire to possess or acquire things that we believe will shelter us from the abyss of nothingness. The emptier we feel, the more we wrap ourselves in the inauthentic trappings of materialism and consumerism, until we become mummified. The result is an artificial life that, given the norms of society, appears to be thriving. Coveting and grasping naturally lead to aggression as we start to get in each other's way. In time, we create the disagreeable social conditions that are passed as karma from one generation to the next.

In Buddhist thought, karma is a conception of time that connects the past, present, and future. As the saying goes, "The present is a shadow of the past and the future a shadow of the present." Karma is a concept of cause and effect, of action and reaction. Our actions motivated by ego-attachment create the reaction of more pathological conditions for the future. But it does not have to be like this. Healthy motivations can give rise to beneficial actions which create wholesome conditions for the future. We are, both individually and societally, the engineers of our own fate—for better or worse.

We can transform suffering into something more positive if we make the commitment to do so. This means change, and change is something we naturally resist, sometimes vehemently. But identifying the source of our suffering has little meaning unless we are prepared to do something about it—to mindfully transform ourselves with care, attention, and awareness. A commitment to transformation, therefore, directs us to the third noble truth.

The *third noble truth* emphasizes simultaneously ceasing the patterns that have engendered so much suffering by dissolving away the old habits of thought and action that have been engendered by greed, aggression, and delusion, and allowing a new way of life to emerge. With time, effort, and practice, the suffering we create by the way we live our lives can be transformed into an authentic existence that is unfreighted by ego-aggrandizement and is free, joyful, and full of creativity. The process of transformation involves stepping aside from the conditions that make it impossible to pursue livelihoods with a genuine sense of peace or dignity and otherwise keep us wheezing round on the purposeless, mindless hamster wheel of consumerism, acquisitiveness, and malcontent. To make these changes real, however, we need to identify pathways that can guide us toward healthy habits and healthy living.

The *fourth noble truth* is about knowing how to stay on these pathways. As we identify suffering and its habitual causes and work to transform those habits, we need some guidelines. The fourth noble truth is linked to a broader framework to guide mindful action that will lead us down a different path, away from suffering and toward genuine wellbeing. This framework is the *noble eightfold path* as set forth by the Buddha: "And what, friends, is the noble truth of the way leading to the cessation of suffering? It is just this Noble Eightfold Path; that is, Right View, Right Intention [Thinking], Right Speech, Right Action, Right Livelihood, Right Effort, Right Mindfulness, and Right Concentration."[46]

In the broadest sense, the noble eightfold path is a set of strategies that can help us to cultivate wholesome action stemming from the wholesome potentialities that lie within us all. What is considered "right" here is not a set of moral commandments or judgments, but guidelines for healthy and more beneficial living. Each strategy is inseparable from the other seven, like the eight legs supporting a table, and all are wide open to interpretation, depending on the need and context. Here, the particular interpretation is for the purposes of crafting socially engaged Buddhist economics.

- *Right view* comes from a clear mind and the ability to comprehend the truth of things as they are without mental embellishment. As we free ourselves from the fog of greed, delusion, and aggression, we become more capable of viewing things as they really are. With right view there is no need for reality checks or reassurance in moments of paranoid speculation. Reality comes to us in plain sight, and we are able to see which kinds of economic behavior are wholesome and which are not; which actions lead to wellbeing and which do not.

• *Right intention*, also sometimes called right thinking, is the practice of keeping the mind clear and focused on healthy things, with a sense of good will rather than ill will; or with a sense of good health rather than ill health. By staying focused and intent on healthy activities, we can train ourselves to avoid being lured toward destructive behavior. With right concentration (see below) and thinking, we can see more deeply into the purpose or end results of our work. We can benefit from reminding ourselves why we are doing what we are doing, or from asking ourselves whether there is another way. Staying focused on healthy purposes makes it easier to dissolve unhealthy motivations that originate in the three fires. This also develops an awareness of the impact that what we do has on everything and everyone around us.

• *Right speech* is working against tendencies of expression that spill out from a mind fraught with greed, aggression, and delusion. As long as people remain captured by these fires, they will express themselves caustically toward one another and in ways that are intended to offend, manipulate, and deceive. Right speech is the opposite of the all-too-familiar venomous gossip in the workplace and deceitful marketing strategies.

• *Right action* is being observant of the relationship between habits of mind and habits of action. A mind consumed by greed, aggression, and delusion motivates economic actions that are prone to destructiveness—trashing the environment, depleting resources, exploiting people, or creating a toxic and unstable culture of greed. When we talk of right action we are not trying to place judgment or blame on others but, rather, to illuminate cause-and-effect relationships. Stepping away from the greed is good ideology; an entrepreneur blinded by greed and the compulsion to take ever-expanding profits might be compelled to produce things without regard to the damage they might cause—violent video games targeted specifically at children, for example. If violent games foster violent sensibilities in children during their early development, children may develop deeply ingrained habits toward violence for the remainder of their lives. In this karmic way, without a strong sense of right action the entrepreneur is unwittingly worsening a cultural condition of violence and aggression. With right action, we can cultivate a deeper sense of the implications of our economic behavior.

- *Right livelihood*, as E.F. Schumacher observed, is part of the Buddhist way. Originally, right livelihood was conceived as a process of earning a living without violence, slaughter, deceit or trickery, usury, narcotics or alcohol, slave trade, weapons, or prostitution.[47] In a modern interpretation, this can be generalized to earning a living without causing harm to others, to the environment or habitats, or to culture. Narrowing this down to specific provisions would be defined differently in different cultures.

- *Right effort* is diligence or conscientiousness in all aspects of life and maintaining vigilance against unwholesome motivations. Being diligent and working hard is often heralded as a virtue in itself. But can we really say that without also knowing toward what end all this work is? If the entrepreneur who produces violent video games is working hard, the effort is wasted because it does not lead to anything beneficial. We will be deluded or cynical to think that our hard work constitutes healthy diligence when that work ultimately leads to unhealthy results.

- *Right concentration* is staying focused and giving the task in hand our full concentration. As we will see, this is closely related to mindfulness in that it involves a kind of total immersion or absorption. It is a true skill to be impervious to distractions when most of us live in societies that are full of short-lived fashions and lacking in clarity of purpose—aside from profit making. Right concentration is the living verification of right view of things as they are without distortion or delusion.

- *Right mindfulness* is the most powerful of the eight pathways and is at the very heart of the Buddha's teachings.[48] Right mindfulness is a state of mind in which people become aware of their thoughts and actions and are fully occupied in the present moment. To be mindful is to be fully and calmly engaged in the here and now. It is a state in which our minds are not cluttered with a running mental commentary or the noise and confusion that hums with the millions of things that can capture our thoughts. It enables us to be openly and directly engaged in the activities before us. It is thoughtfulness without superfluous mental baggage, and the thoughts are clear, open, directly focused, and lucid.

Mindfulness is central to socially engaged Buddhist economics and is something that we will explore in much more detail later on. The four noble truths and the noble eightfold path would be a hollow doctrine without mindfulness, which brings them to life in practice. Mindfulness is the tool that we use to chip away the layers of junk that delude our minds and compel us to actions that cause suffering and damage—particularly those actions that arise from greed, aggression, and delusion. Mindfulness can help us gradually to disentangle ourselves from all kinds of ego-based attachments, including those things that reside nowhere else but in our own minds.

Mindfulness is presence of mind and being wholly in the moment with a clear, attentive awareness. The mind is deliberately kept at the level of bare attention, a detached observation of what is happening within us and around us in the present moment. All judgments and interpretations have to be suspended, or, if they occur, just registered and dropped.[49] A delusive mind captured by defilements and clouded by mental formations creates distortions of thought. These distortions of thought lead to actions that are at odds with the reality of the situation or circumstances. Without mindfulness, we can easily be prone to sinking into a deluded and troubling state, like finding ourselves to be drowning for no other reason than that we stumbled into water but are unable to swim. Mindfulness is the way toward wisdom, as sought by Schumacher in his vision for an economic life based on a spiritually informed way of being that transcends the specific aspects of daily living. Informed wisdom helps us to see clearly which life actions lead to true wellbeing and which do not. In this sense, mindfulness perhaps is the closest approximation to Schumacher's eye of the heart and is the very substance of Buddhist economics.

Mindfully dissolving the old and leaving it behind, kicking the habits of thought and action that make us suffer, and seeking a path away from all this suffering and toward true wellbeing is the key to realizing genuine socially engaged Buddhist economics. The Buddha taught, "Having consumed food, energy is regained, sensual urges are quieted, all unwholesome tendencies are quieted ... and equanimity is the cause of a state of pure mindfulness. When our mind has reached absorption, it is pure, clear, without unwholesome tendencies, unclouded, supple, well-suited for work, and free of apprehension." There is a true being waiting behind all the stuff and noise of the hamster wheel that, once discovered, will be spontaneously joyful. "This is a mental state that is conducive for seeing clearly that 'this is suffering, this is the arising of suffering, this is the passing away of suffering, and this is the path to putting an end to all suffering.'"[50] As we will see in a later chapter, meditation is a key part of this process of unclouding the mind. The process is fairly simple to understand, but the practice takes time and effort. Try for a moment to simply sit on a cushion or chair, breathe, ungrasp, and dissolve all that occupies your mind. It is not as easy as it sounds. In time, if it is practiced well and diligently, we can dissolve the attachments that give rise to so much anguish and become free. From this liberation come the spontaneity, true sense of joy, and authenticity that spring naturally from the very nothingness that we needn't fear.

If all of us were to strive to make our living in a way that follows some or all of the guidelines in the noble eightfold path, our economic systems would be transformed and we would change the momentum of history. We would not only change the kinds of goods and services people enjoy, we would also transform the collective mindset because, as we do things in a different way, we will be thinking in a different way. Habits of thought and habits of action are inseparable. With a mindfulness practice we can develop a greater awareness of our state of mind with some measure of objectivity. If we can be in the moment, and recognize aggression or greed as agitated states of mind when they arise, we can become more adept at not becoming so possessed by them that they control of our lives. When we change our minds, we change our actions, and when we change our actions, we are actively changing society, even though we may not even be aware of it.

The choice of this Buddhist approach to social change is specific. Greed, aggression, and delusion are not just defilements of an individual's mind, they are deeply rooted in our dominant economic institutions and in our collective psyche. Socially engaged Buddhist economics faces these defilements head on, but in a compassionate and practical way. As we look around us and see the raging pathologies of global warming, resource depletion, and massive economic instabilities, we can see the need for considering a new and very different approach to economics. David Loy makes this case succinctly: "Buddhism can provide what the modern world most needs: the spiritual message that may yet awaken us to who we are and why we as a species have such a penchant for making ourselves unhappy."[51] And the modern world needs practical things that people can do and by which they can see the results of their efforts.

The first and second noble truths are about the existence of suffering, and the third and fourth noble truths are about the processes of making practical changes to end this suffering. As we look deeply into the causes of our suffering, we cannot help but make discoveries, one of which would obviously be that we would have to change. We would have to face the difficult challenge of changing the way we act in the world and changing the way we think about the world, which means changing our habits. From the socially engaged Buddhist view, this means transforming both individual selves and the society in which we live.

Transformation means changing from one form to another—a fundamental shift in being. While on his journey, the Buddha did the hard work of searching inward for truth, and what he discovered was that the inner work itself is the truth. This work is the essence of a mindfulness practice, which is a veritable instrument of change and liberation.

Buddhism stems from the experiences and arduous journey of a mn, who was neither a god nor a messenger from a god. He was one of us. From his often excruciatingly painful experiences, the Buddha discovered a path toward healthful, joyful living and away from the suffering caused by deep psychic defilemens,d a path that each of us can follow regardless of our religious or metaphysical beliefs. In so doing the Buddha developed a skillful and unencumbered way of living and coexisting. Living in this way is itself a kind of ethical code—a lived ethics.

Buddhist economics as lived ethics

The middle way, the four noble truths, and the noble eightfold path together provide a basis for practical and healthy living. Together they constitute a framework that is centered on the understanding of the existence of suffering and of ways to end suffering through mindfulness. Through a meditative, intelligent, and mindful practice, individual consumers, producers, and entrepreneurs can liberate themselves from the three fires and set out on the path from greed to wellbeing. What emerges from such a practice is keen awareness, and from awareness comes the wisdom to see clear how to change our economic lives toward the healthy and away from the pathological. In this view, each individual is capable of exercising free will and each can choose to follow a more wholesome way of being in which they lift themselves out of the fog of ignorance and overcome the deep, gnawing tendencies of grasping and craving. Consumers, producers, and entrepreneurs have a chance to change their habits of thought and behavior by taking another direction, the way of the non-self, through nonattachment. An economic society liberated from greed, aggression, and delusion would look radically different from the hamster wheel system we have now.

Such a framework is also radically different from conventional economics. Schumacher was bold enough to take the lead in making this contrast and many have since followed. Buddhist economics became something of a community primarily in Western Europe, North America, and Thailand. Not all who have been inspired by a Buddhist approach agree that the baby of conventional economics should be thrown out with the bathwater, but there is a near consensus that standard economics presents a deranged picture of economic reality. For this reason, socially engaged Buddhist economics is a dissident approach.

Apichai Puntasen, a contemporary dissident from Thailand, notes that a clear understanding of the evolution of the human mind is something that is largely lacking in modern science and completely absent from modern economics. Since the industrial revolution, scientists have been preoccupied with technology, instruments of warfare, and general tinkering with how things work. Yet there has been little attempt to understand the deeply rooted fear and angst that troubles the individual mind, and even less focus on a process of liberating ourselves from these troubles, outside of prescribing pharmaceuticals. "Mainstream economics," Puntasen contends, "has virtually nothing to say about living authentic lives and true happiness aside from its self-proclaimed axioms of self-indulgence." Much of what Buddhist economists write about is their concerns with mainstream economics in this regard—an inability to answer, or even explore, basic questions about what will it take for people to live genuinely happy lives beyond material consumption. Puntasen concludes that Western economic systems and ideologies (which have taken over much of the East) culminate in a state of existence that is characterized by a dangerously bad combination of "... more purchasing more but with inadequate mental development."[52]

Prayudh Payutto, also a dissident Buddhist economist from Thailand, puts conventional economics in perspective: "... economics has become a narrow and rarefied discipline; an isolated, almost stunted, body of knowledge, having little to do with other disciplines or human activities."[53] Payutto's contribution, however, goes far beyond criticism of economics. He developed a system of ethics that discerns between two categories of economic motivations. One category is "tanha," or small-minded motivations that are limited to individual ego-gratification. The other category is "chanda", or big-minded motivations stemming from a desire to contribute to wellbeing.

Tanha economics, for Payutto, is like smoke billowing from the three fires. It is derived from the compulsions of the egocentric consumers, entrepreneurs, and financial market speculators who remain in a kind of dark prison of insatiability and self indulgence.[54] Experience is limited to the immediate thrill or self-gratification, such as the rush of hitting it big on Wall Street or the excitement of buying a new car, and sees little meaning in anything else. Tanha economics flows from a river of craving that the Buddha saw as boundless: "even if one could magically transform one single mountain into two mountains of solid gold it would still not provide complete and lasting satisfaction to one person."[55] Aside from the corporate empires constructed for the few, there is little genuine good that comes from tanha economics and therefore, in Payutto's view, it has little or no ethical value. Chanda economics, on the other hand leads to overall wellbeing not only for the individual producer or consumer, but also for society and our natural habitat. In that case, Payutto defines the activity as "morally skillful" and holding ethical value.[56] Actions holding ethical value in this sense derive from "non-defilement" as having roots in non-greed, non-aggression, and non-delusion. Payutto implores us all to make this effort which, in time, "leads to a more skillful life, and a much better and more fruitful relationship with the things around us."[57]

Payutto's message is that, with a sound practice, ignorance turns to wisdom, greed turns to wellbeing, aggression turns to compassion, and economic activity becomes centered on the pursuit of the genuine wellbeing of humanity rather than ego gratification. Buddhist ethics, in this sense, is not a set of commandments and pronouncements about what is good, bad, evil, or sinful. It is centered on an understanding of how things can be better if we take action to free ourselves. Defilement and ignorance give rise to motivations that lead us astray from our natural being and peaceful existence, but mindfulness and wisdom brings us back.

Collin Ash, a scholar from the University of Reading, compiled data showing how people suffer from a kind of mistaken identity developed in a consumeristic and materialistic culture.[58] That is, our economic system creates mental impairment as we obsess about things, and mistake those things for ourselves. The money and cars and things we covet become our self-identity such that our normal life experiences become warped and distorted. Those afflicted in this way develop neurotic habits of mind that are similar to gambling addiction or to the way that addicts believe that drugs or alcohol will bring them more wellbeing. The end result, according to Ash, is, "a permanent state of unfulfilled desire, manifesting in the economic sphere as a mood of restless dissatisfaction about what we have got and who we are so that we therefore pursue income, consumer goods, and status at the expense of more valuable relationships ... [and commit] the ultimate cognitive error with the self-deception of defining our identity by what we earn and consume."[59]

The principles set out in the noble eightfold path provide guidelines for our behavior. Most effective among them is right mindfulness. The Buddha stated succinctly, "If you act with a corrupt mind, suffering will follow. ... If you act with a peaceful mind, peace will follow."[60] But this view of economic change based on mindfully changing the way we think and act remains highly individualistic. Doubtless, if all the individuals who are engaged in the economic processes of production, consumption, investment, and finance were to practice mindful change, the economic world would be a far different place than we now know it. But there is an important social dimension to this that extends beyond individual choices and that must be addressed as well.

John B. Cobb, Jr., the co-founder of the Center for Process Studies in Claremont, California and author of volumes of work on transdisciplinary approaches to ecological studies and economics, makes a case for how a system of lived ethics should extend beyond individual adherences to certain principles ir choice-making behavior. He rejects individualism in the sense that there is more to economic activity than a mere random collection of individuals making contracts, and buying, and selling things. Rather, people live in communities and within cultures, which play a role in moderating economic behavior. He finds inspiration in the Sri Lank's Sarvodaya movement of A.T. Ariyaratnet which focuses on the restoration and strengthening of village life, rooted in Buddhist philosophy and practice, as a viable, countervailing effort against the corporatized, globalized economy that transforms spiritual beings into beings with insatiable wants and egocentric behavior. Cobb cautions against romanticizing village life in poor countries and, rather, points to an important message for socially engaged Buddhist economics: while we need to be aware that individual behavior does matter, social institutions also matter. Real change takes place both inward–individually and outward–socially.[61]

The compulsions of greed, aggression, and delusion are not only supported in mainstream economics; they are, in many ways, celebrated in our cultures, even though the consequences are often quite destructive. Greed and acquisitiveness have found a comfortable niche in Western Europe and, most prominently, in the United States. Deborah Gregory emphasizes that, "The national culture of the United States," which has so much emphasis on hustling for money, "has supported the rise and continued existence of Wall Street and its affiliates over centuries."[62] Accordingly, we have to continuously and mindfully examine our motivations as well as our social arrangements and to make clear the distinction between those motivations that stem from greed and those that stem from an impulse for creative self development, of which healthy entrepreneurship and business enterprise building can be a part.

TWO

Buddhist economics and socially engaged Buddhism

Working out a set of ethical principles or precepts to guide individual economic behavior is important for positive change, but it is not enough to make the change lasting and effective. Social structures are muscular forces in every society. They shape our values, worldviews, and ideologies. They influence what we eat, buy, and feel. They shape our innermost thoughts and daily behavior, and assert what is considered to be true or not. These social forces need to be seriously addressed for any Buddhist project of social transformation, particularly economics. As such, socially engaged Buddhist economics must have a vision for social transformation that extends beyond individual choice-making behavior. It needs to extend our understanding of the behavior of individual producers, investors, and consumers within the purview of social systems comprised of banking, financial, labor, corporate, market, and government institutions.

Skilled, healthy living based on mindfulness is key, but there are social forces pushing us in the opposite direction. Large multinational corporations and their partners in government exert influence that in many ways spread the three fires of greed, aggression, and delusion around the world with emphasis on conquering markets and dispersing American-style consumerism. From this, conflict and instability are inevitable.

The more people are motivated by the three fires, the more they feel they must manipulate their surroundings to get what they want. Manipulative behavior inevitably leads to feelings of alienation as each person begins to see how they are being manipulated by others. Society becomes awash with mutual distrust and pathology.[1] Recent studies in psychological pathology indicate that societies everywhere are moving in the direction of permitting, reinforcing, and actually valuing some of the traits listed in the "psychopathy checklist," including such traits as impulsivity, irresponsibility, and lack of remorse.[2] These conditions are continuously accentuated through the corporate institutions that thrive like predators in such an environment. Zen teacher Philip Kapleau writes about the widespread suffering that is created in corporate capitalism: "Capitalist industrial society has created [among the human population] conditions of extreme impermanence, terrifying insubstantiality, and a struggling dissatisfaction and frustration. It would be difficult to imagine any social order for which Buddhism was more relevant and needed."[3]

The power of corporate media and advertising to propagandize a certain obsessive/compulsive lifestyle is obvious to anyone who cares to take a critical look. But most of us choose not to think about it. There is comfort in surrendering to a kind of sleepy acceptance of corporate influence and not bothering to seek truth outside of what we are told. This acquiescence stems in part from the fact that corporate society has created its own systems for regulating social behavior. Sulak Sivaraksa reflects on this: "We have to see the relationships between social structures, self-surveillance, and self-censorship. To enforce social constructions, institutions intimidate us ... The media—almost all are for-profit corporations—are expert in legitimizing the actions of those in power."[4] David Loy also draws the conclusion that "the problem is not only that the three poisons [three fires] operate collectively but that they have taken on a life of their own."[5] Institutionalized greed, aggression, and delusion is itself a powerful beast.

Established corporate institutions are indeed powerful, but this does not mean that economic change is impossible. Everything is constantly changing. In a karmic sense, collective habits of thought and action do solidify into social structures, but these structures are impermanent, like everything else. They evolve and change with time. We have inherited a responsibility to give shape to this process of change in the direction of authentic wellbeing. The principal challenge in working toward change from greed to wellbeing is the struggle against the three fires at both levels—the beast within the individual and the beasts wielding social/institutional power.

Recall, the Buddha stated succinctly that "If you act with a corrupt mind, suffering will follow. ... If you act with a peaceful mind, peace will follow."[6] To extend this logic to the social realm would be to say *if you act with a corrupt mind, social institutions become corrupt and widespread suffering will follow; if you act with a peaceful mind, social institutions become peaceable and widespread peace will follow*. To the extent that socially engaged Buddhist economics stems from the noble truths of the Buddha, the first and second noble truths entail acknowledging that the institutional conditions of suffering exist, and the third and fourth noble truths entail doing something about it.

Socially engaged Buddhism

Socially engaged Buddhism is derived from an awareness of karmic cause-and-effect relationships. What we do and how we do it affects others now and in the future. We are always bringing about change in one way or another, and because of that we are always engaged. As historian Howard Zinn says, "You cannot be neutral on a moving train."[7] Awareness of dependent origination is important in this way. When we attest to the basic condition that everything is connected to everything else, we also become aware that our actions affect everything else, giving rise to a kind of karmic sense of responsibility. How we act in the world is the same as how we are in the world, which is the same as how we make the world. The starting place for socially engaged Buddhist economics, therefore, is with the recognition that suffering exists as part of the conditions of society and that to work toward genuine wellbeing we must change those conditions both individually and societally. This involves the hard work of mindfully crafting new and quite different economic institutions that will help to steer behavior in a new direction, away from the greed-inspired corporate institutions. For the transformation toward wellbeing, institutional transformation has to be part of the movement.

Philip Kapleau teaches us that the process of changing society begins with work on the self, but at the same time doing the same kind of work to bring about positive social change. "To help people without hurting them at the same time, or hurting yourself, means that we must first work on ourselves." He uses the term "middle way" as a kind of metaphor, "A Middle Way that alternates between the life of inward meditation and the life of action-in-the-world ..."[8]

Buddhist critique of consumerism

Considering the middle way in this sense, Buddhist and environmental studies professor Stephanie Kaza identifies the problem of greed, aggression, and delusion as it is manifest in consumerism, particularly among Americans. She addresses corporate marketing strategies and notes that advertisers coax consumers by deliberately creating within them a delusional sense of inadequacy and dissatisfaction that can be "fixed" only with more shopping. Moreover, this compounds into social ill will: "by setting up idealized stereotypes, advertisements foster greed, status-envy." Self-identity based on possessions "generates a shadow side of aggression. Gated communities for the wealthy, security guards for shopping malls, burglar alarms ..."[9] For its protection, consumer society needs its own security state. For Kaza, a Buddhist practice can help individuals to challenge this agenda by letting go of this possessiveness and fostering a different lifestyle and mindset. Also, with an understanding of interconnectedness and dependent origination, she argues, that through a keen awareness of what stimulates desire in consumer behavior, we can mindfully make better choices that can lead toward a more ethical marketplace.[10] The idea is to foster more awareness of the forces that influence consumer behavior. Manipulative advertising and glitzy shopping malls overwhelm the senses and load the dissatisfied ego with junk. With mindful awareness, "one can choose to avoid materialist overstimulation or to reduce self-identification with products."[11]

Kaza also points to the four noble truths as conceptual tools that individuals can use to dismantle the grip that consumerism has on the ego and perhaps relieve suffering. Suffering in this sense exists in the form of a manufactured feeling of lack. Nurturing greed and envy is a cornerstone of marketing psychology, as are the conditions of ignorance and delusion as consumers are manipulated into thinking that buying and more buying on the hamster wheel will make them happy. The futility in this is like trying to grab hold of a shadow by lunging toward it, only to have it move further away. For Kaza, liberation from ceaseless suffering is possible if people, particularly the consumers in the marketplace, begin to make better shopping choices by following a specified set of guidelines patterned after the eightfold path.[12]

Undoubtedly, if consumers in general began to make better shopping choices as a result of liberated minds, our economic society would begin to change. There is, however, a limit to how much we can rely on individualistic consumer choice-making behavior. Socially engaged Buddhist economics needs also to see consumerism itself as a cultural phenomenon that was created as part of the bottom-line imperatives of businesses. Profits from sales are the source of returns to shareholders and investors, and these returns cannot be sustained if people do not sustain high levels of consumption. The relentless drive for profits has created the consumer culture that fuels the economic machine. In his description of America in the early 20th century, cultural historian and author William Leach writes, "After 1880, American commercial capitalism, in the interest of marketing goods and making money, started down the road of creating … a set of symbols, signs and enticements …" He asserts that desire and longing were given shape specifically to meet the needs of business. "And since that need was constantly growing and seeking expression in wider and wider markets, the aesthetic of longing and desire was everywhere and took many forms."[13]

The problems surrounding consumerism and the social and environmental damage it does are much more institutional problems than they are problems of individual choice. Nhat Hanh compares corporate media advertising to pollution: "Television, films, and newspapers are forms of pollution for us and our children. They sow seeds of violence and anxiety in us and pollute our consciousness, just as we destroy our environment ..."[14] Relentless profit-seeking is a corporate imperative and, in fact, a national imperative because our economic systems are built around this fundamental principle. Corporations did not invent greed, aggression, and delusion, but they make sure that they stay as permanent fixtures in our culture. As such, it is natural to expect a certain amount of aggression to follow.

Buddhism on peace and conflict resolution

Virtually all those involved in the socially engaged Buddhist movement are also advocates of nonaggression and nonviolence. Payutto notes that peace activism is central to engaged Buddhism primarily "because Buddhism itself, the whole of it, is concerned with peace." Echoing Kapleau, Payutto speaks of both the individual's internal condition of peace and society's external condition of peace. Both are necessary, "In order to have peace outside we must have peace inside ... those who have happiness inside tend to radiate happiness outside also."[15]

Christopher S. Queen sees the application of Buddhist philosophy and practice as a possible key to the resolution of social problems. He sees that for many Buddhists "it is no longer possible to measure the quality of human life primarily in terms of an individual's observance of traditional rites ... or belief in dogma ..."[16] The scale and complexity of social, economic, and environmental crises have motivated Buddhists to engage in public service or political activism in nearly every area of social experience as a way to serve the ultimate cause of peace both within and among peoples.[17]

Peace activist Graeme Macqueen highlights that nonviolence movements need to do more than just renounce violence. He draws a distinction between what he calls "renunciatory nonviolence" and "engaged nonviolence."[18] For Macqueen, it is not enough to forsake violence. Rather, active steps need to be taken to eliminate the conditions that create it in the first place.

Similarly, activist John McConnell argues that a dharma practice "is not a set of dogma to be believed, but a way of beginning, here and now, with the mess we have made of our lives, and turning things around."[19] He and others turn to the "tool of mindfulness" as a way to develop the will and concentration to help resolve conflict.

Social and economic change

These socially engaged Buddhists are doing important work of raising issues of consumerism, status envy, and violence, but there remains a broader question of how to bring about social change. Their work remains heavily situated on individualism and misses the importance of institutional forces. This not only needs to be addressed specifically, but also needs to be elevated as a priority. For true liberation from the three fires, the seemingly invisible barrier that separates individual choice-making behavior from institutionalized behavior needs to be dissolved. An important step in this direction would be to acknowledge that the hamster wheel we all seem to be treading is itself an institutional structure, and at the same time to acknowledge that lasting change will involve creating an alternative to it.

Helena Norberg-Hodge demonstrates a step in this direction. Norberg-Hodge directly addresses engaged Buddhists' efforts toward building new economic institutions. She sees that some traditional Buddhist communities with their own set of economic institutions exist with deep roots in their natural interdependent relationship with their environment. Corporate dominated Western societies tend to be more dismembered— from person to person and from person to nature. Here we depend heavily on technology, and perhaps even have come to believe that technology keeps us alive, rather than water and food. "[M]odern society is based on the assumption that we are separate from, and able to control, the natural world. Thus the structures and institutions on which we depend are reification of ignorance ..." With decades of economic globalization, hamster wheel economics has effectively enlisted the entire planet and has brought much ruin to communities that share different values and social structures. Norberg-Hodge sees the global homogenization of hamster wheel economics and its greed and consumerism as a product of corporate business interests using populations everywhere as their clay to fashion the world in their own image, driving alternatives to extinction. The corporate agenda runs roughshod over every continent, looking for opportunities to profit. The damage is palpable, with the destruction of ecosystems, community vitality, and cultural identity, as well as polarized incomes and social turbulence.[20] For Norberg-Hodge the solution lies, at least in part, with institutional change. She argues that economic localization is a possible antidote to the ravages of corporate globalization. Her suggestion for change is to create specific institutional alternatives such as alternative, locally controlled money systems and Community Supported Agriculture (CSA).[21] Although her suggestions are neither new nor particularly Buddhist in nature, they nonetheless raise awareness of the formidable power of transnational corporations. However it is carried out, working peacefully and mindfully for institutional alternatives is a step closer to realizing a true socially engaged Buddhist economics.

One of the most direct and original examples of engaged Buddhism is the creation of the Order of Interbeing by Thich Nhat Hanh and others during the Vietnam War in the 1960s. These young Vietnamese, pioneers in engaged Buddhism, did not wait for someone else to come and change things for them or to pass a new law or regulation; they took action directly and mindfully. They crafted new institutions and restructured existing ones for no other reason than compassion. They worked tirelessly to help those who were suffering from the ravages of the war in their country by organizing volunteers in the rebuilding of bombed villages, creating farmers' cooperatives, and establishing health clinics.[22] They saw the need for institutional alternatives and they went straight to work creating them.

The connection between interbeing and peace in this effort is important. Interbeing, or interconnectedness, is a point of understanding that the defilements that afflict any one of us can afflict all of us. There is no divisiveness between "us" and "them," there is only "us." During the war Nhat Hanh was asked by some Americans why he did not hate them for what they were doing in his country and he replied, "You were not the only ones responsible ... Our individual consciousness is a product of our society, ancestors, education, and many other factors ..."[23] Warfare is an institution and, like any other institutional force, it has a karmic volition of its own. Nhat Hanh went on to say, "If we divide reality into two camps ... and stand in one camp while attacking the other, the world will never have peace. We will always blame those we feel are responsible for wars and social injustice, without recognizing the degree of violence in ourselves. We must work on ourselves and with those we condemn to have a real impact."[24]

Rebecca Solnit, although not necessarily an engaged Buddhist, expresses a similar sensibility. In *A Paradise Built in Hell: The Extraordinary Communities That Arise in Disaster* (2009), Solnit chronicles events in which people experience a certain purposiveness and fulfillment when they are actively responding to real-time disasters—such as nuclear explosions, earthquakes, or mass violence. An extraordinary consciousness takes over and, Solnit contends, this can "bring out the best in us and provide common purpose. Everyday concerns and society strictures vanish ... people rise to the occasion." People reveal a deeper sense of compassion and empathy and genuinely want to help each other. The implications are that such instances give us a "glimpse of who else we ourselves may be and what else our society could become."[25] Such empathy and compassion can be cultivated in an effort to change society. With a mindful awareness of interbeing and a sense that we are always in these things together, people can and do make positive change. This applies equally to the hardships that unfold from economic crises.

In the immediate aftermath of the banking crisis that began in 2008, there was much finger pointing and casting of aspersions in the news media. The problems that underlie this crisis will never be resolved as long as we feel that "they" are to blame, not "us." To paraphrase Nhat Hanh, we could say that we will always blame those who we feel are responsible for greed-inspired financial meltdowns and economic instability, without recognizing the degree of greed in ourselves. Journalist and author Matt Taibbi exemplifies this in one of his familiar rants:

Sometimes what's required for a real social catastrophe is for one or two ingeniously obnoxious individuals to rise to a position of great power – get a one-in-a-billion asshole in the wrong job and a merely unfair system of government suddenly turns into seventies Guatemala ... Former Federal Reserve chief Alan Greenspan is that one-in-a-billion asshole who made America the dissembling mess that it is today.[26]

Taibbi's message serves no real purpose except to create more divisiveness, anger, and a headlong plunge away from right speech. As we will see in later chapters, the conditions for a massive banking industry and financial market crash went far beyond Federal Reserve policies, and culpability ran deep and wide. It would be absurd to claim that one person, no matter how powerful, was the cause. The hard truth is that greed, aggression, and delusion are pathological conditions that can potentially possess us all if we do not work against them. Interbeing is such that we are all co-responsible for the things that happen as a result of universal, undivided human tendencies. Nhat Hanh expressed this notion of non-divisiveness in these lines from a poem,

I am the frog swimming happily in the clear water pond
And I am the grass-snake that silently feeds itself on the frog[27]

Nhat Hanh has inspired people from all over the world because of his deliberate focus on social issues and transformation. He also inspires by personally modeling how to be engaged in complex and daunting issues such as violence, environmental destruction, and social injustice from a position of compassion and joy rather than anger, blame, and fear.

As part of his understanding of interbeing and non-divisiveness, Nhat Hanh chose not to speculate on metaphysics. Although metaphysics is something that is a preoccupation of many within the Buddhist community as well as other traditions, he sees the truth as the Buddha taught as a product not of the intellect, but of experience. "In conceptualizing we cut reality into small pieces that seem to be independent of one another … wisdom is the fruit of meditation. It is a direct and perfect knowledge of reality, a form of understanding in which one does not distinguish between subject and object."[28]

Roshi Glassman and the Greyston Mandala

Another socially engaged Buddhist who is committed to peace through direct action is Roshi Bernard Tetsugen Glassman, more popularly known as Bernie Glassman. Glassman is most noted for establishing the Zen Peacemaker Order and the Greyston Mandala projects. Formerly a mathematician at McDonnell-Douglas corporation, Glassman developed a distinctive style of engaged Buddhism based on "the creative use of traditional Buddhist metaphors and images … and the emergence of a distinctive new dharma of social service." As Kapleau, Payutto, Nhat Hanh, and others teach us, Glassman also holds that a socially engaged Buddhist practice is predicated on doing the "self work" first.[29] He follows the Soto Zen approach to Buddhism, which emphasizes sitting in "shikantaza" meditation, which literally means "just sitting" and nothing else.

Shikantaza is a term used interchangeably with "zazen," and either term means to wholeheartedly devote oneself to sitting, usually on a cushion in a particular posture, and to being fully aware of what is going on in one's mind. It is not about going into a trance or deep relaxation but, rather, is diligent alertness to the mind, yet being unattached to whatever arises in the mind during meditation. Sitting in this way is a key aspect of a mindfulness practice and we will return to this in more detail in a later chapter.

For Glassman, meditation is an exercise in cultivating what he calls "bearing witness" as a kind of window onto the wholeness of life, without judgment or preconception. It is a process of dissolving attachments in the ego-based mind, letting go of preconceived notions, and simply being. Like Nhat Hanh, Glassman avoids metaphysics and teaches that true liberation is not to be "idolatrous about or bound to any doctrine, theory, or ideology, even Buddhist ones."[30] This may seem paradoxical, but it is a familiar sensibility among many Buddhist teachers to encourage others not to become overly attached to their own beliefs, even when they accept them with deep faith. In this respect, they are following the advice of the Buddha, who urged his disciples not to become angry or upset when others spoke critically of his teaching and not to become elated when others spoke in praise of it, but to maintain an equal, open mind in the face of both criticism and praise. Toward the end of his life the Buddha told his followers, "In these forty nine years I have not said a single word,"[31] so as to discourage his disciples from becoming attached to his teaching. He wanted them to practice the teaching and realize the truth for themselves, rather than grasp onto verbal and conceptual formulations.

For Glassman, nonattachment and bearing witness breaks down social divisiveness and naturally fosters an inclination to engage compassionately in the world. It was from this compassion and openness that Glassman, starting in the 1970s and 1980s, devoted himself to founding various Zen-based institutions. After becoming ordained in the Soto Zen Buddhist tradition in 1976, he sought to build a particular brand of Buddhism that holds social engagement and social transformation to be as important as self work and personal transformation. He became one of the founders of the Zen Center of Los Angeles. Perhaps most notable in terms of social change, however, are the Greyston projects he started after moving from Los Angeles to New York in the early 1980s.

Glassman found inspiration from the earliest Zen masters. As Buddhism spread from India to China in the 6th century, ever larger numbers of people were arriving at monasteries to study and practice meditation. This presented a challenge to the monks and abbots in that these people needed to be fed and housed. Buddhist monks started placing more emphasis on daily chores. The Zen tradition began to take on a new element involving meditation not only when sitting on the cushion, but also when engaged in the tasks of everyday life. The contemplative monastic life extended beyond study and meditation to doing whatever other work needed to be done such as tending to the garden or rice fields, cleaning rooms, preparing meals, and gathering firewood and water. Meditation thus extended beyond the self, to work and social structures. The work itself became a kind of meditation or mindfulness practice. For Glassman, this extended to a business enterprise with Buddhist guidelines—from right mindfulness to right livelihood—both to serve as a way to support a Zen community and to positively effect social change.

In 1982, Glassman opened Greyston Bakery in The Bronx, New York (relocated five years later to Yonkers). The idea of the bakery was to create a business that could support a growing community, provide training and opportunities for personal growth and spiritual transformation, and help to alleviate homelessness among the underprivileged. Glassman notes, "As a Zen community, we didn't want to engage in anything that fell outside the Buddhist definition of right livelihood. We didn't want to produce anything that would harm people. ... In terms of social action, we needed a labor-intensive business that could create jobs for a lot of people."[32]

Greyston continues now as a for-profit social enterprise and became the first Certified B Corporation in the state of New York. Instead of profits going to some absentee owners' pockets as would be the case with a standard C corporation, they go to the Greyston foundation to help fund social progress.[33] As a social enterprise, Greyston pursues multiple objectives: providing baked goods for consumers and other businesses, employment, job skills and training as an anti-poverty measure, and an "open door" hiring system. According to its website, it has an open-door hiring policy geared toward offering employment opportunities regardless of educational attainment, work history, or past social barriers such as incarceration, homelessness, or drug use.[34]

Greyston's business has expanded significantly since the late 1980s, when it contracted with ice cream manufacturing giant Ben & Jerry's to make brownies for the latter's ice cream. The social enterprise's mission has expanded to include developing affordable housing, child care facilities, community gardens, and workforce development projects.[35] These are specific economic institutions that have been created from Greyston's mission.

Glassman's principle of bearing witness, embracing the wholeness of life, is the guiding philosophy of the Zen Peacemakers Order (ZPO), established in 1980. ZPO is an organization of socially engaged Buddhists that Glassman cofounded with his wife, Sandra Jishu Holmes, in 1996 as a means of continuing the work begun with the Greyston foundation, "expanding Zen practice into larger spheres of influence such as social services, business and ecology but with a greater emphasis on peace work."[36]

Self work and social change

A great many stories about social entrepreneurship begin with a question of motivation. Even when we feel that what motivates us is wholesome or ethical, if we are driven by a compulsion to self-aggrandize, our actions will inevitably be taken over by impulses that lead to problems. We become trapped on the hamster wheel and are no longer in control. The compulsion takes over. For this reason, a big part of socially engaged Buddhist economics must start with the self work—the work toward liberating the self from the three fires—and subsequently work outwardly toward a broader project of transformation. But, regardless of these motivating factors, the work of going against powerful institutional forces can be stressful, exhausting, and result in burnout.

Christopher Titmuss notes that "In the movement for social change and justice one of the biggest factors contributing to stress and burnout is that there is a dependency on result."[37] Admittedly, this can be hard to avoid, since we live in a results-oriented society. Nonprofits receiving grant money from foundations are accountable in terms of the results of their work. For-profit businesses, of course, are heavily chained to bottom-line orientation, which in most instances is the single most important criterion for raising capital and establishing bank credit. These challenges are more effectively met when the self work of liberation is done first.

A common theme that runs throughout socially engaged Buddhist projects is the liberation of the mind from ego-attachment and from dogma-attachment. Joseph Goldstein, in an essay titled "Three Means to Peace," echoes the sentiments expressed by Nhat Hanh and Glassman that, "Rather than take religious views and teachings to be statements of absolute truths, they might be better understood as skillful means."[38] Skillful means in this sense is what Payutto referred to as cultivating the means to be a force for good in society by doing the self work of transforming from a egoistic, small mind (tanha) orientation to a compassionate, big mind (chanda).

However it is done, Glassman and many others who are not Buddhists have proven that there are other ways to develop economic production off the hamster wheel. When people can dissolve the blockage of the grasping ego, the world opens wide to possibilities for social change in an infinite number of ways. For Glassman, one such way was simply "to start a business that could also provide jobs and job training outside our community." But beyond that, he tells us, "I was looking for a way for business itself to become a force for social change and a way of spiritual transformation."[39]

And if this can be successfully accomplished in a bakery, why not in a bank, or a even network of banks?

The socially engaged Buddhist projects we have explored here have focused on individual initiatives based on doing the inner work of mindfully liberating ourselves from the three fires, and the outer work of liberating ourselves socially through social engagement. But these projects, and many others like them, are anecdotes. What is notably absent is a more comprehensive view of economic institutions and systems. As we practice mindfulness and develop an awareness of things as they truly are, we clear the fog from our minds and allow reality to simply and calmly come to us. This clarity of perception applies not only to our own behavior, but to an awareness of the social forces around us.

This awareness is crucial for socially engaged Buddhist economics. We will never be able to understand how economies function if we do not understand the institutions that comprise them and how they influence our daily lives on the spinning hamster wheel. The third and forth noble truths are about making lasting and beneficial change. In economics, this must include institutional change and transformation. Crafting new institutions that lead toward systemic change is a long-term, evolutionary process which may seem daunting, but it is no more daunting than doing the self work of liberating ourselves from greed, aggression, and delusion. Accordingly, when we talk of socially engaged Buddhist economics and the process of transforming economic institutions and systems, we have to be very clear about what this means.

A Buddhist-institutionalist view for action and reflection

As I argue here and in my other work, I contend that societies will never get to the other side of recurring financial and environmental crises unless we address the institutional nature of economics. Every economy that has ever existed in history, including the current global economy, is a coordinated system of institutions. In the broadest sociological sense, institutions are social structures that prescribe human behavior. Institutions are established social practices or structures that are characteristic of a particular society and exist to direct or control human social behavior. An institution is a human creation, but it is mysterious in the sense that its origins cannot be traced to a specific invention or to a specific person. Rather, institutions are structures that have their roots in social customs, conventions, symbols, and the daily lives of people which establish the "dos and don'ts" of social behavior.[40] Some are rigid and rule-based structures armed with "or else" consequences and others are nothing more than loosely established shared strategies. But it is within our institutional social structures that economic activity is carried in one way or another.

Economic institutions and social change

Institutions as rule-based structures are relatively easy to see once we understand them. A family is an institution in which parents create the rules and parameters around the behavior of their children—do this, don't do that. In educational institutions teachers require students do math, even though many kids would prefer not to. Neighborhood associations impose rules for residents, and sports leagues place strictly enforced strictures on teams and players. Social institutions are ubiquitous, which means that much of our behavior is institutionalized. Governments, religious organizations, banks, corporations are all around us and each has its conditions for what is acceptable social behavior and what is not. The "or else" consequences are commonly understood: punishment, fines, incarceration, excommunication, foreclosure, or being fired. Living, working, or playing within the confines of these rule-structured situations is what nearly all of us do every day.

Not all institutions are rigid and punitive. Some are less formal and take the form of simple shared strategies among a self-identified community. Individuals who share a vision, a set of values, or goals might adopt rules or guidelines without codifying them formally. A shared strategy that lacks specific "or else" sanctions is more likely to work as an informal institution and can be just as effective as formal institutions if it garners enough support, has enough legitimacy in the eyes of community members, and exacts compliance. That is, advising cooperation or compliance to achieve a goal are informal institutional rules that are rooted in a community who share a common set of values.

Most of us find that compliance is relatively easy to do. Institutions are such an integral part of human social life from childhood on that they become nearly invisible forces in our repertoire of automatic, habitualized behaviors. They are deeply embedded in our cultures and ways of thinking, and as such they are scarcely called into question. They script how we interact with one another, how we drive our cars as we commute to and from work, the manner in which we treat our co-workers or boss, the way we recreate or participate in social activities, how we play sports or music, how we communicate, and how we shop. In the socially engaged Buddhist economics movement, we must have a sound understanding of how institutions work—like hands molding clay—to shape our economic behavior.

Economic institutions are the specific ruled-structured situations that shape our economic behavior. Walton Hamilton, an early 20th-century scholar who coined the term "institutional economics," describes: "Institutions fix the confines of and impose form upon the activities of human beings. ... The world of [human activity], to which imperfectly we accommodate our lives, is a tangled unbroken web of institutions."[41] In this web, we find financial institutions, including the Federal Reserve and the Bank of England, that control our money and systems of credit. Corporations, organized exchanges, media, and other structures set codes and rules regarding when and where production is done, how much it will cost, how products are distributed among the population, public attitudes about consumption, contract negotiations, and everything else that is involved in making a living. The unbroken web also contains other institutions such as organized labor, which sets rules for collective bargaining and working conditions, and government agencies that stand guard over the natural environment and the public sphere, and the list goes on—indeed a tangled web, but palpable and quite real.

Economic institutions are layered together into this unbroken web to form an integrated system that imposes forms upon our economic behavior. As we come to understand the primary role of institutions in our economy and how they work together systemically, we begin to understand the economic system itself. Once we understand the institutional nature of economic systems, and we can see more clearly the broader purposes they serve, we can better discern whether or not these purposes extend to actual wellbeing.

Although economic institutions create some sense of order out of chaos, the order is not always fair, just, or healthy. Institutions themselves, depending on the rules, can exist to serve greed or wellbeing. As Joel Bakan has noted, the economic and political landscape of the global economy has evolved into a system in which virtually every major industry, including banking and finance, telecommunications, manufacturing, pharmaceuticals, retail, is dominated by an elite club of massive corporations. The large corporation is the centralized bastion of the global economy and has conscripted nearly all other social and political institutions to its purpose of single-mindedly pursuing wealth accumulation.

Corporate institutions are shrouded in cultural mystification that covers their agenda with propaganda and apocryphal stories such as how the magic of deregulated markets and how greed leads to social progress, advancing prosperity, and even ecological sustainability.[42] Accordingly, the pathological fires of greed, aggression, and delusion are fanned quite vigorously in this institutional environment.

Institutional economics and Buddhist economics

A school of unorthodox economists known as "institutionalists" provide insights into how such pathology has become habituated in modern capitalist societies. Institutional economics was originated in the United States at the turn of the 20th century by what David Hamilton characterizes as "a herd of dissidents seeking company in misery"[43] and has largely been ignored by mainstream economics and academia. Nonetheless, institutionalism is unique and exceptional, and its core concepts have a natural affinity for socially engaged Buddhist economics as they are grounded in practical problems, the quest for genuine wellbeing, and a holistic view of life.

The term "institutionalism" was first used to describe the work of Thorstein Veblen, the grandfather of institutional economics. Veblen was an eccentric figure in American intellectual history and his career was very erratic; not the least because of his boisterous and often irreverent behavior. The honesty and originality of his work, however, inspired generations of economists and other scholars, particularly his poignant criticisms of the privileged classes in America in his classic, *The Theory of the Leisure Class* (1899).[44] Fundamental to Veblen's view of economics is the separation between creative elements and greed-inspired elements—a distinction between those who contribute to the creation of wealth and those who extract wealth.[45] Each group has its own behavioral traits, and in certain social contexts these traits can become outwardly manifest as patterns or habits. Over time, such habits of behavior become the substance of social structures—institutions. Veblen held the United States particularly to be a place where the greed-inspired and predatory human potentialities could thrive.

The tycoons who monopolized the American economy, such as John D. Rockefeller, Andrew Carnegie, and J.P. Morgan, lorded it over their industries like feudal barons. Their companies were near-perfect embodiments of the fires of greed, aggression, and delusion. American capitalism became a value system in which materialism and wealth accumulation ascended like a druglike substitute for true wellbeing. Rewards and trophies were bestowed on those who could aggressively build corporate empires as monuments to their own egos and who could successfully wage wars of aggression against their competitors. Veblen launched a scathing critique of the predatory corporate society that America had become. He lampooned the wealthy segments of America's population as they ostentatiously displayed their affluence by flaunting their ownership of expensive consumer goods signifying the winners in the hustlers' game. He also highlighted how the average working person on the street had been swept into the game and would go to great lengths to emulate the wealthy. The barons of capitalism became heroic figureheads and their legends were woven deeply into American culture, mindset, and, above all, institutions. Over a century ago, Veblen identified what David Loy now sees as the global problem of the institutionalization of greed, aggression, and delusion.

Institutional economics overlaps with Buddhist economics in other ways. As does the Buddhist view, it illuminates a holistic and karmic view of economic systems. Economic historian David Hamilton summarizes that "To the institutionalist, the individual acting in economic society is subject to permanent alteration by a cumulative series of actions. In fact the actor becomes the product of the cumulative series."[46] By this, Hamilton means that the whole of our entire culture is constantly changing and, as a result, so are we as individuals. This cumulative series of social habituation is, in other words, karma. We act in a world we inherited, and through karmic volition we pass it on, with our particular brand of changes, to subsequent generations.

The implications are that if we develop healthy habits in our economic behavior, then we can expect to bring improvements to the wellbeing of future generations. If our habits are fraught with the three fires, then we can expect to bring the opposite. As Karl Marx noted, "Men make their own history, but they do not make it just as they please; they do not make it under circumstances chosen by themselves, but under given circumstances directly encountered and inherited from the past.

The tradition of all the generations of the dead weighs like a nightmare on the brain of the living."[47]

In the institutionalist view, each of us is born into a world surrounded by cultural signs and symbols with their particular meanings. These include institutionalized forms of social organization accompanied by symbols of status and prestige—the symbol of the dollar or the pound, or the title of CEO—and most of these are just taken for granted as they have stood the test of time and, as such, require no explanation or justification.[48] These symbols also become the normative stuff of the collective mindset; that is, the notions of what is true or not, what is right or wrong, or what is important or not. Habitual action leads to habitual perceptions and ideas. Ideas become typified in a shared consciousness and, with time, are normalized as common sense and taken for granted. From one generation to the next, we habitually and unquestioningly pass on what is collectively exalted as success as if the trappings of affluence, no matter how they were accumulated, are synonymous with wellbeing.

In both institutional economics and Buddhist economics our sense of self and our actions are products of *both* intrinsic being *and* social context. The self and society are inseparable parts of the same complex whole. Our sense of being in the world, our mind, how we act in the world, how we view the world, and how we view others are all inseparable parts of the same organic whole. Over the centuries of modern capitalist development, this organic whole has evolved into a massive structure that is saturated with the idolatry of financial wealth. This is not hard to see if we pay attention to its ubiquity: continuously updated stock market indexes, corporate logos plastered on nearly every surface, television commercials blasting at high volumes in every possible nook, and the cultural avalanche of all the other symbols of sought-after lifestyles on the hamster wheel.

For institutionalists and Buddhists alike, hamster wheel economic life is captured in an institutionalized web of delusions that equate high material standards of living with happiness. In this state people seek to obtain all the trappings of affluent lifestyles, which they believe is the only way to become happy. Veblen identified this kind of delusion using the now famous term "conspicuous consumption."[49] Conspicuous consumption has become ubiquitous consumption, and the result is a nearly universal acceptance of greed in the collective mindset. Through habituation, such a culture conditions our way of thinking, which in turn further conditions our habitual ways of acting in society. We become trapped. For Buddhists, this trap is a root cause of human suffering—pathos.

Even though the monumental crises of global warming, injustice, and instability are looking us squarely in the face, the fog of justification remains normalized as common sense—literally a sensibility held in common—and is accepted without question. It takes little effort to drift along on this tide, yet pathology of mind and pathology of action lock into a mutually reinforcing dynamic, and we and our planet get sicker.

To see our economic society in this critical way is not intended to pass judgment. Nhat Hanh reminds us that these are conditions that potentially affect each of us: "We may think that our agitation is ours alone, but if we look carefully, we'll see that it is our inheritance from our whole society and many generations of our ancestors. Individual consciousness is made of the collective consciousness, and the collective consciousness is made of individual consciousnesses."[50]

People assert themselves in a world they inherited, including a collective consciousness, and by doing so they have an impact. Through karmic volition and time, they change the world that will be inherited by those who follow. When we look into our own selves and we do the self work, we are looking into a sense of self that is continuously changing and at the same time changing the word in which others will live. The individual and collective consciousness are inseparable—and over time. The implication of this is that as we change ourselves in terms of how we act and think, we are changing the whole of society—for better or for worse. The task for socially engaged Buddhist economics is to work for the better.

Socially engaged Buddhist Ken Jones shares the image of Indra's Net as a metaphor for this holistic approach. Indra's Net is often referenced in Buddhist literature to exemplify a interconnected worldview. Rooted in the principle of dependent origination, the image is of a celestial net that extends infinitely in all directions. At each intersection where the strands of the net cross resides a sparkling jewel. Upon close inspection, however, each jewel is merely the reflection of light from all the other jewels in the net. There is no single, ultimate source of light. The whole web is not only greater than the sum of the parts, but is self-sustaining through interbeing or a process of mutual co-arising of all formations. In essence, individual formations have no existence separately from all the others. Jones writes, "From the standpoint of an engaged Buddhism the net is valuable as a working ideal for society and its organizations, in which we are brothers and sisters in mutuality."[51] He is reflecting on Schumacher's economic development model, which he calls "Two Million Villages." This is a decentralized model in which there exist a multitude of semi-autonomous businesses and households situated in local culture, with roots that "lie outside the economic sphere, in education, organization, discipline and, beyond that, in political independence and a national consciousness of self-reliance."[52]

The implications for socially engaged Buddhist economics are important. One is an implication for change. As we change small things, such as our own individual thought patterns and behavior, we are also changing everything else at the same time. The third and fourth noble truths are about change and transformation. From an institutionalist view of economic systems, this means evolving. The institutionalist economists, like many of the most notable scientists of the 20th century, were inspired by Charles Darwin, Alfred North Whitehead, and others who were building an interdisciplinary and holistic framework of analysis. Economic historian Allan Gruchy notes that "The assumptions of the holistic economists relating to the nature of human behavior are in conformity with their view of the economic system as an evolving cultural complex."[53]

Veblen identified that the evolution of economic systems takes place within a process that he calls "invention and diffusion."[54] As people act in the world, they invent and change things. This could be a new form of technology, a new word, a policy, or a business model. However large or small the invention, it results in a shift in how people act and relate to each other. These new things and actions become diffused through social interaction and eventually new habits are formed around them. Eventually these new things become part of the evolving cultural complex while the old habits fade, in a continuous process of renewal and change.

The internet, or the creation of the Federal Reserve System, for example, are inventions that have had significant impacts on our economic system. But smaller inventions, such as a new recipe, or Glassman's Greyston projects, are invented and diffused just the same, and they have an impact on the whole system proportionally—some in sudden and revolutionary ways and others in more subtle and gradual ways. With a mindfulness practice, people involved in socially engaged Buddhist economics can develop a deep understanding and awareness of how they can bring about change in ways that go far beyond an individual's immediate circumstances. Economic systems are thus open-ended processes of a continuous and cumulative state of evolution and change, and we are all agents of perpetual change, which is the uncertain world of economics.

In other words, the manner in which systems change is indeterminate. There is no single direction of social evolution. Invention and diffusion either can cause evolutionary change for the benefit of society, or they can cause things to get worse. Generally speaking, when we talk of technology and progress, we think of these instances of change as an improvement in the means of production. In the Darwinian sense, inventions that result in advancing the means of producing knowledge are more likely to take root and survive, and those that are encumbrances to this advancement will either thwart progress or be eroded by it. If technology and progress are thwarted, then society is destined to remain backward; if they are allowed to grow, then society will evolve and advance. Institutionalist David Hamilton argues that "Economic progress increases the power of the means to achieve given ends, but it says nothing about the ends,"[55] which then begs the question as to why productivity is held to be a measure of progress.

For well over two hundred years, mainstream economists have anchored their conception of economic progress to technology and productivity. At the center of their vision of productivity is capital accumulation, where capital is defined as "produced means of further production." With more capital, greater productivity is realized, and more goods can be produced with a given amount of non-technological resources. With more goods, the standard of living of people rises. In this sense, economic and cultural progress is necessarily identified with capitalism and capital accumulation. This sentiment is exemplified by Austrian economist Joseph Schumpeter: "There is the growth of rational science and the long list of its applications. Airplanes, refrigerators, television, and that sort of thing are immediately recognizable as results of the profit economy."[56]

We need to be continually asking the question of purpose, as did E.F. Schumacher when he made his case for economics "as if people mattered." This question of priorities will surface again when we look at metrics such as Gross Domestic Product (GDP) or gross national happiness (GNH). Is the purpose of all our economic activity directed toward improving the wellbeing of the population? Healthy and functional economic systems can be genuinely responsive to the needs of people, grounded in wholesome values, and attest to secure livelihoods of people in their communities. More often than not economies—capitalist particularly—are functioning to keep the hamster wheel spinning at all costs, even if that means environmental ruination, instability, and violation of basic human rights.

Cultures in which capitalism is the dominant social system of production are permeated with a normative sense of the rightness or correctness of capitalist profit making and accumulation. It is seen as the source of material progress and higher standards of living. Under this rubric, the necessities of capitalism become the environment for selecting which practices are to survive and which will become extinct. As such, these practices become integrated into cultures and, with time, have become the cultural norm. This normative formation gives direction to the development of specific institutions and directs the economic activities of people. As people's activities are directed by the needs of capitalist growth as such, they are heralded as part of human progress.

Now, however, the twin crises of global warming and global resource depletion are forcing us to question these standard assumptions. As growth and accumulation are held as standard functions in a culture dominated by capitalist institutions, people within this culture are unlikely to see their destructiveness. Such cultural blindness stands as a significant barrier to building non-pathological economic alternatives. Getting through this barrier will require both an understanding of the source of the pathology as well as deliberate action to break out of pathological habits of thought and action.

The underlying economic structure and mindset of capitalist institutions are driving habitual and continuous economic growth. This is hastening the decline of our planet's resource base and ecological integrity. These are systemic problems, as is the increasing instability of our financial systems. What is possibly the most sobering reality about such systemic crises is that systems cannot be fixed. As much as we would like it to be otherwise, economic systems are too complex to be repaired or overhauled like lawnmower engines. The concept of fixing is mechanistic and just does not apply. We can no more fix the relentless drive for economic growth consumerism than we can fix human culture. Economies are systems of interconnectedness. Each aspect is connected to all other aspects, and each problem is a reflection of all other problems. As we see the problems of economic instability, global warming, and resource depletion intensify, we also that there is one single cause or culprit. These are systemic problems can be solved only by evolving systems, institutions, and collective consciousness. Many of us cling to the idea that our economies can always grow larger because we have been believing this for a very long time.

Economic activity has little meaning apart from the larger social context in which it takes place. People are not merely occupied in the gaining of a livelihood to the exclusion of everything else; our efforts to make a living are directed and conditioned by a whole spectrum of life, including core values, mores, and attitudes about what constitutes a good life, which are in turn conditioned by economic activity. Institutional economist Russell Dixon notes that, "Economics is, therefore, not a phase of life but a point of view – a way of studying human activity. To understand modern economic activity, which has become the dominant and directive force in our industrialized world, one must appreciate its place in the social entity called culture."[57]

The question of the broader purpose of an economic system has to arise within this entity called culture if it is truly going to change. Our engagement should be not to only strive to understand the purpose of economic systems, but to also attest that systemic change can alter the direction and purpose of the system—hopefully for the better. An individual today inhabits a world that was created by individuals who lived before this time. As we interact with this world, we can develop a certain karmic consciousness, such that certain things are categorized and typified in our individual minds, and we largely remain clueless of the fact that this is a collective phenomenon. Habit of thought can be rigid and going against the tide; however, will always have to be justified in a discursive context as members of society cling to the established way of things.

In this karmic sense, clinging to delusions can send us deeper into trouble. Institutions, societies, and cultures can sweep themselves into ruin by sheer karmic momentum. In the systems or holistic view, changes or events such as economic crises cannot be ascribed to any one particular element in the system. They are always perfect storms resulting from the multiple interactions among all the elements of the system: crises of consciousness as much as institutional and systemic.

In socially engaged Buddhist economics, there is hope. Just as there exist the seeds or instincts for pathological behavior in each of us, there exist also the seeds for healthful behavior. Veblen noted that just as people have the instincts to act in predatory ways, so too they have the instincts to act non-predatory ways. That is, Veblen saw that all people have the potential to be creative and to work toward advancement and wellbeing. Non-predatory, creative instincts foster inventiveness, technology, science, and genuine workmanship. For Veblen, however, these developments come about not as a result of desires for self-aggrandizement but, rather, by a kind of mindfulness toward wanting to create a better world. For this instinct to widely permeate contemporary culture and be free of institutionalized greed, aggression, and delusion in our consciousness, it would be necessary to have a radical shift in consciousness. That is, positive change would require a fundamental shift in ways of thinking about our world. This shift can be brought about through mindful practice and wisdom.

With this shift, healthy and creative ways of being will gradually be developed, and greed, aggression, and delusion will lose their grip and fade away. Nhat Hanh, Glassman and others who have done the self work *and* the work of crafting new institutions see that this work flows naturally once the individual self is liberated from the three fires.

THREE

Happiness failing on the world stage

In mainstream economic jargon, there is a long-established practice of referring to an economy as something analogous to an aircraft or locomotive. It is something that takes off, speeds up, slows down, overheats, and crashes. The central banks of the world are presumably at the controls, and are often reported as pushing and pulling monetary levers in order to control the momentum of the machine. Many economists, including those who stand outside the mainstream, talk of a "dashboard" of economic indicators. The image is one of a console of gauges or dials like those found in the cockpit of an aircraft, and there is much debate among economists and policymakers as to what things should be included on the dashboard. From the socially engaged Buddhist economics perspective, any dashboard would be a collection of indicators that best represent priorities established by the dominant economic institutions. In our current system, ongoing economic growth and wealth accumulation have been clearly established as priorities virtually everywhere. Naturally, the indicators that track this economic growth measured in financialized, market-oriented terms have become a priority.

Economic historian Dirk Philipsen traces the development of national income accounting and the rise of Gross Domestic Product (GDP) as *the* paramount indicator—the biggest and most central dial on the dashboard. GDP is a measurement of the market value of all finished goods and services produced and distributed in a country. Its development followed the rise to dominance of corporate capitalism. Philipsen writes, "Anything that could not be turned into a commodity, to be sold at a profit, became a cultural orphan, living precariously on the outskirts of the market." As the corporate agenda became society's agenda, the values of the market became the values of society. Buying, selling, financialization, commodification, self interest, and greed all rose in an upward swirl with conspicuous consumption, and in the collective mindset "neither good nor service, neither person nor skill, neither land nor resource, had value unless it was financialized in the market."[1]

Swept along with the drive to commodify everything is the standard assumption that more money means more happiness. Philipsen continues, "Indeed, the very definition of happiness and misery was increasingly reduced [in economic theory] to a cost–benefit analysis. ... The pursuit of happiness shriveled into the pursuit of purchasing power. The many flavors of life vanishing behind the stench of greed."[2] Profit accumulation and the culture of consumerism that serves it have become rationalized and normalized as necessitated by the priorities of capitalism, while other things like community, intellectual or spiritual development, and stewardship of the land essentially become irrelevant. The accumulation of money and profits presides as the taskmaster that drives growth in real production and all else is secondary and becomes marginalized on the dashboard of indicators.

But the growth imperative is much more than a standard valuation. It is a systemic necessity. The acorn from which the system has grown is the corporate imperative to generate returns for investors, but as this is diffused into the complex whole of culture not only are individual businesses driven to show bottom-line growth, but the entire hamster wheel system has come to depend on it. If corporate sales growth were to slow down, the source of funds for capital investment would begin to evaporate and new investments in capital stock would begin to fall. Falling investments would lead to an overall slowdown in production and sales. With falling sales, incomes would fall and a downward vicious circle of contraction would follow.

Contraction or recession, if sustained over time, can turn into a depression, and depression signifies systemic failure.

Recall the Buddhist concept in which everything in a system is dependent and contingent on everything else. In the economy, every economic element is dependent and contingent on every other economic element. If economic growth is the primary scorecard of success, then as sales activity grows there is a chorus of cheers from everywhere. Consumers look to growth because it means more goods and services available in markets. The labor force will experience growing job opportunities and rising incomes, public agencies receive more tax revenue to pay for police, schools, and roads. Nonprofits receive more donations and grants from rising incomes, bank loans are repaid, and, most importantly, investors' profits are realized. When growth turns to contraction (recession), however, trepidation is felt by all. Workers experience layoffs and default on their bank loans. Falling profits and share prices in the stock markets deplete the value of pension funds. Bankruptcies soar, along with government budget deficits and budget cuts. Without steady growth, the economic system withers away as a plant deprived of water and sunlight. For this reason, most observers are very hesitant to question this growth imperative and it is very difficult to envision life without the hamster wheel.

Economic growth indicators are artifacts in our evolving cultures. They are part of a two-way process in which the indicators both reflect and reinforce the underlying priorities of the economic system. The standard acceptance of ongoing economic growth has become deeply infused in Western culture and thought. Most would rather ignore the inevitable environmental damage that ongoing growth causes than question it. As long as people are feeling the benefits of growth, and those benefits outweigh the damage it causes, people are likely to embrace the idea that ongoing economic growth is always benign. If this changes, however, and if it becomes clear that the damage outweighs the benefits, then a crisis and reversal of perception will emerge. Such a shift in perception is bound to occur at some point because of the scientific fact that ongoing growth is simply not possible. Countries everywhere now share the same financial system booms and busts, and it is evident that most people seem to be more willing to accept illusions of growth such as financial market bubbles rather than directly face and reconcile this contradiction. In fact, as we will see in the next two chapters, managing and sustaining financial market bubbles has become the primary task of central banks everywhere.

To put this in perspective, if an economic system were centered around the institution of slavery, as in the 19th-century American South, for example, then established media would be reporting all kinds of statistics pertaining to chattel labor, such as conditions of slave labor markets, resources needed to maintain a slave labor force, and so on. By contrast, in an economic system structured around institutions that foster true environmental sustainability and social justice, the indicators would include stats on topsoil conservation, carbon dioxide emissions, alleviation of poverty, and closing wealth and income gaps. Indicators become key only when they reflect the established priorities of the dominant institutions, and as they do so, they reinforce and perpetuate those institutions.

As a reflection of priorities of the current economic system, GDP is reported quarterly, data on price inflation is reported monthly, and on the stock market is reported throughout every working day. Futurist and iconoclast Hazel Henderson notes that "Statistical indicators are the structural DNA codes of nations. They reflect a society's values and goals and become the key drivers of economic and technological choices."[3] Government agencies and nonprofits produce and maintain other statistical indicators of economic activity, although these are not exalted like GDP growth, which for nations everywhere stands on par with state security as a priority.

Gross domestic product

GDP accounting originated with the creation of the National Bureau of Economic Research (NBER) in New York in the early 1920s. Under the leadership of institutionalist economist Wesley Mitchell at Columbia University, the NBER was founded as a nonprofit corporation for conducting empirical research in economics and other social sciences.[4]

Although he was a student of Veblen's, Mitchell's work was quite different. Whereas Veblen's work is largely cultural criticism, Mitchell's work is directed toward the quantification of economic studies. He believed that quantification—statistical data gathering and modeling—could lead to the discovery of patterns of economic behavior and provide policymakers with the knowledge necessary to navigate a course of economic development. Mitchell was primarily concerned with business-cycle fluctuations as the system moved in up-and-down swings between periods of growth and recession. Mitchell devoted his life's work to gathering data on business-cycle swings in the interests of general human wellbeing, as wild booms and busts can cause severe and lasting hardships. Moreover, the timing for his work could not have been more ideal.

The newly elected American president, Herbert Hoover, expressed jubilant optimism about the benefits of capitalism in a speech given at Stanford University in 1928: "We in America today are nearer to the final triumph over poverty than ever before in the history of any land. The poorhouse is vanishing among us.... Given a chance to go forward with the policies of the last eight years, we shall soon with the help of God be in sight of the day when poverty will be banished from this nation."[5] On October 17, 1929, one week before the largest stock market crash in history, Yale economist Irving Fisher famously announced that "stock prices have reached a permanently high plateau and will rise a good deal higher within a few months." In the years and months leading up to the Great Depression, the economic machine was moving fast and hard.

Their jubilance was coming off the heady stock market boom-and-growth spurt of the Roaring Twenties in North America and Western Europe. But lurking just below the surface of all the happy talk was an extremely fragile system that eventually failed dramatically, and by the early 1930s the economic machine broke down. In response to the onset of the Great Depression, Mitchell sought to expand his research beyond business cycle movements to include a more comprehensive set of national economic data. To this effort he enlisted one of his graduate students and protégé, Simon Kuznets.

Kuznets, also an institutional economist, joined the NBER and embarked on the daunting task of defining the methodology and data collection necessary to compile and maintain comprehensive research on overall national economic activity. The young Kuznets was the perfect fit for this job as he shared with Mitchell a passion for rigorous mathematics and statistics, as well as the institutional economists' concern for the general wellbeing of the population. Kuznets, like Mitchell, was an advocate of social progress flowing from science, math, and technology, which would include rigorous social statistics.[6] He was genuinely concerned about the conditions of poverty that mounted in the depression years. Kuznets saw that the needs of the population provide the "touchstone by which the results of economic activity are to be judged ... serving the prevailing economic organization in terms of its returns."[7] The returns, for Kuznets, were quantifiable performance measures specifically defined in terms of human wellbeing. Rather than mine for data that would provide justification for the institutional status quo, which was the tendency of most economists at the time, Kuznets sought to hold prevailing institutions accountable to a comprehensive data set that measures performance in terms of the wellbeing of the population, not just profits and market expansion. This appeared particularly important for government policy, given the conditions of economic instability that had caused real hardship for a wide segment of the population. Kuznets' intention was to assess whether or not the system of established economic institutions was serving the people. And as it became clear that it was not, he would press for institutional change.

Kuznets' effort was herculean. Part of what made the effort so arduous was that the NBER survived on a very constricted budget and received little support from government, at least in the early stages. Leaders in government and the corporate world were not keenly interested in compiling data on social welfare, particularly when they indicated that capitalist institutions were failing spectacularly in this regard. That attitude changed somewhat, however, with the arrival of the Franklin Roosevelt administration in 1933.

By 1933, the US Department of Commerce had been given a mandate from Congress to provide a report on national income.[8] The purpose of the Congressional mandate was to provide statistical information about the economy so that policymakers could make informed decisions on what to do about the Depression, which seemed to be getting worse. Commerce began working in collaboration with Kuznets at the NBER, although with limited in staff and resources, to construct a national income and product accounting system. The main challenge for this project was that its mandate was not clear on what specific things needed to be measured that would provide both diagnostic and prescriptive data. What defines things like recessions, depressions, or systemic hardship, or even economic collapse had yet to be defined outside the Marxian categories of exploitation and class conflict, which were certain not to gain traction in the US Congress or Commerce Department.

From the outset, Kuznets was aiming to establish a very comprehensive system of accountability measured in terms of social welfare and social justice, to include things like opportunity, workplace conditions, safety, child labor practices, and consumer satisfaction. But the federal government vacillated because prioritizing what was to be included in the data set was becoming increasingly problematic and ideological. In other words, what Kuznets proposed to measure appeared radical, as compared to the one, single most important element in the capitalist universe—income growth. Kuznets became increasingly unsettled by what he perceived as the government and business community's indifference toward the genuine wellbeing of the population and that the project was sinking into a bog of political recalcitrance. Ultimately, given lack of support, Kuznets was forced by the US government to settle on what were prioritized as narrow criteria of market-based estimations of spending: consumer spending in the marketplace, business investment spending, government purchases in the marketplace, and international merchandise trade.

What was initially conceived by Mitchell and Kuznets as a tool for guiding policy directed toward helping people who were being trampled by economic crisis became coopted as a stethoscope for tracking business money making—wellbeing was to be inferred.[9] What it was decide to include or not to include in the measurement was not arbitrary, it was based on what passed the litmus test of relevance. And relevance in this case was determined by whether or not it served the effort to prop back up the fallen institutions of the dominant capitalist establishment. Nonetheless, Kuznets continued to press for the inclusion of information about income distribution. In the early Depression years, labor income was hit much harder than property income; blue collar more than professional; nonwhite more than white. But these and many other social indicators were ignored by the government.[10] Kuznets was exasperated that his work was becoming used as an instrument in the service of nothing more than "an acquisitive society."[11] Greed, which was still assumed to be the prime mover of economic growth, prevailed over wellbeing.

Kuznets' objections put to one side, his group produced a report in January, 1934. The contents of the report were devastating. Notwithstanding their limited resources, Kuznets and his group had compiled staggering amounts of data, and pursuant to their congressional mandate they published their report unpretentiously titled "National Income, 1929–1932." In his summary Kuznets wrote, "The economic changes that occurred in this country during the recent years are sufficiently striking to be apparent to any observer without the assistance of statistical measurements. There is considerable value, however, in checking the unarmed observation of even a careful student by light of a quantitative picture of our economy."[12]

What was shocking to the nation was the magnitude of the economic avalanche they had endured in the last five years. In *Table One* of the report, the data showed that income produced in the US economy (not adjusted for inflation) had moved from $83.0 billion in 1929 to $70.3 billion in 1930, $54.6 billion in 1931, and $39.4 billion in 1932.[13] That amounted to a 52.5 percent collapse in the span of four years. Another way to view the scale of the crash is that by 1932 the US economy was producing about 47.4 percent of what it had been producing in 1929 on the eve of the stock market collapse.

Immediately after its publication the report became a high-profile talking point in national policy discourse. Yet, Kuznets' own concerns about the fact that the report was an incomplete picture of economic wellbeing continued to be ignored by the academic and government establishments. The best that it could be hoped to gain from this work was that wellbeing could be inferred from market oriented data. The Commerce Department's position was that only material production based on market transactions would be measured, and from this narrow facet within a multifaceted spectrum of things, wellbeing would be inferred. From that point on, GDP became a symbol and priority of hamster wheel economics.

The war effort provided another institutional priority for national income accounts. During World War II, every nation involved in the conflagration had established an industrial policy of providing material support for the war effort. Historian Paul Kennedy, in his classic *The Rise and Fall of Great Powers* (1987), noted that the relative efficient utilization of a nation's economic resources among warring nations has a tremendous bearing on the outcome of the conflict.[14] Under the leadership of the Roosevelt administration, a monumental drive to expand the munitions industry was underfoot in the US. Again, Kuznets' team provided substantial statistical information about industrial capacity and what was possible, or not, in the manufacturing sector. The statistical data proved invaluable and it then became clear to other nations that such metrics were not just about fighting economic depressions, they were an integral part of modern wars of aggression. In the immediate post-war period, political and industry leaders everywhere began looking to GDP accounts and economic growth metrics as being of paramount national importance as well as a new ideology. In the GDP ideology, growth is seen as a panacea for nearly every social, economic, or political problem. Maldistribution of income, poverty, and even environmental problems are problems that can be solved or ameliorated with GDP growth. In this view, not only does a rising tide lift all boats, it is salvation for us all.

It is understandable that national leaders would draw such conclusions. No one wanted to revisit the horrors brought on by the Depression. It became clear to those looking in retrospect that the structural collapse of economies, particularly in Europe, created the fertile breeding grounds for the fascist movement.

Political leaders were resolute on their national priority agendas to keep the economic growth machine running round the clock. GDP became a fixture in the established structures of political and economic power. Although Kuznets continued to raise objections about the intentions of GDP calculations, those objections were shoved aside. GDP income accounts, methods, and data developed into an international standard that was codified by the United Nations, the International Monetary Fund, and the World Bank.[15]

GDP growth is now like a scoreboard at a sporting event on which every nation, capitalist or otherwise, tracks its successes and failures. It symbolizes success wrought within a system that prioritizes wealth expansion above all else, even total environmental ruination. Nonetheless, it would seem that only those suffering from the most severe delusional impairment are unable to see the environmental damage that economic rapaciousness has done and will continue to do.

In 2012, NASA scientist James Hansen published an editorial piece on climate change in the *Washington Post* titled "Climate Change Worse Than We Thought."[16] He tells of environmental conditions of heat waves and drought attributed to climate change, as well as extreme weather events that are becoming more frequent and growing in severity. But still, people in general tend to ignore the systemic nature of all this and look upon climate change as if it were something strange, an aberration, even though scientists have been showing us data and issuing warnings for decades. Widespread denial lends credence to the idea that the collective consciousness remains trapped.

Kuznets, Mitchell, and the others who created national income accounting systems did so out of a genuine concern for human wellbeing, but their concerns were swept aside. Not, however, without dissent. It did not take long for thoughtful observers to do the math and conclude that the project of endless growth on a limited resource base is madness. International forums on topics regarding sustainability and human rights began questioning the endless growth model and suggesting that nations should pursue different ways of assessing wellbeing outside the framework of growth in economic output. The

Genuine Progress Indicator, the Happy Planet Index, and Gross National Happiness are just a few examples.

Alternatives to GDP

Ultimately, any attempt to measure the wellbeing of the population is going to be subjective and value based. Take any of these measures and stand them alongside GDP and they will equally show subjectivity in their construction. As Kuznets frequently warned, what national income accounts include or exclude is subjective and heavily calculated with a pro-market bias and ignores significant factors that give a much clearer indication of wellbeing. For example, if a group of people from the same neighborhood build a playground for their children, this community effort is not counted in GDP. If the same work is done by a private contractor doing the work for profit, then this market-based effort is counted. If an oil company spills oil into the sea, then cleans up the spill, the costs of the cleaning are counted in GDP as part of the cost of oil sold in the open market. If people in the area where the oil was spilled do the cleanup, it is not counted. As an alternative, and perhaps to derive a more detailed statistical picture, various organizations have been working internationally on developing alternative metrics.

The Happy Planet Index

One such metric is the Happy Planet Index (HPI). The HPI is a relatively new indicator developed by the New Economics Foundation, an independent think-tank founded in the UK in 1986.[17] The Foundation has published three reports since it began constructing the HPI in 2006. It is an efficiency measure in which experienced wellbeing multiplied by life expectancy is expressed as a ratio to ecological footprint:

$$\text{Happy Planet Index} = \frac{(\text{experienced wellbeing} \times \text{life expectancy})}{(\text{ecological footprint})}$$

That is, it measures the length and quality of human life per unit of anthropogenic impact.[18] The higher the number, the better people's lives relative to the stress they place on the planet. The "experienced wellbeing" component of the metric is derived from data gathered in the Gallup World Poll, which uses questionnaires conducted with representative samples of a country's population. The poll uses simple "ladder of life" questions scaled from 0 to 10, in which 0 indicates that the respondent lives in the worst possible life situation and 10 indicates the best possible situation. The "life expectancy" component is derived from the United Nations Development Program Human Development Report and estimates the average lifespan of people in each country. The ecological footprint component is derived from the data reported in the Global Footprint Networks National Footprint and measures the amount of land and natural resources in a country that is used up by the population. As of this writing, the most recent report was released in 2012. Of 151 countries documented in the HPI, the highest-ranking were Costa Rica, Vietnam, and Colombia. The USA ranked 105th, due largely to is heavy ecological footprint.[19] The New Economics Foundation cautions that its reports are works in progress and important aspects are not counted, such human rights, income and wealth distribution, and access to opportunity.

The Genuine Progress Indicator (GPI)

Another alternative metric is the Genuine Progress Indicator (GPI). An American think-tank, Redefining Progress, first introduced GPI as an alternative to GDP in the US in 1995, and has since updated and developed the indicator. Inspiration for the GPI came from earlier iterations. The Club of Rome economists William Nordhaus and James Tobin published a discussion paper at Yale University titled "Is Growth Obsolete" back in the 1970s. The authors suggested an alternative index called the Measure of Economic Welfare (MEW).[20] MEW sought to modify national income accounting by adding the value of leisure time and unpaid work like household production and subtracting the cost of environmental damage. In 1989 the

Index of Sustainable Economic Welfare, proposed by ecological economist Herman Daly and theologian Clifford Cobb in their path-breaking book, *For The Common Good*, expanded on the MEW and provided the groundwork for the GPI.[21] The GPI starts with GDP data but then adjusts the numbers based on criteria not included in GDP. Certain production that is real but not counted in GDP is added back in, such as community projects (mentioned above) or household or natural production where goods and services are produced but not for the market. It also subtracts real costs not factored in GDP, such as resource depletion, crime, ozone depletion, pollution (most significant being carbon dioxide emissions), loss of farmland, and others. In total there 26 variables that either add to or subtract from GDP to derive the GPI.[22]

The methodological challenges of quantifying such a vast array of pluses and minuses aside, the result is an index of wellbeing that points in a very different direction than GDP. For the US in the years between 1950 and 2004, inflation-adjusted GPI increased from $1.31 trillion to $4.42 trillion, whereas GDP for those same years grew from $1.78 trillion to $10.76 trillion.[23] The principal difference between the two indices indicates the environmental negatives.

Indicators are important as they can tell us how well or how poorly we are accomplishing the things that are established priorities. But they do not set goals, methods, policy, or technology. These stem from social will, or fail to become manifest because of the lack of will. GDP is a measure of output, and as such it is a standard indicator of economic performance on the hamster wheel. But these standard assertions do not arise from the statistics themselves, they arise from the values and institutions of society. GDP statistics do not make people want growth. People want growth because it is part of the popular mindset to demand a share of whatever prosperity that might come from growth. Simply put, more growth is believed to equal more happiness. But there remains much that is not reflected in GDP numbers, not the least of which is what it means to be happy. That is not to say that we do not address quality-of-life issues or try to measure them; rather, it is to say that they are eclipsed by the much more deeply entrenched growth imperative. In this sense, societies must decide what goals are most important for wellbeing and then devise the metrics to track their performance in achieving these goals. This is what the tiny Buddhist kingdom of Bhutan, nestling in the eastern range of the Himalayas, has done like no other.

Gross National Happiness

Recall that Thich Nhat Hanh and Bernie Glassman were inspired by Buddhist philosophy and practice to become agents of change in their society or community. This also was the inspiration for the conception of Gross National Happiness (GNH) by the fourth king of Bhutan, HM Jigme Singye Wangchuck. King Wangchuck became Bhutan's "dragon king," or monarch, at the age of 16 in 1972 and was crowned in 1974, about the same time that Schumacher's *Small is Beautiful* was published.

According to Dasho Karma Ura, president of the Center of Bhutan Studies (CBS) at Thimphu, Bhutan, "GNH should be considered as a Buddhist society's equivalent of the social contract, where citizens pursue collective happiness."[24] The pursuit of collective rather than individual happiness emphasizes the wellbeing of the social whole, and this became codified into Bhutan's law. According to the constitution of Bhutan, the government is responsible "to promote those conditions that will enable the pursuit of Gross National Happiness."[25] GHN as a measure of the overall wellbeing of Bhutan's society thus became institutionalized, with four principles of governance: equitable economic development, environmental preservation, cultural resilience, and good governance.[26] Socially engaged Buddhism in Bhutan is not merely another anecdote, it is a national movement and its goals and priorities stand in stark contrast to those of Western capitalistic societies.

The four principles have become what the Bhutanese call the "four pillars," on which government policy has been built with the aim of making a healthier and genuinely happier population. They are inseparable from Bhutan's Buddhist heritage and GNH has been identified by its king as a way to create a more enlightened Buddhist society in which the happiness and wellbeing of all people is the ultimate purpose of governance.[27] King Wangchuck's view first drew international attention in 1986 when he was reported in the *Financial Times* as saying, "Gross National Happiness is more important than Gross National Product." His comments highlighted the country's commitment to building an economy that would elevate Buddhist spiritually inspired values over Western values based on materialism and consumerism.[28] Ura notes that GNH "measures the quality of a country in a more holistic way [than GNP] and believes that the beneficial development of human society takes place when material and spiritual development occur side by side to complement and reinforce each other."[29] The constitution of Bhutan makes clear that there is a distinction between happiness in this sense, grounded in genuine wellbeing, and the fleeting, pleasurable "feel good" often associated with that term in the Western conception. The constitution states: "We know that true abiding happiness cannot exist while others suffer, and comes only from serving others, living in harmony with nature, and realizing our innate wisdom and the true and brilliant nature of our own minds."[30]

Echoing Nhat Hanh's conception of interbeing, Ura contends that compassion is an emotion that springs naturally from a mindset in which people generally see themselves living in a world where everything is connected to everything else. "By being convinced and informed about interdependence, compassion should naturally arise as a person recognizes that his happiness is dependent on all other creatures' welfare. Without this basic understanding, the individual sinks into poor motivation and weaknesses." Poor motivations in the tradition of Buddhist economics are those that are defiled by greed, aggression, and delusion. Ura concludes that by "recognizing the true nature of interdependence, one can see that all karma is collective, that all enlightenment is collective, and therefore that happiness and the policies required to promote it must be oriented toward collective achievement."[31]

It is from the Buddhist sensibilities of interdependence, wholesome motivation, and the responsibility of government to help alleviate suffering among its people that the CBS continues to evolve its Gross National Happiness metric, using data from questionnaires and sophisticated statistical modelling. The goal of the work is to develop and maintain a metric that more accurately reflects the values of the Bhutanese way of life. It is built on the principle that the development of people and their society cannot be limited to material interpretations of wellbeing derived from economic growth. Rather, it takes a more comprehensive, holistic view that balances standard economic needs with social, cultural, and environmental needs.

GNH is further conceived from the principle of karma. With karmic volition, either healthful or pathological qualities can suffuse the world and future generations, depending on the actions we take now. As such, the GNH model holds that a country's economic activity should not be at the cost of suffering for future generations, other societies, or other sentient beings. Expressing this sentiment, Bhutan's minister of education, Thakur Singh Powdyel, comments, "It's easy to mine the land and fish the seas and get rich ... Yet we believe you cannot have a prosperous nation in the long run that does not conserve its natural environment or take care of the wellbeing of its people, which is being borne out by what is happening to the outside world."[32]

With these insights in place, the architects of the GNH evolved their metric beyond the original four pillars of the social contract to include things like health, education, use of time, psychological wellbeing, and community vitality. Between 2005, when Bhutan conducted its first GNH survey, and 2010, when the most comprehensive report (as of this writing) was compiled, the concept of GNH finally developed into a GNH Index. It functions as a composite indicator covering a wide range of socio-economic data which together shine a light on the wellbeing of the population, clustered into nine domains: psychological wellbeing, use of time, vitality of community, cultural diversity, ecological resilience, material living standards, health, education, and good governance. These nine domains are further broken down into 33 more specific subcategories, which themselves are divided further into 124 variables upon which information is collected through survey research. Each of the variables is weighted numerically according to its estimated impact: the more subjective the data, the lighter the numerical weight.[33]

Psychological wellbeing

This domain has to do with cognitive and subjective evaluation of one's own feeling of satisfaction overall. Although all governments to some degree maintain data on social indicators such as crime, divorce, or drug abuse, it is rare to find a systematic assessment of the population's emotional wellbeing. The CBS attempts to discern between momentary experiences of joy and more structural conditions of life satisfaction, emotional balance between things like generosity, compassion, or calmness and negative things like jealousy, frustration, or greed. Recall that in Buddhist economics there is a strong line of causality between deep psychic defilement and motivations that drive human behavior: "the negative emotions may be more accurately called disturbing emotions during which people cannot think with much clarity and that might lead often to formations of poor intentions." Not surprisingly, therefore spiritual practices, including meditation and prayer, stand as a normative basis for psychological wellbeing for the Bhutanese. To give weight to the data collected, the CBS surveys also try to assess how frequently the respondents experience either positive or negative emotions.

Standard of living

This domain is an extension of the original pillar of equitable economic development. In originates from a commitment to equitable and sustainable socio-economic development. Economic activities are to be guided by conditions of environmental sustainability and social equity. Accordingly, the government targets less environmentally damaging industries for investment. Energy development plans, for example, target hydroelectric power rather than more environmentally damaging industries such as mining or logging. Economic production and consumption are the means to the end of meeting material needs in such a way as to enhance a sense of wellbeing: housing security, assets used for livelihoods, and income to support daily expenditures and food security; hardships are due to lack of these things for individuals or households. The CBS gathers data on the basic elements of food security, housing, financial security or hardship both for individuals and for households. This is explored with the consideration that rising levels of production and consumption do not necessarily correlate with happiness.

Good governance

For GNH, good governance mean having well-functioning governmental institutions that are efficient and free from corruption, and that exist to serve the population. The survey evaluates the population's perception of how well the government provides safety, justice, infrastructure, clean water, education, protection of human rights, and other services. Respondents also evaluate trust, transparency in the use of public resources, and accountability. This assessment also surveys to what extent individuals participate in the political process. As such, accountability and citizen participation are considered inseparable for good governance (it should be noted here that in 2008 Bhutan made the transition to a constitutional monarchy, thus increasing the democratic political enfranchisement to the population). The public good of human happiness is predicated, at least in part, on having a system of government that is committed to genuine wellbeing. It is a long-standing tradition of Bhutan's monarchy that the government holds a mandate to keep its population happy.

Health

Of course the health of the population are inseparable from happiness. Happiness can lead to better health and better health can promote happiness. The CBS maintains a holistic view of these relationships in that good health can be maintained through a balance of body, mind, and social relationships, and relationships between people and their natural surroundings. Respondents are asked questions about their knowledge of infectious diseases and diet. They are also asked to assess their own health, ranging from poor to excellent, and how frequently they experience their condition as good or bad. The surveys probe for indications of depression, disabilities, anxiety, and other factors that can give an indication of overall health.

Education

The CBS takes a fairly comprehensive and holistic view of education. Rather than focusing exclusively on standardized test results, dropout rates, literacy, or math and science proficiency as most countries do, students are asked about their inspiration based on a broader connection to their culture. The student curriculum includes the standard subjects of math, science, history and so on, but these topics are situated on a firm cultural foundation of their cultural heritage, community values, and skillsets rooted in traditional practices specific to a particular region or environment. The assessment probes how well students are trained in language, folk traditions, historical literacy, and artisanal skills. Moral values and creative expression are also emphasized. The focus of the CBS assessment of education is not so much on a utilitarian path toward career success as one would see in the West but, rather, on collective wellbeing through moral education.

Community vitality

This domain assesses the strengths and weaknesses of relationships among people in each community. It assesses for things like the level of trust among community members, sense of belonging or alienation, safety or danger, sharing or selfishness. All of these elements are examined in the GNH rubric as either contributing to or taking away from quality of life and the vitality of a community. A community that measures itself narrowly on the basis of material goods and income (poor or affluent) can potentially lead to diminished sense of collective wellbeing as the Bhutan see these as rather narrow criteria for assessing the vibrancy and life of a community.

Cultural diversity and resilience

Overlapping with the education domain, one of the CBS's primary goals is to assess how well its culture is surviving. For the people of Bhutan, cultivating a living cultural heritage based on Buddhist philosophy and practice sustains a framework that also guides their economic activity and thinking. Compassion, tolerance, and respect for all sentient beings underpin the value of coexistence, both among people and between them and nature. Sustainable living comes naturally in a culture that esteems such coexistence and tolerance as high virtues. The Bhutanese foster these virtues through regular festivals, public events, and other social institutions. Bhutan is not alone in its feeling of a loss of cultural identity in a world where perhaps one of the biggest threats stemming from economic globalization is the threat of cultural homogenization wrought by the hegemony of American media and its associated consumer culture. There is perhaps much that the rest of the world can learn from this domain of Bhutan's GNH. Resilience is the ability to withstand being swallowed up in the incredible homogenizing forces of so-called modernity, but diversity is about respecting cultural heterogeneity.

Time use

GNH incorporates a time diary in which survey respondents provide information on how they spend their time during a typical 24-hour period. Work and productivity are obviously important for any economic indicator, but this metric also places importance on leisure and recreation. The survey administers multiple categories of time use, including work, recreation, sleep, meditation. The results are important for measuring wellbeing as an efficiency ratio like the HPI—how much is being contributed or enjoyed in the material sense, relative to how much time is spent being part of the production/consumption system.

Ecological diversity and resilience

GNH incorporates an ecological impact assessment in its data set. The Buddhist perspective of coexistence is predicated on the idea that we all share the same habitat and the same karmic fate. Humans and nature form a partnership of coexistence. Land, trees, water, and other elements of our natural surroundings are not merely a stockpile of resources to be exploited for human purposes. Rather, we rely on nature for our sustenance, comfort, and aesthetic beauty, but must recognize our own responsibility for stewardship. As such, conservation of forests and watersheds is a national priority in Bhutan and is a fundamental tenet of its economic development philosophy of happiness. The GNH survey assesses respondents' environmental awareness, their sense of responsibility for the preservation of wildlife, and their understanding of predatory or aggressive species. In questions directed at city dwellers respondents are asked about their concerns about traffic congestion, noise, urban sprawl, and pollution. This domain emerges directly from the Buddhist concept of interbeing in the sense that citizens are assessed on their awareness of how they make contributions in a broader sense that leads to individual wellbeing. By doing so, they create an institutional context that encourages citizens to contribute to the protection of the natural environment, conservation of the rich biodiversity of Bhutan, and prevention of all forms of ecological degradation including noise, visual, and physical pollution.

In order to create the final composite indicator, the GNH sets a cutoff at 66 percent. This means that the population must have demonstrated sufficiency in 66 percent of the 124 variables in order to be certified as "happy." The primary objective of the GNH survey is to weigh the information gathered from these nine domains according to significance based on both subjective and objective factors and to derive a composite number between

0 and 1. To derive this composite, the CBS uses sophisticated statistical modelling techniques and sufficiency thresholds for each category that is measured. The composite provides a basic statement about the level of GNH, in which 0 indicates a state of perfect unhappiness and 1 indicates perfect happiness. Of course, the number will always be somewhere between the two extremes.

The 2010 GNH Index for Bhutan was .743. This indicates that within the nine domains and all the subcategories of all the domains the respondents reported that their state of happiness was above what would be considered a sufficiency threshold. The key significance of this number is that is serves as a benchmark for trend data over time.

But there is much more to the surveys in terms of trend data. For example, the 2010 survey also shows that men tend to be happier than women, urban dwellers are happier than rural dwellers (although rural areas scored higher on community vitality), educated people are happier than uneducated, certain professions generate more happiness than others, and certain towns have happier inhabitants than others. In time, as the index either rises, falls, or stays the same, it will provide policymakers with information for setting policy guidelines to replicate success or for channeling resources into areas that need to be worked on. Bhutan's policymaking branch of government, the GNH Commission, uses GNH data to craft policies that are intended to "give physical expression to ensuring that our development is on the GNH path."[34]

Beyond its implications for policy, GNH is a symbol of cultural and institutional significance. It embodies the expression of the former monarch's statement that Gross National Product is less important than Gross National Happiness. GNH is a statement that both sublimates and institutionalizes the preservation of cultural forms, natural environment, health, accountable government, not the endless expansion of national output. Hamster wheel economics and the cynical rationalizations of greed that are so deeply established Western institutions cannot be reconciled with the values that are embodied in GNH.

GNH has attracted much attention in North America and Western Europe among progressive and environmental groups. Many have tried constructing their own versions alongside the HPI and GPI. But this raises questions about the viability of such indexes in countries that lack the cultural and political will to adopt fundamentally different ways of behaving economically. It becomes a chicken and egg dilemma in the sense of determining what steps need to be taken. Can societies change their economic institutions and priorities by changing their national economic metrics? Or must societies first change their economic institutions and priorities, and the appropriate metrics will follow naturally? These questions are open to debate and many in the West who find inspiration in Bhutan's initiative believe that adopting new metrics can lead to changes in economic activity. But I believe it is the latter. Institutional change has to come first.

In 2009, the Organisation for Economic Co-operation and Development unveiled the Global Project, which seeks to help develop similar, alternative indicators of wellbeing "beyond GDP." The project aims to develop such an indicator through mindful reflection on the subjective question of whether or not "life is getting better."[35] That same year, then French president Nicolas Sarkozy gathered a Commission on the Measurement of Economic Performance and Social Progress.[36] As chair of the Commission, Nobel prize-winning economist Joseph Stiglitz emphasizes alternative metrics that will question and evaluate traditional GDP measurements, develop other frameworks for broader measurements, and incorporate into them environmental sustainability. The underlying assumption of these and similar initiatives is that by changing what we measure we will change what we do—hopefully for the better. Stiglitz notes, "We look at numbers that tell us what we are doing. If those numbers don't reflect what we care about, we make decisions that actually make us worse off."[37]

Stiglitz's logic, however, could be like putting wagons before horses. The assumption among so many advocates of alternative indicators is that alternative indicators will inspire alternative policy measures, which will move society toward wellbeing. But Simon Kuznets observed how the original intention of national income accounting was mangled by politics. He concluded that the social metric he wanted to create was not consistent with the "acquisitive society." Greed and wellbeing are not compatible ends, and in an economic society in which greed is held to be the prevailing mover of activity, alternative indicators will always be pushed to the margins—which is where they currently are.

By changing our institutions and transforming how we think and act economically, we will establish new priorities. We will redefine what it is that "we care about," as Stiglitz puts it. It is undeniable that alternative indicators can bring useful information to light and direct policy. But policy changes, in order to be substantial and not merely symbolic, must be structured around real institutional changes with different priorities that will give the alternative indicators relevance. Otherwise, the HPI, GPI, and GNH will continue to stand bashfully on the sidelines.

Institutional changes will give impetus to alternative systems of measurement, which in turn will reinforce the mission of institutional change. This is the key difference from Bhutan. Bhutan's particular culture and legal institutions are such that the GNH project was conceived, implemented, and established to make collective wellbeing a national priority. Collective wellbeing is something that the Bhutanese already care about, which contrasts with the prioritization of endless growth, money-making, and consumer culture in Western economic systems.

The government of Bhutan is socially engaged, and it appealed to the world community by gently encouraging nations everywhere to continue reflecting on their priorities.

Bhutan and the United Nations resolution on happiness

The United Nations seems to have a propensity for convening summits that inevitably lead nowhere. The UN Conference on Environment and Development (1992), the Millennium Summit (2000), the World Summit on Sustainable Development (2002), and the United Nations Conference on Sustainable Development (2012) all have something in common: they all made bold declarations for change, and equally avoided addressing the real institutional forces that prevent this change from being realized. I had a chance to witness this at first hand.

In January, 2012, I received a letter from Jigme Thinley, Prime Minister of Bhutan, inviting me to come to the United Nations headquarters in New York to join a task force. The task force was to meet in April and hold a three-day brainstorming session on stitching together a new economic paradigm as part of the implementation of a previous nonbinding UN resolution titled "Happiness: Towards a Holistic Approach to Development," sponsored principally by Bhutan. By that time the small Himalayan kingdom had been in the world limelight for some years as a result of its GNH initiative.

In 2011, Bhutan and 68 other sponsoring nations, including France, Germany, Italy, and the UK (but not the United States), had sought to develop an "entirely new economic paradigm and not just variations on themes of the old paradigm."[38] The sponsors of the resolution noted that "the Gross Domestic Product indicator by nature was not designed to and does not adequately reflect the happiness and well-being of people in a country." And, perhaps more urgently, the GDP indicator perpetuates economic activity that is damaging and unsustainable. Although it was not stated explicitly, the message was that GDP was becoming obsolete as a measure of wellbeing, for the main reason that growth in output has been pushed beyond the planet's capacity to sustain it. By urging the world community to adopt a more holistic dashboard of indicators that would elevate sustainable development, poverty eradication, and other measurements of human wellbeing, the sponsors hoped to orchestrate a fundamental shift in national economic policies. As they submitted their resolution to the General Assembly for a vote, they encouraged those member states that had already begun the process of developing those new indicators and policies "to share information with the Secretary General as a contribution to the United Nations development agenda, including those who have been working on, and making progress with, the Millennium Development Goals." In July 2011, the resolution was passed unanimously by the 193 member states and formally adopted by the UN.[39]

Once the resolution was passed, the UN convened a task force led by Bhutan and set a two-year timeline for its implementation. The first step in that process was a series of meetings with economists, spiritual and civic leaders, and others at the UN headquarters in New York in April, 2012 to work out the details of this new economic framework for the world community. The three-day session in which I was invited to participate was called a "High Level Meeting on Wellbeing and Happiness: Defining a New Economic Paradigm."

The economist Jeffrey Sachs was among the first to address the session. He presented a mainstream economist's arguments for better technology that would stimulate the rising tide of growth. The problem, according to Sachs, is that we are working with old growth models. Accordingly, with better pro-growth models enhanced by modern technology, nations can always continue to grow toward wellbeing. Following soon after Sachs, Hunter Lovins, an advocate of "natural capitalism," expressed the triple-bottom-line contention that environmentally sustainable businesses are more profitable than others, and spoke about how a new paradigm should be made more inclusive and embrace Wall Street companies like Goldman Sachs—which Lovins considers to be a sustainable enterprise. It soon became evident that with these business-as-usual sensibilities on the table, it would be difficult for a new paradigm to be forthcoming.

Nonetheless, the starting place for the happiness-based framework was based on a rubric of genuinely sustainable wellbeing that is embedded in four foundational principles that mirror the original pillars of GNH: (1) happiness and wellbeing rooted in human health, secure livelihoods, diverse spiritual practices, and vibrant cultural traditions; (2) ecological sustainability in the true sense of keeping economic activity contained within the planet's capacity to sustain it; (3) fair distribution of wealth and resources both within and among nations, and a particular commitment to improving conditions of those living in abject poverty; (4) efficient use of resources as a model of global resource stewardship. With these principles in mind, all participants were asked to submit a general proposal for what elements should be included in the new paradigm, prior to the more specific brainstorming sessions.

For my part, I submitted a five-part proposal based on a Schumacherian, socially engaged Buddhist economics approach. It highlighted the notion that nations everywhere are at a crossroads where they must choose either to begin making a fundamental transition by developing a new paradigm or to brace themselves for the full-blown consequences of global warming, global resource depletion, and financial system instability. Such a transition would have to be based on the solid foundation of an entirely new set of assumptions and principles that would set it apart from standard economics, that would be developed to serve a very different set of priorities, and would be governed by very different institutions from those that currently dominate the global economy. (See Appendix.)

After we had submitted our proposals for the new paradigm, the next step involved forming a smaller group called "experts" to develop the details of what the new framework should look like and how it should be implemented. I and about 50 others who were assigned to this group spent the second day of the meeting hammering out the details of the economic paradigm. We spent the first part of the day discussing general aspects, and later split into subgroups to focus on a range of specifics. My job was to lead a subgroup discussion on developing new financial institutions.

The consensus of the group was that the new paradigm needed to be based partially on a careful consideration of the institutions that govern money, banking, and finance. We suggested that one area of development should be to craft a new set of financial institutions, called "Banks for Right Livelihood," that would be specifically chartered to serve the four dimensions of wellbeing, and that would include an international institution standing as an alternative to the World Bank and the International Monetary Fund, which represent old-paradigm economics. I will return to this Right Livelihood banking in more detail in a later chapter. Briefly, however, our subgroup's recommendation was that Right Livelihood institutions could be chartered with the following provisions:

- To have a clearly defined democratic orientation in which voting rights and decision-making powers are broadly and democratically extended rather than limited to the most powerful economies of the world.

- To provide credit and/or equity to finance initiatives that would help communities become less dependent on fossil fuels, such as renewable and efficient energy development projects, public transportation and infrastructure, and environmentally sustainable technologies, and to foster the development of local or place-based economies, small-scale cooperatives, and microfinancing.

- To create financial instruments that would source funding from both signatory governments and private sector institutions that are committed to the four dimensions of the resolution.

- To explore how local communities can create their own alternative monetary institutions that break away from the ever-expanding mountain of debt and move toward more values based or skills based models.

Virtually all of our suggestions for institutional change were rejected outright by the American and European leaders of the experts' group. Instead, what was adopted favored the expediency of working within the pre-established institutional framework of the global economy, and with conventional, mainstream economics, market-based initiatives, and policies aligned with the Millennium Development Goals.

Prime Minister Thinley's instructions to create an entirely new economic paradigm and not just variations on themes of the old paradigm were ignored and old-paradigm thinking won out. The only aspect the framework that would be considered "new paradigm" was an emphasis on tweaking the dashboard of metrics to include economic performance measures modeled after Bhutan's GNH. Alternative indicators, however, such as the Genuine Progress Index (GPI), have been around for decades and have been largely ignored because they do not cohere with established institutional priorities of endless economic growth and the dream of endless accumulation of wealth.

Dashboards showing social and environmental data already exist in most places. Governments, nonprofits, health or educational organizations maintain vast statistical databases on social, health, and environmental indicators. These statistics are useful tools to be used in efforts to effect change, but they do not change economic systems by themselves: societies do. Statistical evidence abounds for the existence of things like global warming, its anthropogenic nature, global resource depletion, and financial system instability of increasing magnitude. Yet the record of accomplishment of international resolutions to change any of these things remains negligible. The reason for this is not because there are not enough gauges on the dashboard, but because institutional change remains off the table. As long as institutional transformation remains marginalized so will the steps we need to take to affect real change, the damage will continue. This reality was ignored as Bhutan's resolution was folded into the pre-established Millennium Development.

In September 2000, world leaders gathered in New York for a three-day meeting at the United Nations for a conference called the "Millennium Summit." The aim of this meeting was to ratify the United Nations Millennium Declaration, which was passed unanimously and included objectives of peace, human rights, security, and economic development for those countries most languishing in poverty. The Millennium Declaration established eight core Millennium Development Goals (MDGs) aimed at improving health and education, and alleviating poverty. The goals were pious, but the trouble lurked in the details, which stipulate that these goals would be realized through a global system of markets and market based incentives organized through the WTO, IMF, World Bank and transnational corporations.[40]

In other words, the MDGs were set against a backdrop of established capitalistic institutional structures that not only resist change but also are instrumental in causing many of the very problems that the goals were hoped to remedy. We would be hard pressed to find a sane person who would argue against reducing poverty, but it is questionable logic to argue that this can be achieved through more economic growth in a world already facing severe limits to growth and climate change. Without specific plans for reforming or reinventing the institutions that cause these problems, the goals are hollow.

Samir Amin, in an article titled "Millennium Development Goals: A Critique from the South," notes that "A critical examination of the formulation of the goals as well as the definition of the means that would be required to implement them can only lead to the conclusion that the MDGs cannot be taken seriously." Amin reflects the concern that many of who worked on the Bhutan initiative at the UN that pious-sounding declarations are not firm commitments to change, particularly when they are captured in a system dominated by business as usual. He concludes that, "the question must be asked: are not the authors of the document actually pursuing other priorities that have nothing to do with 'poverty reduction' and all the rest? In this case, should the exercise not be described as pure hypocrisy, as pulling the wool over the eyes of those who are being forced to accept the dictates of liberalism in the service of the quite particular and exclusive interests of dominant globalized capital?"[41]

The Rio Plus 20 Failure

Bhutan's initiative was presented at the second Earth Summit in Rio de Janiero in June, 2012, also known as "Rio Plus 20." As they had done at the first Earth Summit 20 years earlier and with the MDGs, the member states of the UN General Assembly signed up to a set of sustainable development goals. The primary goals were to make environmental management stronger and more effective, to strengthen the safeguards that protect our oceans, to lock down good security for the world's human population, and to shift to a green economy. The outcome of the 10-day meeting was a document titled "The Future We Want." Much of the substance of the document is a renewed commitment to the 1992 Rio principles that were acknowledged, and then ignored, along with so many other declarations that have been brought with a great fanfare onto the world stage.

"The Future We Want" also makes a plea for support and participation from the world's population, labor organizations, NGOs, local and national governments, business and industry, and the scientific community, and a special plea to business: "We acknowledge the important role of the private sector in moving towards sustainability. We strongly encourage businesses and industry to show leadership in advancing a green economy ..."[42]

Rio Plus 20 was universally recognized as a failure. The meeting itself was marred by political controversy about the fact that Barack Obama, Angela Merkel, and David Cameron were conspicuously absent. "The Future We Want" report was immediately criticized for its tepid and vague statements and absence of details on how the world would do things differently to avoid the failures following the last Earth Summit. This came into clear view at the Rio Plus 20 conference in June, 2012. Reporting on the Rio Plus 20 meeting for the *Huffington Post*, journalist and activist Sunita Narain asks an important question, "How can the world move towards sustainable production and sustainable consumption while ensuring growth for all?" The most realistic answer to her question is that the world cannot. Given the stark reality of the choice between one or the other, the compass inevitably points in the direction of the priorities established by the world's dominant and most powerful institutions, which means growth for some, but not for most.[43]

After Rio Plus 20, the effort spearheaded by Bhutan to build a new approach to economic development for the world community evaporated. But it would be unfair to say that it was for naught. By highlighting GNH and taking it to United Nations and to Brazil, the metric not only gained much exposure and attention, it raised more questions about what lies underneath its development.

Whether GDP or GNH, these are metrics intended for tracking progress toward a previously defined set of outcomes and priorities. It might be an oversimplification to say that one represents greed and the other wellbeing. But it is fair to say that one represents business as usual and the other represents a different set of practices and values altogether. It is not necessary to adopt GNH as our paramount economic indicator for economic wellbeing, but without a real commitment to changing our practices and values, which is centered on changing our economic institutions, such an indicator remains on the sidelines. Recall that when Nordhaus and Tobin questioned the connection between GDP and wellbeing decades ago, concerns were mostly ignored just as the political establishment ignored

Kuznets. Their ideas of wellbeing were not consistent with established norm and the idolatry of money, profit, growth, and consumerism. If these represent business as usual, then the corroborating "metrics as usual" would be GDP, stock prices, bond rates, and so on that are reported in the daily media.

The realization of "the future we want" would depend on a vastly different set of institutions than those that now govern global economic processes. This would require turning economic priorities away from business as usual steered by corporate executives, speculators, and their servants in government; and looking instead to creative workers and entrepreneurs who are able to envisage healthier futures brought about by institutional and systemic change that aims to redirect economic activity.

That future is still a long way off. In the meantime, according to Dirk Philipsen, "the economy has taken on a life of its own.... Separate from us yet also, in a strange twist of logic, presumably best expressing our needs and wants, the economy becomes both alien and dominant in our lives."[44] This contradiction between "the future we want" and the future that seems to be coming is part of the mass delusion created, largely, by corporate institutions and their powerful grip on the flow of ideas and information.

FOUR

The greed-infected cloud of hot money

GDP growth remains a national priority for most nations. The world's economies remain fixated on money accumulation, market expansion, and the speculator's code to buy low, sell high, and take profits. All of this is largely unquestioned, the ideology prevails that greed is good, and nowhere is this more obvious than in the financial centers of New York and London. Gigantic companies trade stocks, bonds, and derivatives in multi-trillion-dollar batches in organized exchanges where the practice of speculation thrives. Large pension funds, mutual funds, hedge funds, sovereign wealth funds, and insurance companies are the institutional players in high-stakes gambling, collecting money from a broad base of the population and using it to play the markets. Staggering sums are swept together into a colossal mass —a greed-infected cloud of hot money—that rises and settles around the world while trolling for opportunities to maximize investor returns. And wherever the cloud settles, instability and crises follow, creating genuine hardship and economic ruin of ever greater magnitudes. This cloud continues to menace, yet is given a free pass to move wherever it is drawn to quick profit, as if it were perfectly normal part of the global economy. What has made this possible is a perfect storm of technological, cultural, and political developments since the early 1990s. Desktop computing and internet technology allow for far greater amounts of money to be pulled together at the speed of light. Along with that has also come a shift in cultural attitudes about greed.

Market populism

Prior to the early 1990s, the unseemly side of greed was still being noticed in popular film and literature. Oliver Stone's 1987 film, *Wall Street*, epitomizes the so-called "greed decade" of the 1980s in the cold-heartedness of the investment banking industry and the damage to working people that is brought about by corporate mergers and acquisitions. Similar themes were captured in books such as *Liar's Poker* (1989) by Michael Lewis, who relates a personal reflection on the reckless bond-trading industry; *Barbarians at the Gate: The Fall of RJR Nabisco* (1989) by investigative journalists Bryan Burrough and John Helyar, who chronicle the notorious leveraged buyout of RJR Nabisco; and James B. Stewart's *Den of Thieves* (1992) exposé of insider-trading scandals. Social satirist and novelist Martin Amis conveys the decadence of late-capitalist Western society in *Money* (1984) and *London Fields* (1989). The message conveyed by American and British artists and writers of that time was that rampant greed had spread through society like a soul-destroying, life-destroying disease.

By the 1990s, however, these concerns seemed to vanish from the popular imagination, and in their place emerged what historian and critic Thomas Frank describes as "market populism." Market populism was partly a byproduct of a shift in politics in which traditionally progressive political parties embraced corporate influence and free market ideology. "From Deadheads to Nobel-laureate economists," writes Frank, "leaders in the nineties came to believe that markets were a popular system, a far more democratic form of organization than (democratically elected) governments." He notes that markets were being re-envisioned as not just mediums of exchange but mediums of consent in which all socio-economic classes saw themselves as players. "Markets were serving all tastes, markets were humiliating the pretentious, markets were permitting good art to triumph over bad, markets were overthrowing the man, markets were extinguishing discrimination, markets were making everyone rich."[1] Captured by the spirit of market populism, the Clinton and Blair administrations forged a consensus around the belief that the world's economies are best served by free markets shaken loose from government regulation. Trade and banking deregulation policies followed, along with the global presence of institutional investors and hot money. Market speculation became all the rage.

Great masses were drawn to the promise of easy money through speculation. It was as if an epidemic of gambling addiction had spread everywhere and was sustained by a delusion that markets would remain bullish for all time—the delusion that everyone would become rich by playing the markets because the markets will always continue to rise in value. As we can see in the historical record, this delusion is a recurring phenomenon and follows a remarkably consistent pattern. Wherever and whenever the general population is caught up in financial market get-rich schemes, mass instability follows. This reality was brought into full view by a series global financial crises over a few decades, culminating in the epic turbulence that began in 2008. Before we get to these stories, however, we need to refocus on the importance of stable systems of money, credit, and finance. These are extremely important for wellbeing, as they are vital to the legitimate functioning of every economy, and they need to be restored to their original purpose before they became casinos.

The original purpose of money and financial systems

Author and founder of the Occupy Money movement, Margrit Kennedy, identifies the importance of money succinctly: "Money is humanity's most ingenious invention."[2] Money is strange in this sense, however, because it is not really a thing. Rather, money is a peculiar social convention that has existed in a variety of forms for thousands of years in virtually every culture on the planet. What specific things constitute money is determined by time, place, and social context. If a society establishes a practice or convention to accept certain things as money, then those things become the currency of that society regardless of their physical form: cowhides, salt bricks, shells, stones, pieces of metal, paper bills, magnetic strips, or numbers on electronic ledgers. If society does not have the social convention to accept such things as its money, then no matter what they are made of or what they look like, they will not be money. Money is not any particular thing, it is a social construct based largely on the faith people have in it. Regardless of its form, if people lose faith it their money it will quickly cease to function and the economy will quickly break down.

Money's most important function is to serve as a medium of market exchange between buyers and sellers. Without money, every producer would be trapped in a cumbersome barter system in which all exchanges would be done directly as product for product. This would eliminate the division of labor based on specialization. Historically, the productivity and efficiency gains from division of labor and specialization were so tremendous that it arguably has made money one of the most significant institutional developments of all time. If a nation can sustain its faith that its money will hold its value, its currency has a better chance of stabilizing as a medium of exchange. As money stabilizes, broader economic functions can develop. Accounting systems use money as the yardstick by which assets and liabilities are measured and recorded. Money allows the making of enforceable contracts, standardized pricing, tax collection. If it is stable and functioning, money serves as the glue that holds everything together. If the glue dissolves, market exchanges become impossible, production and distribution grind to a standstill. Things fall apart and social and political instability are sure to follow.

But maintaining monetary stability is tricky, as we see that most of what we call money is something that is formed out of thin air by banks. Specifically, money is created when banks make loans. The institutions of money and banking are inseparable, although perhaps not in the way most of us have been taught. The traditional way of thinking about banks is that they collect deposits on which they pay a small amount of interest, and then lend the deposits back out at a higher interest rate and profit from the difference. To a small extent this still happens, but banks do not really lend deposits.

The way banks make their interest income is by simply advancing bank loans to borrowers. The loans are made of money that the banks do not actually have. A bank can simply create a spreadsheet account, enter a number for the loan amount, and lend the money to a borrower. When the borrower takes out the loan it automatically becomes a deposit and new money—money that didn't actually exist before—is put into circulation. The obvious problem is that this can easily destabilize, and this is the main reason why every modernized economic system in the world has a central bank to regulate this money-creation process.

Central banks such as the Bank of England and the Federal Reserve System (the Fed) regulate money creation by stipulating a ratio between the amount of cash reserves held by a commercial bank and the amount of deposits. Banking regulations require that banks maintain a certain ratio between the amount of money they lend and the amount of cash they hold on reserve. By controlling this ratio, central banks can control the amount of money that commercial banks create through lending. A commercial bank can make as many loans as it wants as long as it has the appropriate amount of cash on hand to meet the central bank's reserve requirement. If the central bank lowers that requirement, then banks do not have to hold as much on reserve as a ratio to deposits, which means that they can lend more and thus create more money. Even so, the cash they hold on reserve does not have to originate from depositors, because banks can borrow the cash from other banks, or from the central bank. If banks lend too much and the ratio becomes top heavy with loans, banks can borrow from each other or from their central banks to shore up their reserve amounts. The upshot of all this is that as long central banks make cash available to banks, there is no limit to the amount of credit that can be created in the system. As we will see, this can be very dangerous when the credit is used for speculation.

The institutions of money and banking are only pieces of the larger jigsaw puzzle of the financial system. Taking a holistic, institutional view, the financial system in its entirety serves to assemble and concentrate large amounts of money from widely dispersed sources and redirect them toward various uses. Money flows in and out of various institutions, and is aggregated such that development projects can be financed. As money flows into a mutual fund, for example, it is a source that can then be used to buy corporate stocks and bonds, and the stocks and bonds themselves are the means by which a corporation can finance real capital investments in plant, equipment, and technology. Farmers have always relied on regular flows of credit during the long seasonal cycles between agricultural production and the payments from that production. College students need access to loans for their education. Communities need financing for infrastructure, schools, security in old age, and for building homes. Again, the question raised here is not about whether or not we need money and credit; the question is about the priorities of the systems. Money and credit can be used for real human development and progress; or they can be as leverage for speculation, hostile corporate mergers, endless consumer spending, or to finance wars of aggression by governments. From the perspective of socially engaged Buddhist economics, the difference—like the difference between GDP and GNH—lies in our collective mindset and institutional priorities.

The question for socially engaged Buddhist economics is not about whether we can survive without banks, credit, or finance. We cannot. The question is how to make these institutions stable, how to make them accountable, and how to make them work to help us achieve true economic wellbeing. To do that, people have to reexamine their attitudes toward money and its importance. Margrit Kennedy sees the need to liberate ourselves from habitual attitudes in which we have been trapped: "The fact is we're locked worldwide in a kind of intellectual dungeon because we assume that the dominant monetary system is the only possible and proper one."[3] If people in communities mindfully cultivate a healthy attitude toward money and liberate themselves from greed, this can go further than any other movement I can think of toward positive economic change for the future. In this effort for positive change, the importance of sustaining the stable and true purpose of money and financial institutions cannot be understated. For now, however, these institutions remain stuck inside the hamster wheel economy get us no closer to wellbeing, notwithstanding. As Kennedy tells us, our attitudes toward money remain locked in a dungeon of the mind even though the door can be opened at any time, and perhaps is already wide open if we dare to try stepping out.

Again, the questions raised here are not about the viability of money or credit, they are about what our financial institutions are used for, toward what purposes, and under what priorities. These questions bring us back to the problems of recklessness, speculation, and institutionalized greed, which seem to eclipse all else, as these institutions have become subservient to the greed-infected cloud of hot money.

Speculation

Although the terms are often used synonymously, speculation and investment are not the same. Investment is made with the intention to put financial capital into something that is real, like new plant and equipment, schools, or technology. Speculation is engaging in buying and selling transactions with no expectation other than that this trading activity will yield financial gains. Greed, aggression, and delusion flourish in such an environment, particularly when market conditions are volatile. The more violently market prices swing up and down, the more speculators are drawn in, as they see opportunity to profit.

With the rise of market populism, profit making through speculation has become a normal, expected practice. Everyone, it seems, has come to expect big returns on their nest-egg portfolios managed by institutional investors as an entitlement. As institutional investors pool together vast sums of cash into the cloud of hot money, speculative greed becomes sanctified as an economic norm, even though it is creating mountains of instability. A pattern is evident in which institutionalized greed leads to institutionalized speculation, which leads to wild instabilities, although this pattern remains largely unquestioned in the popular imagination.

It is as if we have all come to expect recurring financial instability as just an ordinary part of how economies work, like bad weather. As such, everything can be commodified, which means that everything is considered fair game for speculation, and nothing is protected from wild volatility—not even the homes we live in.

Robert J. Shiller, Yale University professor and a leading housing market economist, exemplified this mindset. In an article in the *New York Times* he writes about housing as if it were something to be found in a casino. Although his article is about market efficiency, he emphasizes strategies of placing bets on housing price movements and how to profit from them. He notes, "Suppose you are convinced that housing prices are too high. How can you profit from this insight?" When he talks of profit making, he is not referring to income made from work performed in the housing industry, but to gains snatched up from speculation. He lauds how some more cunning players got the game right: "During the financial crisis, some professional investors did manage to profit by correctly forecasting home price declines. They used mortgage derivatives such as collateralized debt obligations to place their bets."[4] At one time, when someone said "placing bets," this would imply some kind of gambling, like a poker game or blackjack. But Shiller uses the term as if it were just a normal function of housing market activity. What he fails to mention, however, is that such placing of bets and speculating in housing and mortgage derivatives were the foundational causes of the colossal housing market/ banking crisis that began in 2008. The damage stemming from this crisis was real and substantial and brought a permanent state of instability and financial ruin to staggering numbers of families everywhere. Today there remains a gloomy atmosphere of uncertainty that hangs over all of us, as we cannot know if our homes will be affordable one year, astronomically expensive the next, and then collapse into foreclosure the next.

Nonetheless, the current establishment treats all of this as perfectly normal. Although speculation is a major preoccupation in the financial world, and market numbers are quoted ceaselessly in news reports, the actual intention of speculation is scarcely mentioned. It is as if it has become accepted yet remains a taboo subject or secret. Symptomatically, this appears as denial, in the sense that financial speculation is a huge and constant preoccupation yet is rarely mentioned as a legitimate function. Perhaps there is also a general assumption that we should not be allowing this, but do it anyway—which is classic addictive behavior. When major crises erupt, which they always do under rampant speculation, they are treated as surprisingly aberrant or anomalous events, rarely as systemic. Occasionally, however, a rare critic will open issue publicly.

David Stockman, director of the US Office of Management and Budget under former American president Ronald Reagan, laments the perniciousness of the speculative greed that has taken over financial markets: "capital markets ... steadily morphed into casinos focused on speculation in a vast [new] array of hedging instruments and markets not capital raising for the main street economy ... The hedging casinos ... consume vast resources without adding to society's output or wealth, and flush income and net worth to the very top rungs of the economic ladder— rarefied redoubts of opulence which are currently occupied by the most aggressive and adept speculators."[5] Stockman points the finger of blame at Wall Street, but, as we have seen through the spirit of interbeing, there is little to be gained by casting blame on this person or that group when all of us are involved to one extent or another. Greed is not a condition exclusive to Wall Street or Lombard Street; it is a human inner drive to accumulate that has become uncontrollable. Whatever it is that some of us obsess about, whether money or cars or real estate, is not as important as knowing the source of the obsession.

Greed-inspired financial market speculation is a deeply embedded aspect of a shared economic culture that has been made nearly invisible by market populism. Contemporary society encourages it as a way to achieve success, even when it means that some individuals make gains by taking advantage of others. It seems that it is only when it leads to instabilities on a very large scale, and only when a critical number of people are damaged, that it becomes culturally unacceptable. But even then, what actually seems unacceptable lasts for only a relatively short time after one crisis and before another crisis starts all over again.

Speculation and the recurring pattern of instability

When the greed-infected cloud of hot money floats around the planet it is searching for high returns for its client portfolios.

Eventually it settles in a place where there are relatively liquid financial instruments that shows promise. The instrument could be a stock, bond, piece of real estate, a derivative, or even flower bulbs. When enough hot money settles on the instrument, a predictable pattern of instability follows.

The pattern begins when the instrument captures the interest of speculators who arrive at the market with intentions to trade and extract profits. This speculative interest can become contagious and draw more speculators into the market, driving up the price of the instrument. Higher prices fuel even more speculative buying, which drives prices higher yet, and soon a boom is underway. A speculative boom will cause prices to inflate into bubbles, which means they rise far above any reasonable value. The bubbles become even more overinflated as speculators use money borrowed from banks to place their bets, and so on until the instrument's price is ridiculously high. Eventually, however, for a multitude of reasons and circumstances, these market bubbles always burst. What was once a greed-inspired boom reverses into a panic selloff. Sell commands in the markets cause prices to fall, which accentuates the selloff; the collective impulses that once drove prices upwards turn into fear-inspired selling and prices fall to some rock-bottom level. At that point, the greed-infected cloud of hot money lifts away from the instrument and drifts elsewhere, in search of another instrument that will capture the interest of speculators. The whole process starts all over again in another location. In every instance, fear and anger turn into amnesia almost as fast as greed turned into fear and panic. Greed and euphoria are part of the speculator's game when assets are rising and value, just as panic and fear are part of the game when they crash.

Capital markets such as stock markets were created so that entrepreneurs could capitalize their business enterprises. The idea was to open a stock exchange so that shares could be sold to a wide segment of the investor population. This was a very expedient way to aggregate large amounts of finance capital so that a company could do something big such as building railroads, auto manufacturing plants, or steel mills. The success or failure of the enterprise would be measured in terms of the returns the shareholders received on their investments. The financial standing of the company would be audited by weighing these returns against debts, and this would determine the fundamental value of the shares. But even though this is the stated purpose of capital markets, what takes place there has very little to do with these fundamentals and almost everything to do with speculation.

Writer and business analyst Doug Henwood writes about this, "fads, bubbles, and panics drive security prices far more than their fundamental value," meaning that the movements of hot money and horde psychology cause volatility.[6] Of course, not all market activity is based purely on speculative buying and selling, and there are people and institutions that still make financial investment decisions based on fundamentals. But comparatively, particularly in the last few decades as market trading has shifted to a global electronic infrastructure, there is a much larger segment of the world's population that trade stocks purely on expected price movements. The trading activity arises not because speculators see strengths or weaknesses in what corporations are doing, but rather around expectations gleaned from gossip, hunches, pseudo information—noise. Henwood concludes, "Were noise traders all truly listening to sounds of their own devising, they might cancel each other out, but instead judgement biases affecting investors in processing information tend to be the same."[7] Hence the horde psychology.

The collective tanha (small, egoistic minds) of the horde of speculators, captured by the lure of easy money, push markets into mass waves of volatility that sum into gigantic crises. People, through their brokers or fund managers, swarm the markets with their get-rich-quick schemes, prices soar, and this unleashes an epidemic of greed-inspired trading, along with the delusion that there will not be a price fall. The human emotion of greed transforms into widespread public mania—a collective pathology of mind. Yet most people are very reluctant to see trading activity in this way. The horde psychology is that continuously soaring prices are the normal state of things; and when prices fall, it is a shocking abnormality, like an unexpected storm. Friedrich Nietzsche reflects on how such collective pathology can be appear to be normal if enough people are drawn in: "Madness is something rare in individuals but in groups, parties, peoples, ages, it is the rule."[8] The historical record of such madness in market speculation is remarkable.

Greed-inspired financial market instability has a history of repetition stretching back about 400 years. In the early seventeenth century Amsterdam there was a commodity market boom and bust in which people went collectively insane over tulip bulbs. In eighteenth-century England and France speculators were swept up into government bond and debt privatization schemes that boomed wildly, and were followed by a deadly crash. Various stock market crashes and banking meltdowns occurred everywhere in the capitalist world during the 19th and 20th centuries, and numerous worldwide financial meltdowns marked the turn of the 21st century. In each of these historical events, there were elements of both comic and tragic theater. They were comical in the sense that the lure of easy money tends to bring out ridiculously foolish behavior, yet tragic in that these events always ended in ruin and the destruction of people's livelihoods. The history of financial market instability is the same drama with the same plot being played over and over again, only changing the characters and costumes. It is played for the same audience, who show up every evening as if they have strangely forgotten the entire story from just the night before. Every time it is the same. It opens with greed, then greed turns to fear, fear turns to panic, panic turns to amnesia, and amnesia turns to back greed all over again.

As we look at this from a socially engaged Buddhist perspective, the problems associated with greed and delusion are not specific to the banking industry, or even to speculators. Greed is a human emotion for which we all have a propensity. What makes these financial crises daunting and epic is their institutional and cultural nature. Part of what keeps this pattern repeating is that it is deeply ingrained in our cultures to keep them so. In capitalistic cultures that have been imbued for a long time with all the symbols of affluence, these symbols become archetypes of the mind. With time and much conditioning, the collective mind nestles into a comforting hallucination that this is all somehow healthy and normal, as long as enough people feel that they might get a share of the takings. But when the promise of gains turns to ruin, the horde become angry, as if they were robbed of an entitlement. Inevitably, they begin demanding government bailouts and central bank largesse to restore the markets to boom times. As we will see in the next chapter, these public agencies are compliant as a matter of routine policy making, which was never what these institutions were created to do.

There is irony in this drama. Since the late 1980s, global financial markets have experienced unprecedented levels of instability that affected every corner of the world. In part this has come to pass through the active role that government institutions play in creating the conditions for such instability. The governments and central banks that people turn to for bailouts and restoration are the very same institutions that created the crises in the first place. These crises were a public-private joint venture in ruin. The central nests of the corporate–government nexus of speculative greed are located in Washington DC and New York. Wall Street companies, the Federal Reserve System, the US Treasury, the International Monetary Fund, and the World Bank collaborated to deregulate financial systems not just in the US, but everywhere. They were the major players in a game of massive speculation which led to a vortex of massive crises followed by massive bailouts, and they swept nearly the entire rest of the world into this vortex.

American-style neoliberalism and more instability

The global stock market crash that occurred in 2000 and 2001 was among the most severe crises in the history of financial market instability. It was emblematic of a trend that started in the late 1980s. That trend was to deregulate markets so that large private sector companies and institutional investors could move their cloud of hot money in and out on their own speculative terms, with governments and central banks standing by with bailout money ready in case their schemes failed. The trend was part of the broader movement of neoliberalism that was centered on a belief in unregulated markets, but not wholeheartedly—thus the bailout backup plans.

Shortly before the crash, billionaire financier George Soros warned about the dangers of an aggressive neoliberalism. His concern was the potential for instability that was certain to follow the recklessness of financial market deregulation. But the neoliberalist agenda had already been in full swing since the era of Ronald Reagan and Margaret Thatcher and was rapidly gaining momentum with market populism in the West and the collapse of the Soviet system in Eastern Europe. Leaders of the public-private joint venture were unrelenting in their push for a kind of market free-for-all both on their home turf and in the financial systems of the rest of the world. Soros's warnings were ignored, and the costs to mop up following one crisis after another were staggering.[9] With neoliberalism, institutionalized greed, aggression, and delusion were cut loose and the greed-infected cloud of hot money enshrouded the planet like never before.

With the onset of neoliberalism and market populism, the will of governments to keep large corporations in check collapsed. Rather than challenge their power, it became far more likely that elected representatives would follow the instructions of their corporate patrons. In this environment of corporate rule, neoliberalism became the dominant ideology of both progressives and conservatives alike. Political parties in the US and the UK began dismantling government regulation of business and markets; they justified it by claiming to be creating more "freedom" by getting the government off their backs so that they could do their job of creating prosperity. Although the Labour party in Britain under the Blair administration and the Democratic party in the US under the Clinton administration were considered non-conservative, they followed the same anti-union, pro-big business deregulation measures as their conservative predecessors. The neoliberal agenda turned out to be quite selective, however, and, ironically, the idea of "small government" often meant just the opposite when it took the form of massive bailouts.

Deregulation, "shock," and "surprise"

As the neoliberal movement unfolded, a new discernible pattern emerged. Deregulation unleashed recklessness, which led to a crisis followed by public expression of "shock" and "surprise," and then solemn pronouncements about how bailouts would be forthcoming to contain the problem. The pattern usually began when major corporations pressured government to deregulate their industries, claiming that regulations were antiquated and at odds with the new realities of the global economy. Once the government conceded, and ignored the reasons for regulation in the first place, it was expected that the companies could become more flexible, competitive, and able to self-regulate in the open market. But instead they became reckless and ran roughshod over their industries. The period of recklessness invariably concluded with troubled conditions and threats of mass bankruptcies— although part of the process was the implicit (ultimately proven correct) understanding that if things go wrong for corporations, government and central bank institutions are there to assist them out of their troubles. Government officials would express an appropriate amount of "shock" while appealing to taxpayers for bailouts. Such is the "moral hazard" of allowing businesses to run amok, yet not be held accountable for their recklessness. In this economic environment, companies are no longer constrained by the notion that excessive greed is a bad thing, and are actually encouraged by government. This environment is the very epitome of the institutionalization of greed and aggression, and is coupled with a widespread delusion that this somehow can contribute to the wellbeing of the population.

One of the first examples of this was the deregulation of the airline industry, beginning in the US in the late 1970s. Following heavy lobbying by industry insiders, the Airline Deregulation Act of 1978 stripped the US Civil Aeronautics Board of its power to control airfares and routes for commercial flights. When the industry regulations were dismantled, a series of rate reductions were implemented and new firms entered the market. Soon, competition within the industry turned cutthroat, and within a decade nearly half of the companies were either aggressively driven out of business or forced to merge with larger competitors.[10] Throughout the 1980s this cutthroat environment forced airline companies to find ways to cut costs, which was predictably followed by labor strikes, and consumer complaints about delays, lost luggage, and poor service in general. By the 1990s, all the major US airline companies were hemorrhaging huge sums of money, and the George W. Bush administration, suitably shocked by the financial misfortunes besetting the large airlines, quickly moved to bail them out. The Air Transportation Safety and System Stabilization Act of 2001 breezily passed through Congress with solemn gestures of patriotism, along with a nearly $19 billion bailout package for the airlines. The bailout notwithstanding, United Airlines filed for bankruptcy the following year. Its $25.2 billion failure is among the 10 largest corporate bankruptcies in American history.[11]

Another early and large-scale example of this pattern was the Chrysler Corporation bankruptcy and bailout in 1980. Oil prices skyrocketed in the early 1970s and Congress mobilized to enact new Corporate Average Fuel Economy standards (CAFE) legislation. The legislation was designed to require certain fuel economy for new cars produced by the auto industry. Although the legislation passed, it was not initially enforced as it was struck down in the pro-business Federal Court of Appeals as "arbitrary and capricious." Chrysler was then free to continue producing its large gas-guzzlers, while competitors for America's auto business streamed in from offshore, as they were selling more fuel-efficient alternatives. As gasoline prices continued to climb, Chrysler's market share plummeted and the company faced bankruptcy. Shock and dismay abounded both in the auto industry and in the halls of government in Washington, and a solemn resolution to provide a $1.5 billion bailout package was passed into law.[12]

The Savings and Loans debacle

Next in line were the American Savings and Loans banks (S & Ls). These banks were originally chartered to exclusively provide mortgages and promote home ownership, particularly in the post-war decades of the 1950s and 1960s. The S & L deposits were insured by the federal government and the government imposed restrictions that these banks could lend only for home mortgages, and imposed rate ceilings on what the S & Ls could pay depositors. Rapid price inflation in the 1970s pushed up interest rates and rates on money market mutual funds (comprised of small-denomination time deposits). Rates were also rising in bond markets. S & L depositors began to pull their money out of these banks and putting it elsewhere to take advantage of higher rates. Running out of deposit money, the industry's lobbying association, the National Council of Savings Institutions, began pushing the federal government to change the rules and to deregulate.[13]

In 1980, the federal government passed the Depository Institutions Deregulation and Monetary Control Act, which was followed two years later by the Garn–St. Germain Depository Institutions Act. Unrestrained by deregulation, the S & Ls embarked on a wild binge of financing dubious high-risk ventures. Journalist and author Frederick Sheehan writes, "S & Ls were an attractive platform for a businessman with a certain turn of mind. Deregulation of the industry permitted a panorama of investment classes that had previously been forbidden."[14] Banks could entice people to bring their deposits into the bank and open checkable money market accounts that paid competitive interest rates. Their money poured into the banks and back out again into a carnival of greed-inspired lending for farmland speculation, shopping mall development, and questionable real estate schemes. The S & Ls were borrowing from depositors at high rates, but also charging even higher rates on the loans, some of which were collateralized by rising land prices. According to author Martin Mayer, the S & L bankers "could raise endless money and take it to whatever gambling table was most convenient. If they won, they kept it … if they lost, the government would pay"—the reason being that the deposits, like any other bank's deposits, were federally insured.[15]

The global recession of 1981–82 began to unravel the whole arrangement as it caused land prices to fall, among other things. The borrowers who were speculating in land deals and using S & L loans as leverage began defaulting on their loans. To make matters worse, the bankers were investing heavily in junk bonds sold largely by the infamous Drexel Burnam Lambert's bond brokers under the guidance of convicted felons Ivan Boesky and Michael Milken. Milken mischievously manipulated bond markets by trading back and forth within his own company to make it look like the bonds were hotly traded instruments.[16] Milken and his gang were caught finally, and by 1987 their fake bond market fell apart, about the same time as the stock market. The industry, of course, fell into ruin. The key point here is that the greed-inspired and aggressively speculative deals made by the S & Ls were based on the delusion that phony bond markets and dubious land speculation ventures were somehow an appropriate use of federally insured deposits.

By 1988, about one third of all S & Ls that were operating in the United States failed.[17] Political leaders in Washington were once again expressing shock, and made grave resolutions to bailout the banks. The bailout plan came the following year when the federal government passed the Financial Institutions Reform, Recovery, and Enforcement Act of 1989.[18] The Act created the Resolution Trust Corporation, which in the industry is referred to as a "bad bank." A bad bank is a government institution that uses taxpayers' dollars to buy the junk or nonperforming assets from private sector banks. By doing so, the government cleans the bad assets off the balance sheets of the banks, the idea being that it will sell off the assets after the crisis has abated. It took a number of years and several hundred billion in losses of taxpayers' dollars before the government finally rid itself of the junk that it had absorbed in its service to the S & Ls industry.[19] The large banking community was taking notice. Further moral hazard and more trouble were inevitable.

Meanwhile, Alan Greenspan, who had just assumed his role as chair of the Federal Reserve Board, and was seemingly oblivious to this emerging pattern, noted that "deregulation was working according to plan."[20] It is unclear whether he meant that part of the "plan" was to turn to taxpayers for a bailout, but by then the pattern had been clearly established. In the case of the S & Ls crisis, leveraged speculation and large-scale crisis left the government in a position where it had no choice but to orchestrate a bailout of depositors at a total cost of approximately $160 billion, which included $132 billion from taxpayers.[21] Emboldened, the banking industry lobbyists pressed for more deregulation even as the world watched stock markets crash spectacularly in October, 1987, for similar reasons.

Speculation and instability go global and the crash of 1987

The crash of 1987 revealed some instabilities that were building in the financial system. One factor was the growing market for derivatives. These instruments were poorly understood and were sold to the investor public as a way to protect their investment portfolios against risk, although in actuality it was the opposite. Another factor was that computers were being programmed to make trades in such a way that they could respond to bits and pieces of information at lightning speed, which served to intensify selloffs when they occurred. A third factor was the Federal Reserve itself under the leadership of the newly appointed Alan Greenspan.

Part of the reason why derivatives were a fast-growing segment of the financial industry was that the industry itself was becoming less focused on raising capital for real investment purposes, and more on how to deal with the risk in speculative ventures. The traditional notion of speculation had always been that the speculator gambles on two fundamental principles: potential gains and the risk of potential losses. The two principles are inversely related, which means that higher gains usually implies higher risk. This began to change as Wall Street tried to foster a mass delusion that risk no longer existed, with the invention of derivatives.

The particular derivatives that played a role in the crash of 1987 were called "portfolio insurance."[22] As with most derivatives, these were contracts created to hedge against unwanted price movements of underlying assets. Grain buyers, for example, can hedge against a price spike by purchasing futures derivatives based on contracts to deliver grain at certain price in the future. This hedging principle was applied to the stock market with portfolio insurance rooted in the ludicrous notion that investors would be insured against losses in the stock market.[23] The basic idea was that if there were unwanted moves in prices in one direction, the derivative allowed a trade in the opposite direction.

With these instruments, at least in theory, speculators would have a built-in mechanism to adjust to any unwanted shifts in the markets. They were led to believe that they could automatically preempt a market panic. Investment bankers and fund managers created and brokered these instruments as elixirs. But like all magic tricks, it was an illusion. The risks and potential instabilities were not eliminated, only hidden. In the imagination of portfolio managers for institutional investors—mutual funds, pensions, endowments, and trust funds—derivatives nullified the risk side of speculation, leaving only the sky as the limit to the gain side.

Because risk was hidden in this way, the prices expressed in markets were becoming divorced from any real meaning of underlying fundamental value. In other words, it was becoming very difficult to see whether stocks represented anything real in terms of the value of a company's assets, its debts, or its earnings.

Markets were becoming opaque and abstract. The cloud of hot money was becoming larger and dense, like a fog. The strange thing about these derivatives is that when stock prices started to fall in a big way, those who owned the derivatives could simultaneously exercise their option to buy at those lower prices *and* sell the stocks to make a profit. In other words, portfolio insurance derivatives made sure that speculators would profit enormously from downward pressure on stock market prices if they exercised their options the moment the market appeared vulnerable. The only thing that could possibly have happened after that was a crash, and it did dramatically.

The advent of computerized trading hastened the process. Institutional investors and brokers were increasingly employing people with backgrounds in math and computer programs to write algorithms to automatically execute these trades based on bits of information. The programs, not people, dictated what stocks and futures were to be sold. As stock prices began to fall, this automatically triggered sell orders from computers.

Various bits of bad economic news started streaming in throughout 1987. In the weeks leading up to the crash, the stock market took a series of tumbles. These tumbles were the triggers to the computers to make a programmed trade. Since the use of computers was widespread, the programmed trades were synchronized and responded massively in like fashion—to sell. Institutionalized greed turned into institutionalized fear and computerized panic in seconds. The system was overwhelmed by a trading frenzy on October 19, and by the end of the day, the Dow Jones Industrial Average had lost 23 percent of its stock value, which amounted to about $500 billion in paper wealth.[24]

The leaders at the Federal Reserve expressed surprise, but were unmoved. Market crashes "always come as a surprise, otherwise they wouldn't be crashes," says former Fed governor Robert Heller,[25] although it is remarkable that one who had ascended professionally to one of the highest and most powerful positions in modern banking could be so uninformed about a pattern that had been replicated consistently for a very long time. Frederic J. Sheehan admonishes Greenspan, "it is unfortunate that this real-world, real-time opportunity to understand the misleading promises of derivative manufacturers passed him by."[26] Similarly according to Stockman, "the Greenspan Fed misunderstood the most thunderous wake-up call in financial history."[27] These criticisms may be accurate, unless the official central bank position was to be deceptive and publicly deny that such bubbles even exist; which was the temperament of the Fed from the Greenspan years forward. The central bank of the United States, a major force in financial system regulation, showed indifference in public testimony to the instabilities caused by an overpriced stock market or leveraged computerized trading, nor did it show interest in regulating the increasingly volatile derivatives industry.

As we will explore in the next chapter, Greenspan established a trend for central bank policy called the "Greenspan Put." The basic strategy of the policy is to turn a blind eye to speculation and greed, deny the existence of greed-inspired bubbles, but when they inevitably burst to try calming the markets by tossing unlimited amounts of bailout cash into the banking system. The Greenspan model has been emulated by central banks everywhere, with all its hallmark characteristics: an outward denial of the existence of market bubbles although inwardly pushing policy measures directed at keeping them from collapsing at all costs, and perpetuating the illusion of paper prosperity so that the bubble itself can be the drive wheel of growth for the rest of the economy. In other words, the model is to make people feel happy on paper so they will spend more on GDP and keep the hamster wheel running at full tilt.

After 1987, the predictable patterns of neoliberal deregulation and financial market instability not only continued, they worsened. Hot money began moving more rapidly around the world as the worldwide electronic trading infrastructure developed and speculators feverishly scoured for new opportunities and new markets. The electronic herd of speculators and institutional investors once again nestled into a "this-time-is-different" belief that somehow large-scale financial market crises would not happen again. That belief, of course, changed with the onset of the financial crisis in East Asia and the stock market crash of 2000–01.

Both crises were instances of financial market instabilities that could be traced to two significant developments in the 1990s: the development of computer technology and the internet, and the post-Cold War hyperbole of the "New World Economic Order." These developments, moreover, were not mutually exclusive. The so-called "emerging markets" in countries whose economies appeared to be on the cusp of developing opportunities for investment, particularly in East Asia, were a magnet for speculation. At the same time, tremendous developments in computing power and internet technology brought these markets much closer together and dramatically facilitated the movement of finance capital around the world. This combination of promised prosperity in emerging markets stemming from an infusion of capital, along with advances in computer technology, set in motion a speculative boom and bust unlike any other since the 1920s.

The similarities between the 1920s and 1990s are striking. The euphoric optimism of the 1920s was given the dramatic name of "The New Era," and the euphoria of the 1990s was similarly dubbed, "The New Economy." Both eras came at the end of global conflict, as the New Era followed the end of World War I in 1918, and the New Economy emerged after the end of the Cold War in 1989. Both were boom periods characterized by get-rich-quick schemes, flurries of technological innovation and growth industries, and media hype.

The New Economy of the 1990s promised miracles. Behind these often exaggerated promises were giant corporations and their political adjuncts in government. Millionaires and billionaires were being made seemingly overnight with the meteoric rise of the dot.com sector. New internet companies were sprouting every day and producing everything from electronic greeting cards to online grocery-shopping services. Also at the end of the Cold War, the West began celebrating the notion that capitalism had emerged triumphantly in the world as the premier economic system. With a certain swagger, American foreign policy leaders traveled the globe pressuring countries in Eastern Europe, East Asia and elsewhere to begin restructuring their economies to conform to American-style neoliberalism: cutting government spending on social programs, lowering taxes, reducing government regulations on business activity, privatizing publicly owned businesses, and, most importantly, opening up their economies to global trade and financial investments.

The Washington Consensus

These policy prescriptions came through Washington DC based institutions that collectively came to be called the "Washington Consensus," comprised of the International Monetary Fund, the World Bank, the Federal Reserve System, and the US Treasury Department all headquartered in Washington.[28] The Washington Consensus evangelized to the world a vision of a global system of capitalism in which financial investments could travel seamlessly from one country to another. Behind the scenes were the large Wall Street investment companies that pushed the neoliberal agenda as surrogate foreign policy institutions. In this vision, it was mandatory for countries to open up, or liberalize, their financial markets so that they could become members of the club of modern finance. The principal argument behind policies for capital market liberalization was that finance capital could be allocated around the world most efficiently by following free market principles. Finance capital is scarce in many parts of the world. Scarcity means higher prices, and for finance capital that means higher rates of return. In a global free market environment capital will automatically flow around the world to wherever it is needed the most—that is, where it is scarcest and where it pays higher returns.[29] Everyone, regardless of where he or she is located, could become a stakeholder and could share in the benefits of economic growth stimulated by capital investments. All people of the world would have the opportunity to participate in get-rich schemes, but to do so they had to play by the rules established by the Washington Consensus. Most chose to play along, and the results were tragic.

The December Mistake in Mexico

Countries that followed the recommendations set forth by the Washington Consensus endured some of the worst financial market instabilities in their histories. Among the first was a massive crisis in Mexico, known as the "December Mistake." After the deregulation of Mexico's currency and bond markets in 1994, a binge of speculation and instability followed, and concluded with a $30 billion bailout.[30] Approximately $20 billion of the bailout funds came from the US Treasury's Exchange Stabilization Fund supervised by newly appointed secretary of treasury Robert Rubin and his sidekick Larry Summers. The bailout was widely criticized in the media as a cynical maneuver to bail out Wall Street banks under the guise of helping a neighbor to the south. Nonetheless, American politician Newt Gingrich, soon to become Speaker of the House, expressed the appropriate measure of "shock" and informed the public that the bailout was necessary because it had to stop the crisis before it caused millions of illegal immigrants to surge across the US/Mexico border.[31] The argument was remarkable, considering that the bailout did virtually nothing to improve the living conditions of ordinary Mexican people, although there was a massive benefit to Wall Street hedge funds and banks.

The East Asian Crisis

Shortly after the crisis in Mexico, similar instabilities were building in the financial markets of Thailand, Malaysia, Singapore, Hong Kong, and South Korea after the governments of these countries were convinced by the Washington Consensus to deregulate their controls on international capital flows in financial markets. Again, Wall Street firms were given the green light to move money in and out of these countries as they saw fit. The cloud of hot money drifted to Thailand to speculate on its currency, the Thai baht. It was as if a giant, brand new casino had opened for business and speculators rushed in to place their bets. Most of these bets were in anticipation that the currency would lose its value relative to the US dollar. Speculative bets like this can be a self-fulfilling prophecy if enough money is drawn to them, and that is what happened to the baht. Market players from the US and Europe saw these bets being placed and anticipated that the baht would collapse under the weight of the speculation. They started pulling their money out of Thailand and in 1997 a massive panic selloff occurred in which investors began selling their holdings of Thai securities. The Thai currency collapsed and Thailand's stock market dropped by a staggering 75 percent. Following a similar pattern, the panic spread to other countries, leaving a wake of economic ruin. Hong Kong's stock market tanked by 23 percent, and unemployment in South Korea soared, tripling the poverty rate.[32]

Observing what was happening in Thailand, speculators became skittish in other markets and the panic began to spread to other countries. In October 1997, Hong Kong's Hang Seng stock market index showed a fall of 23 percent and its central bank spent over $1 billion in US dollars—an amount equal to about half of Hong Kong's broadest measure of its money supply—to prevent a collapse in its currency. Unemployment soared in South Korea along with poverty rates. Interest rates everywhere in East Asia spun wildly out of control, and at one point rose overnight to as high as 500 percent. In Malaysia the national currency, the ringgit, also collapsed, the stock market crashed and the country plunged into a deep recession that was felt in every sector of the economy. Malaysia's real GDP declined by 6.2 percent in one year. In Indonesia, the experience was similar: collapsing currency and crashing stock markets followed by a deep recession. Accompanying Indonesia's currency crash was skyrocketing price inflation. Steep increases in food prices precipitated riots and political instability.[33] For all the Asian countries involved, this was among the worst economic downturns in their histories, and people suffered in large numbers.[34] Meanwhile the greed-infected cloud of hot money lifted away from the Asian markets to seek fortunes elsewhere.

It should be noted that Wall Street firms and the policies pushed through by the Washington Consensus were not entirely responsible for these crises. As with other significant events in history, there were a multitude of causes. It is nonetheless clear from the evidence that, had these countries not followed neoliberal policies, the crises could have been averted. Moreover, the countries that did not play by the rules set by the Washington Consensus and that were still part of the global trading system were spared. According to Joseph Stiglitz,

> I believe that the capital account liberalization was the single most important factor leading to the crisis ... Indeed, in retrospect, it became clear that the IMF policies not only exacerbated the downturns but were partially responsible for the onset: excessively rapid financial and capital market liberalization was probably the single most important cause of the crisis, though mistaken policies on the part of the countries themselves played a role as well.[35]

In an ironic turn of events, the Asian countries had no choice but to turn to the very same IMF for bailouts. The bailout deals were brokered by then UK chancellor of the Exchequer Gordon Brown, who had nonetheless stood by his prime minister, Tony Blair, as they pursued the neoliberal game plan. In the US, Robert Rubin, a former Wall Street investment banker, was Treasury Department secretary at the time and brought representation for the banking and finance industry directly to the White House cabinet. Rubin led the charge to crack open the financial markets in East Asia. Returning to the question of moral hazard, the element of risk in speculation was largely nullified, as companies knew that the IMF, the US Treasury, and the UK Treasury would be standing by to bail them out if things went badly. The IMF distributed tens of billions of dollars in loans to the governments of East Asia so that they could pay back their obligations to New York and London firms. In retrospect, Robert Rubin commented that he was "shocked" and had never seen anything like this before, which is remarkable, considering that he had just finished administering the bailout deal in Mexico for precisely the same reasons.[36]

The Asian crisis could very well be considered a triumph for institutionalized greed and moral hazard. Speculators enjoyed high rates of return while they lasted, and enjoyed the welfare of the IMF, which stepped as lender and bill collector on their behalf. Those who lost were not speculators, but the poor people of these countries who were just beginning to experience improvements in their lives, only to find themselves thrown back into poverty as their economies tumbled and the IMF imposed its austerity strictures.

This process was characterized by then prime minister of Malaysia, Mahathir Mohamad, as a new form of capitalist imperialism: "In the old days you needed to conquer a country with military force, and then you could control that country. Today it's not necessary at all. You can destabilize a country, make it poor, and then make it request help." The help, in this case, would come from the IMF, which subsequently took control over the policies of the country. "[And] when you gain control over the policies of a country," Mahathir asserted, "effectively you have colonized that country ..." He called specifically on the international community to take note that the international financial institutions were acting in accordance with their own greed, not the wellbeing of people. The institutions, he argued, "are not in the business of attending to the social needs of people. They are only thinking about their profit, and if you allow the market to go free, unregulated, then the world will face monopolies of giants who will not care at all about what happens to people ..."[37]

The dot.com crash

Not long after the Asian crisis had run its course, the cloud of hot money drifted back to the stock markets, where a major stock market crash began to boil out of the tech sector. From the peak of the stock market boom to the trough of the bust, the dot.com crash between 2000 and 2001 was among the most startling stock market crashes in the history of the world.

By that time, desktop computing power had become more affordable and user friendly. No longer were personal computers merely a hobby for techies; they had become a regular tool for businesses as well as a common household appliance. Consumers began spending huge amounts of their disposable income on newer and faster machines, and on multiple generations of new software packages. By the mid-1990s, technology was a red-hot growth sector and this found expression in the stock market. Alan Greenspan appeared obsessed with this technology and the enhanced productivity that came with computing power. In virtually every public forum where he was invited to speak, he referred to the miracles of technology and enhanced productivity to make a case that markets were not over-inflated into bubbles. This argument was used as a means to side-step warnings that instabilities were once again building in the financial system. With his tech-optimism, Greenspan became the paramount spokesperson for what came to be called the New Economy. In the New Economy entrepreneurs came out every corner of the world to create dot.com service sector companies that sold online travel and dating services, music, books, banking services, pornography, retail services, and practically every other thing imaginable that does not require a physical human presence. Most of these companies were not very profitable at the time, but their stocks were publicly traded and their prices skyrocketed with speculative fervor. Blinded by delusion, the horde of individual and institutional speculators seemed not to notice, nor wanted to acknowledge, that tech stock prices were overinflated.

Beyond technology, there was a demographic dimension to the dot.com crisis. Baby boomers were entering their prime income-earning years and by the 1990s and had collectively amassed a substantial sum in their retirement and mutual fund nest-eggs. With the accessibility provided by the internet and the speed wielded in desktop computing, online amateur speculators were drawn to the market en masse as "day traders." Financial gambling addictions and delusion spread like epidemics. A massive bubble in the stock market was seemingly unavoidable.

In 1991, London's FTSE 100 was indexed at around 1,200, depending on when you take the measurement. In a tremendous boom-and-bust swing, the index rose to 3,000 that same year. Also in 1991, in New York, the Dow Jones Industrial Average was at 2,600 and had risen to 11,302 by 2000—an increase of 337 percent in 10 years. The Nasdaq, which is heavily weighted with stocks of businesses in the computer and internet sectors, rose from 414 in January 1991 to a peak of 5,250 in March 2000—an overall increase of 1,168 percent in the same 10-year period and an average annual increase of 32 percent. The 1990s showed the largest stock market increase over a single decade in the history of capitalism.

As the likelihood of a crash became more evident, the delusional hype became increasingly shrill and aggressive. New Economy euphoria reached a high pitch with the publication of books such as *DOW 36,000: The New Strategy for Profiting from the Coming Rise in the Stock Market*, by James Glassman and Kevin Hassett (1999). Glassman and Hassett asserted that "The stock market is a money machine.... The Dow should rise to 36,000 immediately, but to be realistic, we believe the rise will take some time, perhaps three to five years."[38] But, as with every other bubble in financial market history, when masses of people and cash are swirled up in get-rich-quick speculation, trouble inevitably follows. Institutionalist economist John K. Galbraith observes, "For built into this situation is the eventual and inevitable fall. Built in also is the circumstance that it cannot come gently or gradually. When it comes, it bears the grim face of disaster."[39] Within a year of the publication of Glassman and Hassett's book the stock market crashed with a resonance that could be heard around the world. In a single day of trading the Nasdaq lost 2.8 percent of its market value, and by October, 2002 it had fallen to near 1,100, which amounted to a loss of 78 percent from its peak. In London, the overall market capitalization of stocks fell by 4 percent—over £800 million.

We will return to the conditions and implications of this market crash in the next chapter. What is important here is to note that this was just another avoidable and unfortunate disaster, made to happen in a very familiar pattern. Millions of workers worldwide lost their jobs in the aftermath as economies everywhere were plunged into recession. Millions more saw the hemorrhaging of their pension funds and the obliteration of their retirement nest-eggs. Yet, undaunted, the horde of individual and institutional speculators turned away from stocks and began looking for new, promising opportunities for their gains. The greed-infected cloud of hot money lifted itself up from stock markets and settled on new ground—real estate and mortgage derivatives. The Asian and dot.com financial crises were profoundly damaging, but they stand as minor disturbances when compared to the next round of crises that were looming on the horizon.

The meltdown in 2008

While the aftershocks of the crises in Mexico and East Asia continued to wreak havoc around the world, political leaders continued to push hard for even more financial system deregulation. Hardcore neoliberals in government, with the financial support of their friends in the banking industry, continued to ram through a series of deregulation initiatives that by 2008 had set in motion a series of crises that destabilized the world.

In the years and months leading up to the crisis of 2008, all the institutional elements for a colossal financial crisis were set in place. Central banks created an atmosphere conducive to easy money policies by understating price inflation and making credit widely available for speculative ventures. More banking-industry deregulation allowed commercial banks, investment banks, and hedge funds to merge into leviathan institutions now referred to as "universal banks." And new derivatives were spawned and traded in multi-trillion-dollar batches.

Banking deregulation allowed previously separate institutions to merge into one. Commercial banks, investment banks, insurance companies, and hedge funds all combined together into a single house. Commercial banks are what we typically think of as banks that take deposits, make loans, and offer checking account services. Investment banks are companies whose principal activity is to assist in raising finance capital by providing consulting and brokerage services to corporations that seek to issue stocks or bonds in order to raise capital. Unlike commercial banks, whose earnings come from interest on loans, investment banks' earnings come from the fees they charge for these services, and from capital gains made from brokering stocks and bonds. They create and broker stocks, bonds, and derivatives and help to facilitate high-profile corporate mergers. Hedge funds are a special kind of privately held mutual fund reserved exclusively for the wealthiest individual or institutional investors. Typically, hedge funds are small in terms of the number of people who are investors, but they control disproportionately large amounts of investment funds. These institutions are now merged as universal banks, concentrate enormous amounts of assets, and as a result have centralized tremendous amounts of risk. More eggs in smaller baskets, and the baskets themselves are very unstable. Moreover, their size and scope anointed them with "Too Big To Fail" status, making possible the moral hazard of allowing these companies to pursue ridiculously unstable practices with the assurance that central banks would bail them out if things went wrong, which is precisely what they did. For those of us who bothered to look and question what was going on, it became clear that these mergers were leading toward something quite dangerous. The universal banks were able to suck up vast amounts of hot money that was pouring in from various widely dispersed institutional investors that were attempting to recoup losses incurred in the dot.com stock market crash. Banking firms like Lehman Brothers and Northern Rock were securitizing mortgages and trading them as safe investments to these institutional investors. They also borrowed heavily to cover these transactions and soon buried themselves under a pile of dubious speculative ventures and debt. Hubris, greed, and an enormous concentration of money combined to erect an upside-down financial pyramid constructed out of fragile real estate markets, subprime mortgage contracts, dubious securities backed by those same mortgages, massive debt collateralized by those dubious securities, and questionable derivatives that were gambles on an assumption that somehow all of this was low risk. It was like an upside-down pyramid of bubbles layered on top of each other. At each level, a bubble below would help to inflate an even larger one above. It was inevitable that that the whole edifice was going to crumble and the costs and the damage to people's lives would be staggering.

The cracks in the edifice began to show when housing prices began to decline between 2006 and 2009. Home prices in the US, measured by the Shiller Index, fell by a devastating 33 percent. Home sales plunged by 13 percent in 2007, which up to that point was the biggest decline in 25 years, and continued plummet by 22 to 24 percent in each of the years following.[40] Subprime mortgage payments stopped flowing, equity values collapsed, and soon the trillions of mortgage-backed instruments were collapsing in value. In other words, the bubbles that had inflated the inverted pyramid had finally started their long-awaited burst. Soon, banks and investors who had borrowed heavily to invest in mortgage-backed instruments discovered that their portfolios of these instruments were being obliterated. The universe of fictional financial value that these institutions had created disappeared back into the thin air from where it had come.

Among the first to experience large-scale trouble was the UK bank Northern Rock. As Northern Rock's assets dried up, so did its cash flow and it became incapable of servicing its debt obligations. It eventually turned to the Bank of England for emergency bailout funds. But once the news of the bailout became public, panic spread among its depositors and run on the bank ensued in which the depositors literally demanded their money out of the bank. This was the first bank run in the UK in 150 years. At the same time, Wall Street giant Lehman Brothers for the same reasons moved into bankruptcy and broke the record as the largest corporate failure in history. Until then, the record bankruptcy had occurred in 2002 with the $104 billion collapse of telecommunications giant WorldCom. Lehman Brothers surpassed that record and wiped out $639 billion in assets.[41]

When financial crises become extreme like this they can set in motion a chain reaction of troubles, as every aspect of the economic system is linked to every other. As the crisis spread from the banking sector to other sectors of the economy, the economic machine began grinding gears and falling apart. Business failures and layoffs soared. The numbers that revealed the magnitude of the economic crisis that followed were stunning. In the US, foreclosures soared everywhere and increased by 55 percent during the year from summer 2007 to summer 2008 (an increase of 76 percent over the previous year). During the third quarter of 2008, 1.35 million homes fell into foreclosure. New home sales collapsed and lending companies took over properties that were collateralized with real estate holding market values that had fallen far below the outstanding debt on the mortgages. Banking business associations reported that the first quarter of 2009 showed record levels of credit delinquencies—the highest since 1974—and attributed the cause of these delinquencies to mounting job losses.[42]

Unemployment in the UK soared from about 5.5 percent in mid 2008 to almost 10 percent by the end of 2009. In the US, the Department of Labor shocked the nation when it announced a 597,000 net jobs loss for the month of November, 2008, which was the worst monthly loss in 34 years. This was followed by new records, with losses of 681,000 in December, 741,000 in January, 2009, 681,000 in February, 652,000 in March, 519,000 in April, and 322,000 in May. People saw the May numbers and began to sigh with relief that the worst was over. But then the Department of Labor reported another 467,000 jobs lost in June. By July, 2009, total payroll employment had fallen by 6.5 million jobs in less than a year and half. Job losses caused more defaults, and foreclosures in the mortgage industry continued to rage, hitting hit a record of 2.5 million in 2009.

What was happening in the US and the UK was happening worldwide. Most European countries fell into financial trouble as they had to bail out their banks, which were reeling from the crisis as it spread everywhere. Just like other investors caught up in the mortgage instrument schemes, European governments invested public funds as they were duped into believing they were high-quality, low-risk instruments. The value of instruments was obliterated and countries in the Eurozone plunged into financial crisis and recession in the spring of 2010. Many of the countries in the Eurozone had been piling large amounts of debt over many years, although this had gone largely unnoticed as the speculative bubbles in securities and real estate remained inflated and the economies were growing. But when the crisis and global recession hit, their debts suddenly became very high-profile problems, and they remain so. On April 23, 2010, Greece's prime minister, George A. Papandreou, declared his country a "sinking ship" and requested financial aid from the IMF and the European Central Bank. The IMF makes loans but it does so under strict conditions of austerity, which means that governments must significantly lower the debt by cutting their spending programs. Greece is a country that has sustained a tradition of much public employment, so when the IMF spelled out its conditions and the government cut its budget, massive layoffs of public employees followed and people rioted in the streets.

Virtually every industry in the world remains dominated by fantastically large corporations fraught with institutionalized greed, aggression, and widespread delusion; complex and opaque derivatives continue to be traded in a financial system that has lost its connection with the true purpose of a legitimate financial system. The only thing that seems certain now is that any attempt to impose new regulations or restrictions, or even to enforce existing ones, will be met with costly litigation from industry giants with deep pockets for lawsuits. Serious attempts at new regulation are destined to become little more than what *The Economist* calls "a boom time for lawyers."[44] Even so, the truth is that governments cannot legislate away greed.

Bubbles, boomers, and consumerism

Since the 2008 crisis and its aftermath, critics, media pundits, and others in the political establishment have been calling for restitution for what happened. The financial instabilities of the last two decades had multiple causes, but these were not limited to court cases and legislation. Although the Wall Street–

Washington joint venture stands out as the primary culprit, culpability stretches farther and runs deeper in the cultural milieu. One factor in particular was demographic, and the rise of a cohort that was eager to jump on the market populism bandwagon.

By the mid-1990s, when the stock market bubbles started to take off, the baby-boomer generation was beginning to make its way through the income-earning population. The boomers are those born between the years 1945 and 1965, which meant that by 1995 they were between 30 and 50 years old, a time when most people are in their prime-income earning years. They were also more inclined than previous generations to be involved in financial market speculation. Deborah Gregory notes that, "since 1987, individuals have become responsible for their retirement savings through defined contribution plans, the funds of which are tied up in the markets."[45] William Fleckenstein, journalist and author of *Greenspan's Bubbles: The Age of Ignorance at the Federal Reserve* (2008), elaborates: "The year 1995 marks the start of the biggest stock market bubble this country has ever experienced. Baby boomers, captivated by the Internet and the new financial networks like CNBC, believe they possess the know-how to invest for themselves and had earned the right to be rich."[46] Alan Greenspan, testifying in a routine report to Congress in May, 1994, also noted that, "[Lured] by consistently high returns in capital markets, people exhibited increasing willingness to take on market risk by extending the maturity of their investments." To interpret his typically opaque language, Greenspan is saying that people were inclined to take long-term positions in the stock market and were shifting substantial amounts of money away from short-term money market accounts and savings deposits. He continued, "it is evident that all sorts of investors made their change in strategy—from the very sophisticated to the much less experienced."[47] According to Fed estimates, Americans moved approximately $282 billion from their piggy banks to the stock market in 1993 so as to get in on the bullish money-making phenomenon.[48] As Frederic J. Sheehan notes, "Money chases an inflating asset."[49]

If people at this time felt that they were entitled to become rich, it was not through wage growth. Former Federal Reserve governor Lawrence Lindsey repeatedly reported to the Fed's policymaking wing, the Federal Open Market Committee, that the wages and salaries of the working population in the 1990s were stagnating, while the wealthiest 1 percent were taking the majority of income growth from their investments. People on the rat wheel were falling into debt because, as Lindsey noted, "the non-rich, non-old live paycheck to paycheck, quite literally. That's where all their income comes from. Remember, virtually none of the capital income or business income goes to them. They have to live on their wages and that wage share is also declining ... The middle-class, middle-aged people who are borrowing are really getting their income squeezed."[50]

Nonetheless undaunted, people in significant numbers were drawn into market speculation as a way to get what they considered their fair share. Equity growth, not wage growth, was fueling expenditure on personal consumption. Increasingly, Americans were seeing their net worth, at least on paper, rise proportionally with expanding retirement portfolios and home equity. These were used as collateral to support consumer debt, and consumer debt was driving real economic growth measured in terms of GDP. The US economy was resting on a squishy foundation of equity bubbles. Lindsey warned again in 1996 that "there is a long-term social cost we are going to pay from all this.... Consumption has expanded more quickly than the income of the great majority of American households." Lindsey was referring to the dangers that awaited as a majority were using bubbles to keep the economy alive, and reiterated, "the long-term costs of a bubble to the economy and society are potentially great. They include a reduction in the long-term saving rate, a seemingly random redistribution of wealth, and the diversion of scarce financial human capital into the acquisition of wealth. As in the United States in the late 1920s and Japan in the late 1980s, the case for a central bank ultimately to burst that bubble becomes overwhelming." In other words, Lindsey was suggesting that the Fed should take the air out of the bubble before it became any bigger, and thereby lessen the magnitude of the crisis that would follow. Chairman Greenspan responded, "On that note, we all can go for coffee" and, after the coffee break, moved on to another topic. Lindsey's warnings were ignored and the public thereafter was subject to a seemingly endless feat of financial log-rolling.[51]

Greenspan not only ignored Lindsey's warnings, but believed that equity extraction, particularly from real estate, was a viable economic model. Sheehan tells how "Greenspan was living for the moment: 'I believe that equity extraction from homes will continue to be a source for positive growth in personal consumption expenditure.' Greenspan then extolled some Fed model ... that calculated 20 percent of personal consumption came from consumers cashing out their 'wealth.' Rising house prices were essential to America's continuous shopping spree."[52]

The implications of all of this for socially engaged Buddhist economics are profound. Both the institutionalist economists and Buddhist scholars have taught us that life on the hamster-wheel of economic life is one captive to delusions of a kind of happiness that can be attained only by more and more affluence. Our long-term habitual acceptance of greed has evolved to become firmly embedded in our social institutions, our cultures, and our collective thought processes.

Once we see the institutional dimension to these problems, then we also see that institutional transformation has to be part of the solution. Institutions are social structures that script social behavior with rules, norms, and shared strategies. If we seek to truly evolve from greed to wellbeing, we will have no choice but to create new social structures that will script our social behavior with entirely different rules, norms, and codes. In the next chapter we will explore this process of institutional transformation as a wholesome and creative process flowing from insight, compassion, and an approach to this work that is liberated from the dungeons of greed.

Perhaps one place to start the process would be to examine our individual attitudes, while simultaneously recognizing that we got ourselves into these messes together and we can work together to get ourselves out. There is no one "out there" to blame because in our state of interbeing "they" are our own mirror reflections. People everywhere enthusiastically embraced market populism in the 1990s. A broad segment of the population supported the Clinton and Blair administrations and their continuation of neoliberal policies inherited from conservative predecessors. People applauded the appreciation in real estate markets and the stock markets with a delusive expectation that this would continue for all time. Institutionalized greed is a shared human phenomenon, and to demonize those involved is the same as demonizing ourselves. Labeling others as culpable for the latest round of financial havoc only creates more divisiveness and makes it harder for us collectively to work for resolution.[53]

As we do the inner work of liberating ourselves from greed, aggression, and delusion, the hamster wheel will no longer keep us captive and subject to endless crises that continue to grow in magnitude. It is important to remember that we need financial systems and money and credit as they were originally created, and we need them to have a true and wholesome purpose. Modern economic systems cannot function without them. Therefore, before we can get to the next steps of changing our behavior, we need to reconnect to that true purpose by sweeping away the fog of delusion. This could, and actually does, involve creating alternative institutions through action and reflection—including new forms of banking that are chartered as if people and communities matter.

FIVE

If the Buddha chaired the Federal Reserve—banking for right livelihood

Recall that the first noble truth in Buddhism is to see that suffering exists. When hundreds of thousands of people are thrown out of the workforce each month and see their life's savings obliterated, they suffer. The second noble truth is to see the underlying causes. In the last chapter we uncovered a repeating pattern in which banking and financial systems are thrown into chaos and instability caused by institutionalized greed, aggression, and delusion. The image of a greed-infected cloud of hot money is a metaphor for how these things have become suffused into our most powerful economic institutions, society, and the popular mindset. To most people, speculative buying and selling and taking gains seem like perfectly normal aspects of how economies work. It is as if we have all unwittingly normalized an epidemic of gambling habits. But normalizing speculative greed in the popular imagination does not necessarily mean that it is healthy any more than the burning of fossil fuels is good for the environment, though it too is normalized. For those who are willing to look, the pathological aspects of both are plain to see: global warming and instabilities that are occurring with ever increasing magnitudes of severity. The pathology will continue until we are ready to change—or are forced to change—our habits.

The third and fourth noble truths are about change. There is a way to transform suffering into wellbeing by finding the ways to end the habitual thoughts and actions that bring us trouble. The eightfold path (see pp. 35–38) helps with some practice guidelines in daily life for establishing different and healthier ways of thinking and being, including mindfulness. Mindfulness is a way to cultivate the skillful means we need to change ourselves and to be effective agents of institutional change. This leads to a simple although sometimes daunting challenge. If we conclude that it is true that greed, aggression, and delusion are institutionalized and the cause of economic instability and suffering, then mindful individual *and* institutional transformation must be part of the solution.

From the socially engaged Buddhist perspective, we can see both our internal condition of habituated greed and the external, institutionalized greed that reinforces it. As we work to liberate ourselves from the endless cycles of instability, it is imperative to work against both these forms of greed. Recall that Zen master Philip Kapleau teaches us that this work involves a special kind of middle way in which we alternate between the inner work of mindfully dissolving the grip of the three fires and the outer work of taking action in the world around us. In the economic world, this means swimming against a powerful current. Decades ago the philosopher Herbert Marcuse identified the nature of this struggle. Although he was not a Buddhist, Marcuse identified the challenge of this work of transforming the mind—consciousness—and the institutional power structures that hold the mind under their grip. He writes: "Now it is precisely this new consciousness, this 'space within,' the space for the transcending of historical practice, which is being barred by a society in which ... the supreme promise is an ever-more comfortable life for an ever-growing number of people ... whose life is the hell of the Affluent Society."[1] Transforming deeply entrenched historical practices is obviously challenging, but it is the challenge itself that makes it all the more important. In Buddhist terms, this is breaking the cycle of karmic volition; that is, extricating ourselves from, and transforming, the pathological conditions that we inherit from history. Transforming the space within through mindfulness is inseparable from transforming the society out there.

In socially engaged Buddhist economics the inner and outer worlds are inseparable. This means that the moment we begin changing ourselves, we are changing the world around us at the same time. For this reason, mindfully cultivating awareness and compassion has to be socially informed and socially effective. As we work to make things better for others and future generations, sometimes creating a small, humble example is all we can do, yet this can gain positive karmic momentum in ways that we could never have imagined. If we understand this, the prospect of making real social change becomes less daunting. Developing the power of mindfulness and the willingness to use that power to break from destructive habits, including socially constructed habits, leads to a radical transformative social activism.

Recall that Bernie Glassman did the hard inner work of sitting in meditation, clearing himself of the three fires, and then set out to build new economic institutions from a place of compassion. He and others provide us with a model of this kind of Buddhist inner–outer transformative social activism. Glassman's Greyston Mandala projects, initiated with the founding of a single bakery decades ago, and are still going concerns. This is inspiration for us to consider the vast possibilities for undertaking similar projects, including starting a community bank, a financial cooperative, or a credit union, and from these initiatives to build networks of financial alternatives that will naturally gather the like-minded. Slowly and incrementally, we can begin to gain the skillful means to leverage control over the economic lives in our communities. As we gain control, we can direct our work away from the pathology of greed, aggression, and delusion, and toward creative self development and genuine wellbeing in our communities. Such communities will become empowered and form a base from which, through democratic means, people can push upward for real changes in the broader economic system—including our central banks.

In this chapter we will see that we do have the ability to change the financial climate around us by creating institutional alternatives—what I call right livelihood banking. Although I always emphasize that the best starting place is on a small and local scale, it is important to also emphasize that large-scale institutions like central banks are still necessary and important. As much as people would like to tear down enormous structures of power like the Federal Reserve System, we need central banks for stability in our national economies; but we need for them to be democratically accountable. It would be unrealistic to suggest that we must infuse institutions such as the Federal Reserve, the Bank of England, or the European Central Bank with Buddhist principles. It is not unrealistic, however, to say that we can mindfully cultivate new, healthier principles of economics in our own community based institutions, while pressuring these large-scale institutions to be more accountable and to support things like Bhutan Commission's platform of right livelihood. But before we get to all that, we need to see the importance of responsible, true-purpose central banking. As a case in point, we now turn to a brief story of how the United States tried miserably to have an economic system without a central bank.

America's terrible experiment

Throughout most of the 19th century, the US economy floundered without a central bank. America's first central bank, the Bank of the United States (BUS), was chartered in 1791 in Philadelphia and was patterned after the venerable Bank of England (chartered in 1694). Both institutions were originally created to issue money and credit, and to function as the custodians of public funds. They were created to be a stabilizing force in societies that were experiencing the paroxysms of modernity and the ascent of secular nation-states. The BUS was given a 20-year charter that expired in 1811. But the bank was caught in a tangled web of political and ideological conflict over the role of government in economic affairs, and it took another five years before the US government renewed the bank's charter. The bank's second 20-year charter expired in 1836. Once again, the charter was not renewed, as the result of and initiative taken by president Andrew Jackson, from Tennessee.

Jackson came to Washington from the agrarian, slave economy of the American South. He feared that the BUS represented the power, wealth, and influence of northern states that would encroach on the economic independence of the South, and he denounced the BUS as "the Monster," to which his opposition became something of an obsession. In 1832 Jackson vetoed the bank's recharter Bill, later explaining that "A bank of the United States is in many respects convenient for the Government and useful to the people. [But it is my] belief that some of the powers and privileges possessed by the existing bank are unauthorized by the Constitution, subversive to the rights of the States, and dangerous to the liberties of the people." To the accompaniment of strong attacks against the bank in the press, Jackson presented himself to the public as an economic populist who was fighting against the arbitrary power of big government. His movement gained momentum, and when the BUS's second charter expired in 1836, it was never again renewed.[2]

Though he presented a populist image to the public, Jackson had a private plan for speculative ventures with public funds. After the BUS was dismantled, Jackson sequestered all of the federal government treasury funds that had been deposited in the central bank and moved them to what became known as his "pet banks," located in south. The funds were subsequently used to finance land speculation deals in areas that later became cotton plantations.[3] According to historian Edward Pessen, "Many of the new banks were speculative ventures pure and simple, whose managers were operators [speculators] in the worst sense of the word."[4] Jackson's cronies made themselves rich by exploiting cheap money that otherwise belonged to the taxpayers. But the real, lasting damage had only just begun.

What followed from 1836 to 1913 was a banking system comprised mostly of state chartered banks that were poorly regulated and unstable. The most glaring problem was that there was no nationwide standard for maintaining capital reserves. This meant that banks lent too much and lost depositors' money by lending money for dubious speculative ventures. "Wildcat Banks," as they were known, would collect deposits, keep a small amount of cash on hand, and use the depositors' money to finance get-rich-quick deals on the stock market, in commodities, or in precious metals. These were highly risky ventures, and most failed. Although the federal government attempted to create more stability through new legislation, the system experienced one crisis after another. Each banking crisis was followed by a deep economic depression: one in 1873, another in 1882, and again in 1893.[5]

The final crisis that set in motion the movement to create a new central bank was the Panic of 1907—yet another chapter in the long story of greed-inspired pandemonium. In the years between the economic depression of 1893 and 1907, the stock market steadily lost value. At the same time, some of the large national banks were caught up in stock market speculation and siphoned off bank reserves from across the national landscape to play the stock markets. State and national banks started to abandon their true function of financing agriculture and industry and instead turned to gaming the markets. In the summer of 1907 a number of leveraged ventures in the stock market failed and a rash of bankruptcies spread through Wall Street brokerage firms. By October of 1907, the stock market had fallen to about 50 percent of its peak the previous year. A general panic began and frightened mobs of depositors showed up at the banks, demanding to withdraw their deposits. Many banks tried to sell off their holdings of bonds in order to raise the money needed to pay off depositors, but this boomeranged, as it caused bond prices to crash. For the bondholders, which included many banks that had not played the markets, falling bond prices caused a steep decline in the value of their holdings. Since there was no central bank, there was no lender of last resort to which legitimate bankers could turn for help. Eventually, banks resorted to calling in loans from business clients. These clients, who were themselves hoping to find bank credit to keep afloat, instead had their funds pulled away and were forced out of business.

The panic spread from New York City banks to smaller banks across the nation, until it became a full-blown national crisis resulting in a significant wave of bank failures, along with the destabilization of the dollar. To make matters worse, people began to fear further banking collapses and began hoarding gold. The US currency was at that time fixed to gold as part of the Bank of England's international gold standard. As the panic became widespread and people demanded redemption of their Treasury notes in gold, the supply of gold held by the Treasury declined. This led to an even greater shortage of money precisely at a time when it needed to expand—but it could not expand because there was no central bank.[6]

In the aftermath the Panic of 1907 the damage to communities everywhere was severe. What seemed to matter politically, however, was that the collapse of bonds had punished the more powerful, wealthier classes. Even though populists and progressives had been clamoring for change, striking, boycotting, forming unions and political parties, and pushing for monetary reforms for decades, the call for thoroughgoing banking reform began only after the violent booms and busts in the financial system had brought ruin to significant numbers of the wealthy. In any case, the entire nation was exhausted by economic chaos, and sought reform.[7]

After the Panic of 1907, the federal government passed the Aldrich-Vreeland Act (1908). The Act established a National Monetary Commission that would investigate strategies for monetary and banking reform. The Commission's report, published on January 9, 1912, was not flattering to the banking system. It included a long list of criticisms charging that the system was antiquated, had no provisions for shoring up funds in times of trouble, and lacked means of interbank cooperation. One point that the commission noted in particular was, "We have no effective agency covering the entire country which affords necessary facilities for making domestic exchanges between different localities … or which can prevent disastrous disruption of all such exchanges in times of serious trouble."[8] Elsewhere the report also noted that, "We have no power to enforce the adoption of uniform standards with regard to capital, reserves, examinations, and the character and publicity of reports of all banks in the different sections of the country."[9] The report made it clear that without a central bank and monetary authorities, the banking sector would languish in chaos.

The Commission also took issue with the political mischief that was the legacy of Jackson's pet banks: "Recent efforts to modify the Independent Treasury system by a partial distribution of the public moneys among national banks have resulted, it is charged, in discrimination and favoritism in the treatment of different banks." The Commission therefore concluded,

"The methods by which our domestic and international credit operations are now conducted are crude, expensive and unworthy of an intelligent people"[10] Its recommendation was to charter a new central bank that it called an independent "National Reserve Association," and which would eventually become the Federal Reserve System.

President Woodrow Wilson signed a law granting a 20-year charter for the Federal Reserve System on December 23, 1913. The Fed's charter was amended and made permanent in 1927. The Federal Reserve Act resolved to modernize the system of revenue collection and disbursement for the Treasury Department, to stabilize and make flexible the money supply, to stabilize the check-clearing process, and to make the financial system generally more stable. The main obstacle to creating this central bank, however, was the deeply entrenched ideology of laissez faire and the widely felt distrust of "big government." Accordingly, to appease the Jacksonians, who were distrustful of big government, the Act called for a somewhat "decentralized" central bank; that is, not a single, government-owned and controlled bank, but a system of 12 Federal Reserve district banks, each owned by private banks. In other words, the Federal Reserve System, the Fed, came into being as a privately owned institution with a public mandate. Within this structure there are as of now 25 branch banks extending from the district banks. According to its website today, the Fed was founded by Congress in 1913 to provide the nation with a safer, more flexible, and more stable monetary and financial system. Over the years, its role in banking and the economy has expanded. It falls into four general areas:

- conducting the nation's monetary policy by influencing the monetary and credit conditions in the economy in pursuit of maximum employment, stable prices, and moderate long-term interest rates;
- supervising and regulating banking institutions to ensure the safety and soundness of the nation's banking and financial system and to protect the credit rights of consumers;
- maintaining the stability of the financial system and containing systemic risk that may arise in financial markets;

- providing financial services to depository institutions, the US government, and foreign official institutions, including playing a major role in operating the nation's payments system.[11]

Take a look at the mission statements of the Bank of England or the European Central Bank, and you will see they too are centered on the same goals of soundness, stability, and containing risk.

The function of containing systemic risk is of particular importance. Recall that when the banking crisis of 2008 began to unfold, central banks everywhere acted swiftly to contain the damage by making massive amounts of bailout funds available to banks that were in trouble. In the US, bailout costs passed the one trillion dollar mark in the summer of 2009. The UK government made approximately £500 billion (roughly $700 billion) available to the financial sector, with a plan to "restore market confidence and help stabilize the British banks."[12] The Republic of Ireland posted up about £435 billion (roughly $600 billion), which amounted to about 230 percent of its GDP. Since 2008, the Fed has pumped around $4.5 trillion into the financial system. The Bank of Japan and the European Central Bank each poured close to $700 billion into the crisis.[13]

In each of these places, the story of these bailouts and many others like them is simple: banks lost money on the speculative bets they placed on risky mortgage derivatives and they needed to borrow money. They were like gamblers who needed money to cover their gambling debts. If we look at this from a broader, systemic perspective, the bailouts made perfect sense in that the central banks were not going to stand by and watch the entire financial system go up in flames, which could precipitate a global depression—which is precisely what the Federal Reserve had done after the stock market crash in 1929, and the results were catastrophic. But what is often left out of this story is how the same central bank institutions that came to the rescue, most notably the Federal Reserve, were culpable in having allowed the problem build to such gargantuan proportions in the first place.

When central banks say that they are trying to "restore market confidence" or "contain systemic risk" what they are really saying is that they are trying to keep market bubbles inflated by pumping massive amounts of cash into them. Bubble management as a kind of monetary policy began at the Greenspan Federal Reserve in the 1980s, although the central bank was never chartered for this purpose and, as we will see, was explicitly warned against it by the National Monetary Commission.

After the market crash of 1987, the Federal Reserve discovered that if it could keep market bubbles inflated it could also fabricate an illusion of paper wealth. With that illusion fixed in the popular imagination, people spend money on goods and services, and this ratchets up GDP numbers to indicate growing prosperity. This model of financializing consumption, which came to be called the "Greenspan Put," became a de facto form of monetary policy for the global economy. As such, central banks are not only increasing systemic risk in the financial system but spreading it to every other sector by propping up economies on a squishy foundation of greed-inspired speculative bubbles. And one thing that we know for certain about speculative bubbles is that they always burst.

The Greenspan Put and bubble maintenance

Financial markets are always potentially unstable, but this is seen as a bad thing only when they are on the crashing side of the instability. On the booming, bubbly side, mass delusion, greed, euphoric optimism, and feelings of prosperity take root in the collective imagination. The plan for the Greenspan Put was hatched with the idea that as long as the bubbly optimism could be maintained, it would not matter that it was an illusion, as long as the final outcome was more GDP.

Although bubble maintenance was never the purpose of central banks, it has the outward appearance of effectiveness through keeping economies from sinking into the abyss of recession and mass unemployment. Thus, the hallmarks of Greenspan Put were to maintain debt driven spending at full force by fueling it with cheap and plentiful credit, and to keep the nerves of speculators calm by flooding the banks with bailout cash at every sign of trouble. But to do this, they also had to create another illusion, by convincing the public and government policymakers that there is no such thing as price inflation. This was because pumping fresh new cash into banks not only inflates stock prices, but can push up the prices of everything else as well.

As early as 1994, Greenspan admitted to maintaining elevated stock prices as a policy objective. In a testimony before the US Senate, he claimed that the Fed's position was cautious about tightening the money supply and raising interest rates, for fear that it might send messages of uncertainty to the stock market. Greenspan testified, "we at the Federal Reserve were concerned about sharp reactions in markets that had grown accustomed to an unsustainable combination of high returns and low volatility." Greenspan was admitting to sustaining a customary delusion that speculation yields high returns with low risk. He added that if they were to raise interest rates, which speculators are also not accustomed to, the "shift could impart uncertainty to markets, and many of us were concerned that a large immediate move in rates would create too big a dose of uncertainty would could destabilize the financial system, indirectly affecting the real economy."[14]

His testimony was the Greenspan Put in a nutshell, and the financial press took notice. Journalist Frederick Sheehan noted that soon there developed a widespread belief "that if markets ever tumbled, Fed Chairman Greenspan would flood the market with money, which would truncate investors' downside risk while launching a new speculative fury."[15] In this way, the Fed officially became a sponsor of speculative bubbles throughout the 1990s, though denying in public that inflating bubbles existed. Throughout the latter half of the 1990s, leading up to the big stock market crash of 2000, and with very few exceptions, the Greenspan Fed's position was to make cash readily available to speculators at low interest rates. William Fleckenstein wrote: "As 1996 draws to a close, with rates holding at 5.25 percent, it had been almost two years since the Fed has stopped tightening (though it had eased three times) and the stock market was now 60 percent higher than when the Chairman began to briefly use the word bubble [two years prior]." Easy money flowed into the financial system, stock prices inflated and systemic risk continued to build in the system. Greenspan admitted again, "What we are trying to avoid is bubbles that break, volatility and the like …"[16]

Even the Fed was acting like a financial market speculator and was trying to outguess speculators with interest-rate shell games. At a Fed meeting held in March, 1997, Greenspan commented, "I conclude … that 25 basis points [a quarter of one percent increase] is enough for now [because] … at this stage, the market is expecting 25 basis points. It has discounted such a move, frankly, but it has done so in a positive way, not a negative way." This was the first interest rate hike in two years, and would be the last one for another 15 months as the Fed carefully pandered to stock market speculators. The game of speculation was being treated by the Fed as business as usual, and in fact was embraced by it as a positive force in the system. The Fed kept up its appearance of being friendly to the markets for the endless stream of cable news media. At the same meeting, Greenspan further stated, "The stock markets are up this morning; the bond market is up. I think that if we were to move 50 basis points today after a long period of doing nothing, through being vigilant if you like, we suddenly would shock the market into thinking that we must feel that we are behind the curve. We are not behind the curve."[17]

By July of 1998, the stock market was 160 percent higher than it had been at the end of 1994. Recall, however, that by the late 1990s there had been a series of global crises stemming the greed-infected cloud of hot money menacing financial markets everywhere. To calm the market jitters, the Fed moved to drop target interest rates in September, then again in October for no apparent reason, as encouraged by former Fed governor Alice Rivlin, who noted in a Fed meeting, "Now, we can wait until our next meeting, but that would involve a long wait. The risk of waiting in my view is that we may be forced into a reactive position. The beauty of doing something now is that nothing much was happening."[18] In response to the arbitrary interest rate cuts, the markets soared, and this trend continued well into the following year. In July, 1999, the Dow Jones Industrial Average rose 72.82 to close at 11,139.24, easily topping its previous record close of 11,107.19 on May 13. In the week of May 9–15, 1999, it rose 5.6 percent or 586.68 points, the biggest weekly point gain in its 103-year history.[19]

Speculators came to see the Greenspan Fed as their true benefactor. Whatever the greed-infected cloud of hot money wanted, the Fed seemed willing to accommodate. Author Justin Martin reflects on the calming effect Greenspan had on the markets at the time of East Asian crisis: "During those dire days in 1998, it often appeared inevitable that the crisis would overtake the United States. But it never did. The boom just kept on booming, and for that Greenspan was about to receive considerable acclaim."[20] Risk appeared to vanish from capital markets and stock market speculation became a national pastime, particularly in the technology stocks. Tech-heavy indexes such as the Philadelphia Semiconductor Index and Nasdaq soared. For speculators, Greenspan was a true friend of speculators—someone who would enable their gambling addiction –they need not be concerned about consequences. Jerry Jordan, former Fed official from the Cleveland district bank stated the Fed's position succinctly: "I have seen – probably everybody has now seen – newsletters, advisory letters, talking heads at CNBC, and so on saying there is no risk that the stock market is going to go down because even if it started to down, the Fed would ease policy to prop it back up."[21]

In its newly self-proclaimed role as the container of systemic risk, ironically, the Fed worsened it substantially by letting it build to dangerously high levels. Greenspan rationalized this by making speeches about how stock prices were not overinflated, due to the magic of technology and the high levels of productivity it induced. In a series of testimonies before Congress in 1997 and 1998, Greenspan unveiled his standpoint that there was neither inflation in stock prices nor general price inflation, due to technological developments, particularly in high tech. He testified that "Clearly, impressive new technologies have imparted a sense of change in which previous economic relationships are seen as being less reliable now ... An acceleration of productivity growth ... would put the economy on a higher trend growth path than have [the Fed previously] projected."[22] And in another testimony he reiterated, "As I noted earlier, our nation has been experiencing a higher growth rate of productivity – output per hour worked – in recent years. The dramatic improvements in computing power and communication and information technology appear to have been a major force behind this beneficial trend."[23]

Greenspan was attempting to foster a consensus around the idea that when technology and productivity measures were properly accounted for, stock prices were not overinflated. With Greenspan's endorsement, market populism became market madness. People were quitting their jobs to so that they could play the stock market and, according to a Montgomery Securities poll, "investors expected a 34 percent annual stock market return over the next decade,"[24] which was basically expecting the market value to double every two years. The same arguments that were rolled out by the Fed to de-bubble stock markets were used to deflate price inflation.

The Chairman testified again before Congress: "The present budget scoring process is already partly dynamic but tends to underweight the impact of supply-side changes," by which he was referring to the technological boosts to productivity. As result, he concluded, government budget "relies on a consumer prices index that may overstate inflation by 0.5 percent to 1.5 percent."[25] Politicians were inspired by Greenspan's words because the implications for their budgets were significant, because certain spending programs, most of important of which being social security payments, were subject to cost-of-living adjustments pegged to the consumer price index (CPI). If they could change how price inflation was measured in the CPI to show less inflation, they could save billions in inflation-adjusted pension benefits paid to retirees.

The Federal Reserve and the US Bureau of Labor Statistics took a series of disingenuous steps to adopt an extremely narrow base from which to estimate price inflation. Nearly all the big-ticket things that people spend their money on— housing, food, heating bills—were warped out of its inflation measurements. When questioned about the seeming disconnect between the inflation index and the reality of what people were paying for food and gasoline, Greenspan repeatedly attributed it to productivity gains, even to the dismay of others on the Federal Reserve Board.[26] The result was a surreal situation in which people continued to pay ever steeper prices for things and housing prices were blazing out of control, yet the Fed was telling them that there was no actual price inflation, even though their grocery bills, rental payments, and transportation costs were rising faster than the value of their paychecks.

Thus, the Greenspan Federal Reserve made sure that all the factors for a major stock market crash were set in place: easy credit for leveraged trading, moral hazard, and the comfort of the Greenspan Put, along with delusional thinking that there was no price inflation and that stock markets cannot be in a bubble because of productivity gains. As Justin Martin put it, "the boom just kept on booming"—that is, until it finally crashed. And as we saw in the last chapter, the crash of 2000–01 was among the very worst in history.

The Fed stepped in once again and poured cash over the markets in an attempt to douse the flames of a bearish market. The stock market unraveled in the usual pattern in which greed turns to panic, and the Fed lowered interest rates 11 times in 2001, bringing target interest rates to their lowest level in about 40 years.[27] The greed-infected cloud of hot money drifted to real estate, which, combined with the low interest rates, set off another speculative boom as the stock market went sour. Greenspan quickly turned to embrace housing market appreciation as the new miracle economic driver. Like so many of these booms and busts before, greed and delusion were epidemic and Americans began, as the saying went, "using home equity as ATM machines." An even more dangerous bubble was born, as we saw in the last chapter.[28]

Home equity soared with a frenzied new bubble in housing prices. People and institutional investors began trading houses as if they were commodities and extracting hundreds of billions in equity each year. Wealth extraction as a model for spending is more like plunder—a one-time phenomenon—and has nothing to do with real production. Nonetheless the frenzy continued. With it came more mania, delusion, and spending binges, which Greenspan celebrated: "First, I think it's fairly evident that unprecedented levels of equity extraction from homes have exerted a strong impetus on household spending … the level of existing home turnover is quite brisk and …

the average extraction of equity per sale of an existing home is well over $50,000. A substantial part of the equity extraction related to home sales, which is running at an annual rate close to $200 billion, is expended on personal consumption and home modernization, two components, of course, of the GDP."[29] GDP, the ultimate raison d'être for the hamster wheel madness.

Coordinating stock market and home equity bubbles was never the intended function of the Federal Reserve or any other central bank. The Greenspan Put represents a wide deviation from its original mandate as specified by the National Monetary Commission in its charter. The Commission had clearly circumscribed the key functions of the central bank: to maintain stable cash reserves, issue currency, provide credit as lender of last resort, and serve as banker to the government.[30]

Moreover, in its report of January, 1912, the Commission had submitted a dire warning against the Federal Reserve becoming a vested player on Wall Street,

> [The] commission has been impressed with the necessity of inserting provisions that would prevent beyond question the possibility of its control by any corporation or combination of corporations, banks or otherwise ... No provision of the bill to reconstruct our monetary system is of more vital importance than this. To-day the financial interests of the whole country depend, in times of trouble, upon what is popularly known as "Wall Street." ... the domination of New York is an accomplished fact ... The responsibilities of continuing this control are too enormous, the risks of failure are too great, for this condition to be tolerated for long. In our judgment the only effective remedy will be found ... with the power to maintain the independence of banks under all circumstances ...[31]

Putting itself in the service of financial market speculation became the defining role of the Federal Reserve during the Greenspan years and thereafter. This role is deftly rationalized in its mission statement with the simple claim that "Over the years, its role in banking and the economy has expanded." This role—maintaining market bubbles—continues to grow with each cycle of instability and has become a policy stance of virtually every central bank in the capitalist world, and each with a very short-term orientation. They perform the necessary function of calming markets and containing systemic risk, although without regard to the long-term consequences of actually worsening systemic risk by making the bubbles larger and too big to fail. The Federal Reserve's role is reactive, and it seems to be unconcerned with preventing or safeguarding against systemic risk; it merely contains it as if it were, vexingly, already there.

Taking a broader view, however, it is pointless to place blame at Alan Greenspan or the Federal Reserve or other central banks. They are enablers of speculative greed and instability, but there is a much larger population of speculators and consumers who demand to be enabled. William Martin, secretary of the Treasury and Fed chairman from 1951 to 1970, warned about the dangers of tethering the economy to speculation and asset bubbles. He held that "it is an economic axiom that goods and services can only be paid for with goods and services."[32] His view was like that of Veblen, in the sense that people who are productive will make the earnings to buy things from others who are also productive. Extraction is simply taking without real creative or productive work. But, had Martin been sitting next to Greenspan making such an argument in testimony, he would have been shouted out of the room by virtually everyone—government officials, bankers, and the general public. The Greenspan Put remains as the principal central bank policy measure, although the banks themselves try to conceal it with remarkably odd terminology.

Quantitative easing: the Greenspan Put under another name

In its self-defined role of container of systemic risk, the Federal Reserve, under the leadership of Ben Bernanke, created over a trillion dollars in cash in order to buy a spectrum of securities, including mortgage-backed junk instruments, from Wall Street. This was a highly unusual measure taken by the Fed, which began in late 2007 and has continued on through to the current period under the leadership of Chairwoman, Janet Yellen. In doing so, it positioned itself as the largest vested player in the mortgage-backed instrument business. It is now impossible to distinguish the line of separation between the Fed's role as a public, regulatory institution and its high-profile role in derivative speculation. Members of the National Monetary Commission would shudder to see how far this central bank has strayed from its original mandate.

Traditionally, Federal Reserve policy was limited to dealing exclusively in Treasury bonds or making loans to banks. If the Fed wanted to expand the availability of credit and lower interest rates, it would buy government bonds from banks. By doing this, it pumped money into the banks, which put downward pressure on target interest rates. If it sought to contract credit and raise rates, it would sell the bonds and pull money out of the banking and lending stream. With the interest income from those bonds, the central bank covered the cost of its operations. Banks getting low on reserves could go to the Federal Reserve and borrow at low rates. The system functioned well, as the Federal Reserve could regulate the money supply and interest rates, and at the same time sustain itself through these bond deals.

This model of central banking continued after the 2008 crisis hit. As early as winter 2007, the Federal Reserve surreptitiously began to open up backdoor programs for large Wall Street banks that were getting into trouble through their dealings in mortgage derivatives. Under the old rules, banks could borrow either from each other or from the Fed when they were strapped for cash. Banks became reluctant to borrow from each other as the crisis began to unfold and they starting writing down tens of billions of assets from their balance sheets. Apparently, going through the front door to borrow from the Fed during times of perceived trouble creates a kind of stigma in the banking industry. To avoid this stigma, and to allow banks access to more credit and cash, the Fed created various backdoor bailout programs that it referred to with peculiar vagueness as "facilities." The overall plan came under the broader and even more peculiar title of "quantitative easing."[33]

Prior to the backdoor bailouts, the Fed sat on its own piggy bank of between $700 billion and $800 billion of Treasury bonds. Starting in late November 2008, the Fed began pouring newly fabricated money—$600 billion—into banks to buy their mortgage-backed securities.[34]

By March of 2009, the Fed's balance sheet had exploded to include about $1.75 trillion of bank debt, mortgage derivatives securities, and the more traditional Treasury bonds. To finance this explosion, the Fed had to create an avalanche of new money that it created out of thin air. In an apparent attempt to dodge scrutiny, the Fed gave these purchase programs oblique names such as Term Auction Facility, Term Securities Lending Facility, Commercial Paper Funding Facility, and Money Market Investor Funding Facility.

With these facilities in place, the buying spree continued for years under the heading of Quantitative Easing I, Quantitative Easing II, and Quantitative Easing III, which included an open-ended program in which the Fed would purchase $40 billion to $85 billion worth of these derivatives each month. Cumulatively, after all three phases, the Federal Reserve's holdings—now comprised of bonds, debt, and derivatives—had risen from around $800 billion prior to the financial crisis to over $4 trillion as most recent buying program concluded in October 2014. The counterpart on the liability side of the Federal Reserve's balance sheet was a substantial increase in banking industry reserves—cash.[35]

All of these facilities, in one way or another, were devices that the Federal Reserve used to fulfill its role as a "bad bank"—eating up as collateral the toxic securities that were accumulated in the private-sector balance sheet—and to pump large amounts of clean cash into the banking system. Of this, former Goldman Sachs banker Nomi Prins writes, "Some argued that the Fed was doing its job to promote liquidity in the system, as explained on its mission statement ... But the scope with which it provided loans for lemons was unprecedented. And, as we've seen, even before the Treasury's TARP (Troubled Asset Relief Program) bailouts the Fed was doing its own bailing. Yet there was no Congressional furor about the trillions of dollars of Fed facility programs as the facilities were spawned, so deft was the body in its motions."[36]

Bubble maintenance as global monetary policy

The Federal Reserve was not alone in bankrolling speculation on the stock market. According to John Kirton at the University of Toronto, "34 central banks cut rates 66 times in the last three months of 1998" and, like the Fed's, their aim was to fight the trend toward bearish markets.[37] The Bank of England and the European Central Bank (ECB) carried out nearly identical monetary policies. Over the period between March, 2009 and January, 2010, the Bank of England purchased £200 billion in securities in its own unconventional program of quantitative easing, followed by another £75 billion in each of 2011 and 2012, although most of these assets were sovereign debt securities.[38]

The ECB did something similar, although it demonstrated a strong bias toward bailing out private sector banks that were caught up in speculative disasters, while shunning governments that were desperately in need of support. As they were unable to escape snowballing debt, Eurozone countries had to turn to the EU and the IMF for help; and to get help from these institutions they had to agree to the usual medicine of austerity, including government cutbacks, privatization of public services, and the "disempowerment of central banks."[39] In addition, the European authorities are trying what the IMF calls an "internal devaluation." This is a process of shrinking the economy and creating so much unemployment that wages fall, so as to have a comparative low-labor cost advantage in free international markets.[40] This is the neoliberal theory, anyway. And in theory it would allow low-wage countries to export more so as to earn the hard currency they need to get themselves out of debt. In the US, economists euphemistically call this "flexibility" in labor markets. The *New York Times* European economics correspondent, Jack Ewing, writes, "To some people, the European Central Bank seems like a fire department that is letting the house burn down to teach children not to play with matches."[41]

These problems are institutional as much as they are ideological. The ECB is bound by the conditions of the EU treaty to create a transnational system in which governments are not allowed to use the central bank for bailouts, which reflects a concern not to monetize government debt. It sees itself as a lender of last resort, as does any central bank. But it is restricted to being such a lender only to banks, and not to governments. To private-sector banks, the ECB provides generously. In 2011, the ECB, under the leadership of Mario Draghi, provided a €489 billion ($640 billion), to over 500 European banks over a three-year period at an average benchmark rate of 1 percent.[42]

The story was repeated in August, 2015, when China's stock market crashed and unleashed another cascade of panic selloffs in world markets. The crash came after a series of bad news about China's seemingly invincible trajectory of growth. In one day of panic trading, China's Shanghai Composite index collapsed by 8.5 percent. Like falling dominoes, European and Japanese markets fell by about 5 percent, and the Dow Jones and Nasdaq indices fell by between 3 and 3.5 percent. Stock market traders habitually turned to their central banks for fallout shelter, and the Federal Reserve, now with Janet Yellen at the helm, came to the rescue. The Greenspan Put remains in place, as noted by the *Guardian*: "It was just as if they had said to themselves: who cares if China's economy is slowing; the 'Greenspan Put', which so famously propped up US stock markets during the 1990s and early 2000s with one interest rate cut after another, is still in operation."[43]

Political scientist Johnna Montgomerie, from Goldsmith's University of London, summarizes the institutional dimension to the problem: "The governments of the 'Anglo-American' economies at the heart of the crisis, the United States and the United Kingdom, have shown a surprising willingness to abandon long held principles of fiscal restraint, independent central banking and rules based economic policymaking in favour of discretionary political interventions to stem the financial crisis."[44] In Veblenian terms, it appears that the financial institutions of contemporary global capitalism are in a state of conflict between the legitimate functions of banks that stem from the instincts to foster stable economic development, and the predatory instincts to speculate and exploit every opportunity, use every bit of information, and devise every cunning stratagem to make a score. As the creative instinct is overtaken by the predatory one, speculation overtakes the legitimate functions of finance and the system becomes unstable.

But, as we strive for creative self development, the need for financial services in the service of is real. Legitimate financial institutions exist for this true purpose, not for predatory speculation. Banks allow people to safeguard their savings as they plan for their retirement or for their children's education. They also exist to help people finance purchasing their homes or to help businesses raise capital to build new industries, or to help governments finance schools and roads. These are the healthier activities that stem from our creative and parental instincts to pursue stable livelihoods. From the socially engaged Buddhist perspective, therefore, the big challenge before us is to restructure our financial institutions and bring them back to these true-purpose functions.

By now, most people have a sense that financial systems everywhere are fraught with greed and deceit, and that the Federal Reserve System and the US Treasury Department are highly corrupt institutions. But, at the same time, people seem to be hoping that these institutions will restore the illusion that the perpetually upwardly mobile elevator of riches is still possible. Most are willing to accept the illusion as real, like being entertained by magic tricks. As people hold on to the idolatry of easy money, they look to the financial sector to restart the gambling casino and while the federal government stands by with stacks of chips.

As long as the public remains complacent and uncritical, there will be no impetus for change and the conditions that led to the crisis will continue to worsen. The large banks are becoming increasingly consolidated and powerful, which means that the amount of resources they can bring into speculation will raise the profile of next crisis. In a case of gambling addiction writ large, our society will keep coming back to the table for more until we have squandered every resource, are crushed with debts, and have brought ourselves to complete ruin. There is not a single person on the planet who can claim that he or she is in good economic shape when they are saddled with gambling debts. This is the condition of the financial systems everywhere. This is particularly daunting when we see that in the immediate aftermath of crashes the banks keep merging with one another and becoming larger, more powerful, and pulling central banks and treasuries everywhere more tightly into the mutual support network of corruption.

It was not merely a bunch of giant Wall Street firms overcome with greed and delusion that brought so much instability and ruin. Private-public teamwork within a highly centralized structure of concentrated financial and political power has created a culture of greed and predation that is a seemingly permanent fixture in capitalist societies. Moreover, the general public is not a mere innocent bystander as people are repeatedly drawn to the delusion that financial systems magically create wealth from thin air. The real tragedy is that in the process, people's livelihoods are being destroyed.

If we reflect seriously on this, we will conclude that gambling and speculation are not a wholesome and stable means to providing livelihoods and comfort in retirement. How healthy is it for a culture to experience wave after wave of crises that bring people to ruin and cause others to scratch and claw to avoid the same fate? Is this the whole of human nature, or is it a manifestation of one aspect of human nature that is brought out by our culture and institutions? Human nature has a wide spectrum of potentialities, of which those that are greed-inspired are only a part.

Everyone becomes shocked and angry when things crash. Yet, rather than recognize that there is something delusional about expecting to enjoy an ever-growing pile of easy money made from speculation, for most people it is easier to hope for another bubble. In a self-reinforcing habitual circle of delusion, our system creates a culture that idolizes easy money and puts everyone on a hamster wheel in pursuit of it; and all the while, the exhausting pursuit itself reinforces the yearning for easy money. It seems to never end.

Banking for right livelihood

Although systemic change has to be the goal over the long term, it is highly unlikely that the greed-inspired financial systems are going to change any time soon. It is also very likely that the global economy will go into another tailspin and the central banks will be ready with cash to do damage control as usual. What is also conceivable, however, is that small-scale alternatives can take root and develop at a local level, and that people will have a better chance of gaining control and determining the direction in which their local economy evolves. In fact, establishing roots at the local level is the historical rule for most businesses, not the exception.

In conversations I have with activists at speaking engagements, someone invariably asks the question, "What can I do as an individual?" My most frequent answer to that is "start a bank." Of course, people stare in vexation at this and are daunted at the thought. Starting a bank is not particularly easy and bringing about real social change never is; but it is a challenge worth taking on because, once we gain control of money, we control the economy by controlling the medium of all exchanges— all the connective tissue in the system. Once we control the economy, we can control our livelihoods in a direct, materially democratic sense.

But money is more than just a medium of exchange. In its special capacity, it can either form the bonds that can define a community or it can tear the community apart. Since the banking crisis of 2008, the pathological conditions of our banking and financial system have come into full view as if someone had taken the lid off of Pandora's box and allowed every possible dismal thing imaginable to escape into the economies of the world. So much of the instability came from rapid movements of hot money ripping its way in and out of markets and tearing to pieces everything in its path. Communities can mend and protect themselves by taking control of the flows of money and financial capital and rendering them a stable and vital part of people's livelihoods.

Making this kind of change will take a long time and much hard work. To this end, each of us needs to find a way to untether ourselves from habituated greed, aggression, and delusion. As we do this, we will gain the ability to step into the flow of a living economy with a clear mind. We also will begin to see creative possibilities for crafting new and better institutions that restore banking services to their original purpose of providing for the needs of people and communities. Once again, the work of socially engaged Buddhist economics is both inwardly and outwardly transformative— a mindful transformation both of the self within the economic society and of the economic society. In that context, perhaps the most direct and proactive first step in this transformation is to work on building alternative economic and financial institutions directed at wellbeing, beginning with a bank.

Creating right livelihood banks in your communities

As first step, those interested in creating a right livelihood bank (RLB) in their community need to form an organization. The purpose of the organization is to see the process through the various stages of development—planning, applying for a charter, raising capital, and, eventually, commencing operations. There are a variety of ways to organize, but the most common for this type of venture is to establish a community based nonprofit, cooperative, or social enterprise. This involves drafting a formal business plan in which members of a community identify a need for a bank, how it will be capitalized and what kind of banking services it will provide, and democratically selecting the individuals to serve on the board of directors.

Once all of those aspects have been clearly delineated, the next step for the organization is to apply for a bank charter. The charter itself is the agreement between the community organization and the government agency that grants banking charters. It is basically the permission to operate a bank. Getting a charter is a fairly complex process that takes time, resources, and patience, due to strict local banking laws, national laws, and central bank regulations.

The information to be included in a charter application will cover things such as the amount of funds needed for capitalization, the number of shares to be sold and at what price, operating cash, where the shares will be sold, and the percentage to be held by principal shareholders. As it would be for any other business, raising capital is key. It is generally assumed that $12 to $20 million in locally raised capital is needed to get started, although very small financial cooperatives can start for much less. Aside from raising capital, the process could also require the organization to submit information on a business model for earnings calculations, building lease information, business or personal affiliations, passport photos, environmental site tests, proposed officer salaries, tax liabilities, and the names of legal representation. If the application for a charter is accepted, which is usually decided in a few months, the bank will have to apply for deposit insurance with the FDIC Federal Deposit Insurance Corporation (US), or the FSCS, Financial Services Compensation Scheme (UK), before it can accept deposits from the public. When all that is done, the bank can open for business.[45] The list of red tape can go on, and the chartering process may take years, but this is the path of social and institutional change for the better: rigorous and gradual.

The idea is to create alternative economic institutions that model economic activity in ways that are quite different from greed-inspired business as usual. Although it may seem surprising, there actually is a measurable demand for these alternatives. We discovered this in the immediate aftermath of the 2008 banking crisis. A widespread backlash against the giant Wall Street banks was the "Move Your Money campaign" spearheaded by journalist Arianna Huffington. Huffington and others exhorted depositors everywhere in the US to take their money out of the big banks and put it someplace else; presumably someplace that is smaller and more accountable. Many followed the call and showed up at local credit unions, financial cooperatives, and community banks to open new accounts. However, a bottleneck occurred because the smaller banks did not have the wherewithal to accept the new business. They were swamped. To give a sense of scale, it would take about 15,000 of these small local banks to equal the assets of one J.P. Morgan Chase, and if everyone in US were to move all of their money out of the four largest banks an additional 40,000 small banks would be needed just to absorb the deposits.[46] There is plenty of work to be done.

Financial cooperatives are similar to other cooperatives in that they are owned by stakeholders in the community. Most commonly, financial cooperatives are organized into nonprofit credit unions of which the depositors are also the owners. Ideally, a mindful system of money and finance would evolve into a network of independent, community based financial cooperatives, with the money and financial services local and free from speculative greed. As a network or association, financial cooperatives could more effectively achieve local control of money and credit by unifying their banking policies to achieve broader community based goals: food production, local manufacturing, land reclamation, education, health cooperatives, and so on.

Fortunately, creating community and values based banks is not an entirely new idea and there are examples and experiences from which we can learn. One example is the Permaculture Credit Union (PCU), a small financial cooperative in Santa Fe, New Mexico. The bank was founded in 2001 and it took two years to evolve from just an idea to obtaining its charter. Its members have placed about $4.8 million in equity into the bank through membership share certificates and member savings. Nearly all of that money comes back to the members in the form of loans to finance projects that are consistent with the ethical principles of permaculture, such as solar energy, water catchment systems, retrofitting older cars to improve mileage or for alternative fuels. The vision of the founders of the PCU is not just environmental. They see the significance of recycling the dollars within the community in order to sustain the vibrancy of the local economy. This bank is living proof that people can create a values based business model and succeed, although how to measure success is outside the margins of convention.[47]

Much of what defines a bank's activities depends on how it is originally incorporated and chartered. The conventional view of a corporation is that it is a business institution incorporated specifically as a vehicle for profit maximization. Jay Coen Gilbert and Andrew Kassoy, members of the progressive leadership think-tank the Aspen Institute and the founders of B Lab, have a different view. Through their work, the people at B Lab hope to unlock investment capital to be used, unlike in conventional corporate institutions, to have a material impact on society and evolve toward wellbeing. Their model of business is that the business itself is a force for social change.

The aspiration of B Lab's founders is to change the economic system from the inside out by certifying a new breed of corporations, B Corporations. The B stands for benefit—social and environmental benefit—and the business model is based on the principle of a corporate entity chartered to be a force for social and environmental benefit, and that force is written into the company's articles of incorporation and bylaws. The people come and go, but the company is bound by its articles and bylaws to stay on its path.

The primary initiative of the B Lab is to help existing companies to become B Corporations through a rigorous certification process. Becoming B certified is comparable to getting products certified as organic or fair trade, but in this case it is not the products or services that are certified, but the company itself. The first step in the certification process is for the company to enroll in B Lab's B Impact Assessment. The assessment is a questionnaire that has evolved from other, more traditional models for evaluating socially responsible investing such as the Global Reporting Initiative (GRI) based in the Netherlands, Conscious Capitalism and others. Most socially responsible investment assessments are based on a single issue, such as their environmental record or profile in fair trade. B Lab had expanded from these models to assess a broader scope of issues, including social equity, community responsibility, and environmental sustainability. The nature and structure of the questionnaire varies depending on the kind of business, and a more rigorous rubric is created for manufacturing companies, which have a greater potential for environmental impact than those in the service sector. Overall, the assessment covers several categories: corporate governance, workers, community, environment, type of business model, and certain disclosures.[48]

The PCU and B Lab are just a couple of examples of what we mean by institutional change, for which the possibilities are endless. Rather than trying to reform Wall Street, people and communities take the initiative to create alternatives cut from entirely different cloth. The business model establishes specific foundational principles that are integrated as part of the DNA of the enterprise. The enterprise can thus remain true to its original purpose of effecting positive social change through business, and it is from this kind of work that right livelihood banks are developed. With varying levels of success, people around the world have been and are doing such things in their communities, and so can the rest of us.

Of course, business enterprises that are created to be a positive force for change do not have to be anchored to Buddhist philosophy and practice in order to be successful. What I propose here, however, are some suggestions for foundational principles for those who are inspired by socially engaged Buddhist economics and are seeking to embark on a project of social change through RLB. The suggestions that follow are a starting place, or template, which people and communities of the like-minded can add to or subtract from in order to keep their activities whole and on the rails. With that in mind, consider the four noble truths as applied specifically to RLB.

The noble truths for right livelihood banking

The first noble truth of RLB is to recognize that suffering exists. In Chapters Three and Four, we took a tour of financial system and banking instabilities since the late 1980s. In each instance, not only did crisis result in instability, but people's livelihoods were brought to ruin as their jobs, savings, businesses, and communities, and in some cases entire national economies, were wrecked in the aftermath of a major financial boom and bust episode.

The second noble truth of RLB is to learn from these experiences and identify the underlying root causes—institutionalized greed, aggression, and delusion. Greed-inspired speculation, an aggressive push for institutional changes that facilitated such speculation on a grand scale, changes in government banking rules and policies, and the shift of central bank duties to bubble management together created the root causes and conditions for epic crises of instability.

The third and fourth noble truths of RLB are about transforming suffering into wellbeing. The primary impetus for change is to extricate ourselves from greed, aggression, and delusion. To achieve this and to stay on a path toward developing new business models, I propose a 12-fold noble path model, or 12 pathways toward RLB. This model is a reordering and extension of the original eightfold path to fit our vision for a business model for the post-greed 21st century.

Twelve pathways toward RLBs

We will assume that a community based organization has completed the preliminary work of starting a banking enterprise. The variations on how this can be done are nearly infinite, and there is no one-size-fits-all prototype . Each community will have different needs, laws, and other factors that will determine the shape and size of the institution. The twelve pathways are merely suggestions for how these newly chartered financial institutions can have a common denominator and common purpose of moving away from the destructiveness of greed-inspired banking and toward a model that is inspired to promote genuine wellbeing.

Right concentration of RLB

Before anyone applies for a bank charter, they must have a clear idea of the purpose for creating such an institution in the first place. This is particularly important for any enterprise whose mission is unconventional. Right concentration is about staying the course and staying focused. It is easy for a project like creating a new bank to be swept away from its original purpose as circumstances in society or communities change. The community organization must stay vigilant, with reminders as to why it is doing this hard work of creating alternative economic institutions, and to that end it must continuously examine its motivation and whether its motivations are true to its original purpose. As most Buddhists will attest, right concentration can be cultivated with a commitment to a mindfulness practice and meditation.

Right thought of RLB

In the Buddhist literature, right thought has also been expressed as right aspiration or right intention. Whatever expression you prefer, the notion is that as the organization provides banking services to its community it stays committed to wholesome practices. People need financial services to build good things for their communities and a RLB can support these initiatives. The right thought behind this banking model is to have a frame of mind grounded in good will for the community rather than in the selfish, greed-inspired ill will that seems to have thoroughly plagued hamster wheel banking.

Right view of RLB

This, more than any of the other pathways, is closest to Bernie Glassman's nondogmatic tenets of bearing witness: "Not knowing, the renunciation of fixed ideas and prejudices; bearing witness to the pains and joys of the world; and healing oneself and all beings in the universe."[49] It is the organization's viewing its projects, its clients, and its community as they are without holding preconceived notions about their rightness or wrongness. Of course, any bank has to deal with risk and assess the credit-worthiness of borrowers, but with right view these are objective assessments for prudent banking practices, not prejudices or judgments. Right view also means being able to assess whether the organization's services to the community are objectively leading away from or toward genuine wellbeing.

Right action of RLB

This is very close to right mindfulness in the sense that by right action we are mindfully observing the interplay between our thoughts and our conduct in the community that arises from those thoughts. The stories of banking debacles in Chapter Three and Four attest to how bankers, inspired by greed, set out to indulge in recklessness. Their actions led not only to instability but also to costly bailouts and widespread damage to the livelihoods of the community.

Right effort of RLB

It is not enough to work hard to achieve right livelihood; the organization must also make assurances that the specific projects themselves are not harmful to the community. A story from my home state of Oregon illustrates this point. In November, 2015, a US district judge in Portland sentenced CEO Harder of Sunwest Management to prison. Sunwest was the third-largest operator of assisted-living homes in the US, and between 2006 and 2008, Harder worked exhaustively to stitch together a vast network of mail fraud and money-laundering schemes in which he milked about $130 million from 1,000 investors, including his own family members, friends, and members of his church community. This was the biggest fraud case in Oregon's history and was inspired by pure greed. According to the press reports, Harder was a CEO who burned through corporate cash as if it were his own, bought luxury cars and six homes, flew groups of family and friends to places like Alaska, Ecuador, and the Cayman Islands, and flew around in a Bombardier jet estimated to be worth $20 million.[50] Harder characterized himself as a "hard working" executive—and joined other criminals in prison who also see themselves as hardworking individuals. Right effort is the commitment to making sure that our hard work is an effective means toward the end of community wellbeing.

Right speech of RLB

Right speech is an important ethical code for socially engaged Buddhist economics. As we saw earlier in this chapter, the Greenspan Federal Reserve conveyed misleading information about the conditions in financial markets that caused a massive buildup of systemic risk and resulted in catastrophe. Right speech is the practice of doing away with deception and adhering to a principle of truth in all banking activities. Truth in lending is part of a US federal law that was passed in 1968 and was entrusted to the Federal Reserve to enforce, but after it became clear to lawmakers that the Fed had violated this trust through the Greenspan years, enforcement, as of July 21, 2011, was transferred to the Consumer Financial Protection Bureau, whose authority was established by new banking legislation passed in 2010.[51]

Right livelihood of RLB

As we have defined it elsewhere, right livelihood is another important ethical code for socially engaged Buddhist economics. It is a broad code emphasizing that livelihoods for wellbeing are trades or professions that, either directly or indirectly, avoid doing harm to other living beings. To interpret this code literally would mean that the organization would not be able to cause harm to any living thing, not even a cabbage, which of course would be impossible for human life. It would also be inconsistent with the Buddha's notion of the middle way because it would lead to starvation. However, we can interpret it in a Kantian sense.

The 18th-century philosopher Immanuel Kant expressed as an unconditional moral law that one should "act in such a way that you always treat humanity, whether in your own person or in the person of any other, never simply as a means, but at the same time as an end." Kant's message was that the rights and dignity of human beings are necessarily to be respected, regardless of the merit of their actions.[52] Kant's moral imperative can be extended not only to human beings, but to all fauna and flora in the natural world—as ends in themselves and not as means to our ends. In the hamster wheel economy, natural plants and wildlife are treated as resources to be exploited for profit. They are valued only in so far as they contribute to the bottom line. The question that arises is whether such a principle must necessarily preclude harvesting natural resources, growing vegetables, or raising animals for food. To respect and preserve natural processes is to respect the balance that nature provides to sustain life. Sustainability does not preclude cutting trees or raising beef cattle or poultry; rather, it places these practices in a broader moral imperative to sustain all life as much as we want to sustain human life, and to not drive living things to extinction for our own gain.

Right mindfulness of RLBs

As I have argued throughout, this is at the very core of the pathways toward wellbeing. It is a commitment to remain fully engaged in the here and now of the activities of the organization. We will return to this, as most of the next chapter is devoted to this pathway, which has many beneficial qualities as a practice.

Right ecology of RLBs

This and the following three pathways extend beyond the traditional eight pathways in Buddhist thought. Right ecology is an awareness of, and commitment to maintaining, a healthy relationship with our natural environment. Recall that the GNH initiative originated from principles of sustainability and proper stewardship of natural resources as pillars supporting GNH. Specific business models such as the PCU and B Corporations have also made these principles into their core business values. Accordingly, an organization that starts a right livelihood bank must also adhere to such values both in its operations and in its decisions regarding the types of projects for which it provide financial services. Ecological sustainability is a term that has been badly mangled by hamster wheel business and business discourse. In order to give sustainability true meaning, it is suggested to make business practice such that it stays within the guidelines established by the Brundtland Commission's original definition of sustainability.

This original and specific definition of sustainability was developed in the 1980s by the United Nations World Commission on Environment and Development (WCED). The WCED became known as the Brundtland Commission because it was headed by Gro Harlem Brundtland, former prime minister of Norway. The Brundtland Commission was convened to address critical issues of poverty and economic development, as well as concerns about environmental degradation. The goal was to institutionalize at a global level certain guiding principles for dealing with world poverty and caring for natural environments.

The report titled *Our Common Future* which the Commission produced in 1987 contained the first widely accepted and practical definition of sustainability as a guiding principle for economic development. This has become the standard definition of sustainable economic development and reads as follows: "[economic] development that meets the needs of the present without compromising the ability of future generations to meet their own needs."[53]

The definition provided a platform from which researchers and scholars began working to formulate more precise principles for a sustainable society. This led to the development of the "Socio-Ecological Principles for a Sustainable Society" by John Holmburg, Karl Henrik Roberts and Karl Erik Erikkson of the Institute of Physical Resource Theory:

1. Substances extracted from the lithosphere must not systematically accumulate in the ecosphere.
2. Society-produced substances must not systematically accumulate in the ecosphere.
3. The physical conditions for production and diversity within the ecosphere must not be systematically deteriorated.
4. The use of resources must be effective and just with respect to meeting human needs.[54]

Right inclusiveness of RLBs

This is a commitment of the organization to fairness and accountability to the community. The implication is that the organization will include local owners because the bank's capital is locally raised, but will extend decision-making powers to the stakeholders of broader community in which the business operates by encouraging members of the community to serve on its board of directors. In this way, right livelihood economics is predicated on a principle of intrinsic democracy. The core institutions that govern, control, and regulate economic activity are themselves intrinsically democratic, in that the democratic will of the people is not externally imposed on institutions, but is inherent in the institutions themselves.

Right stability of RLBs

If there is any one particular defining characteristic of hamster wheel banking it is that it is inherently unstable. As we have seen, virtually every major financial market boom-and-bust crisis has occurred where institutionalized greed predominated. The pattern of financial market instability has always been rooted in the same core institutions and driven by the same motivation of getting rich by frenzied buying and selling. By contrast, right livelihood aims to establish a tradition of locally based systems of economic stability. Community based systems of finance tend to be less oriented toward the Wall Street-style gambling and speculation that have led to much instability and ruin. One of the most damaging aspects of the US capitalist economy is the stress and insecurity bought about by instability. Layoffs and unemployment associated with downturns lead to both sociological and psychological problems. Revenues used to fund vital public services expand and contract with business-cycle instability, leaving schools and other public services vulnerable. Speculation and the instability that it causes have to be systematically removed from any form of RLB institutions.

Right engagement of RLBs

Finally, the organization is an element within the broader holistic movement of socially engaged Buddhist economics. To this end, RLB aligns with the goals for social activism articulated by the Buddhist Peace Fellowship. The Buddhist Peace Fellowship was founded in 1978 to be a catalyst for socially engaged Buddhism. Its stated purpose is "to help beings liberate themselves from the suffering that manifests in individuals, relationships, institutions, and social systems." Its goals are stated as follows:

1. The Buddhist Peace Fellowship works for peace from diverse Buddhist perspectives.
2. Buddhist Peace Fellowship embraces a triple treasure of compassionate action—learning, speaking, and doing.
3. Speaking Communication: Our public voice brings Buddhist teachings into conversation with situations in the world, inspiring and informing action for peace.
4. Learning/Community: Our trainings strengthen Buddhist leadership for peace, and build socially engaged Buddhist communities.
5. Doing/Collaboration: As part of the mandala of social change, we act in collaboration with other organizations and individuals, working together to cultivate the conditions for peace.[55]

With the 12 pathways in place as a foundation, an RLB movement can take root and stay on task in pursuing not a pile of gold, but a kind of chanda return. Recall from the first chapter that in the Buddhist economics view of Payutto and others there are two types of motivations: tanha, which is the motivation that stems from self obsession and ego gratification, and chanda, which is a sense of wellbeing for the broader community or even the whole of humanity. Chanda returns, then, are returns that are not narrowly defined as financial gains from investments as they would be in hamster wheel economics. Rather, such returns are the inherent aspects of wellbeing for a broader community that result from orientation to right livelihood principles. To this end, RLB, as we presented them to the United Nations in 2012, are chartered:

1. to have a clearly defined democratic orientation in which voting rights and decision-making powers are broadly and democratically extended rather than limited to the most powerful economies of the world;
2. to provide credit and/or equity to finance initiatives that would help communities become less dependent on fossil fuels, such as renewable and efficient energy development projects, public transportation and infrastructure, and environmentally sustainable technologies, and to foster the development of local or place based economies, small-scale cooperatives, and microfinancing;
3. to create financial instruments that will draw source funding from both signatory governments and private sector institutions that are committed to the 12 pathways of right livelihood banking;
4. to explore how local communities can create their own alternative monetary institutions that break away from the ever-expanding mountain of debt and move toward more values based or skills based models.

The benefits that come from all of this—local democratic control, access to badly needed financial resources, true-purpose financing, and values rooted in wellbeing—are the chanda returns.

RLB as government utility

With the locally based RLB infrastructure established and a commitment to right engagement, RLB has the potential to become a broader movement for change within the existing banking systems. A right livelihood movement could empower communities to transform local governments into truly democratically accountable institutions that were not captured by moneyed interests and from this basis to build a populist platform to push upward to make state and federal government agencies similarly accountable.

One aspect of this state banking is advocated by Ellen Brown in her book, *The Public Bank Solution: From Austerity to Prosperity* (2013). Brown argues that each state should have its own state bank that functions in a manner similar to a public utility. Brown writes, "By making banking a public utility, with expandable credit issued by banks that are owned by the people, the financial system can be made to serve the people rather than people serving the banks." Brown contrasts a public bank that is chartered to serve the needs of the community with banking in the rat-wheel economy, which she characterizes as parasitic: "The virtues of an expandable credit system can be retained while avoiding the parasitic exploitation to which private banks are prone, by establishing a network of public banks that serve the people because they are owned by the people."[56]

In the US, such a bank exists in the state of North Dakota.[57] The Bank of North Dakota (BND) was established in 1919 by North Dakota's state legislature. It is a correspondent bank, or sometimes called a partnership bank. The BND was originally created as an alternative to the predatory and poorly regulated private bank monopolies that dominated the industry at the time—a time that we have returned to nearly a century later. It was chartered to help improve the economy of the state by assisting the development of local financial institutions. Like US Central in the credit union business, the BND serves as the bankers' bank for community banks located in the state. It is a for-profit institution, although aside from small student loan and business development lending programs, it does not make loans directly to borrowers. Rather as a correspondent bank, the BND is chartered to provide banking services for other financial institutions.

The source funds for the BND come primarily from the state treasury. By law, state government agencies in North Dakota are required to deposit their funds in the BND, although local municipal agencies are exempt from this requirement. (Outside of North Dakota virtually all state and federal government agencies maintain their treasury funds in special accounts with private commercial banks. The private sector is not required to keep these funds within the state and so they can be used outside the state either for legitimate purposes or for predatory or speculative ventures.) In the North Dakota system, the state collects taxes and fees from individuals and businesses, and allocates those funds to state government agencies to cover the cost of running schools and other state services. The BND uses these funds to provide financial services to local community banks to help them, in turn, provide financial services to people and businesses in their communities.

The BND maintains about $4 billion in assets and has a loan portfolio of about $2.8 billion. The bulk of these loans are partnership loans with North Dakota's community banks. In a similar structure to the credit union business, the BND helps to aggregate capital for about 90 to 100 community banks as they make mortgages and loans to small businesses and farmers in their communities. The BND provides a secondary market to which local community banks can sell mortgages to shore up liquidity for more lending. It also underwrites commercial and state bonds for capital investments. It helps community banks to manage their risk with loan guarantees to community banks that extend credit to local entrepreneurs. Although it is a for-profit enterprise, much of its profits are returned to the state's coffers in the form of rebates or dividends. Thus, the money earned in the state and taxes collected by the state are recycled in the state by a state-owned bank. As I mentioned above, capitalizing new, local banks can be an enormous undertaking. To help with this, the BND has a bank stock loan program specifically targeted for expanding its local ownership of banks. In this program, local investors who are interested in buying shares of a community bank in their area can receive financing from the BND.

With any measure of such institutional development, people and communities would be well on their way to creating a genuine alternative. As part of this effort, the socially engaged Buddhist economics movement would be poised to push for national and international reforms, not the least of which would be to revisit the charter of our central banks.

It is over a century since the National Monetary Commission convened and made its recommendations for central banking in the United States. The time for another such commission is past due. Although the Fed was created by an Act of Congress and is subject to some degree of Congressional oversight, the strand of substantive democracy connecting people and monetary policy is a mere hair's breadth. Each district bank in the Fed system is owned by, and has boards selected by, private sector banks. The people who sit on the boards are not elected by popular vote, as would be the case for other public institutions such as school boards or utilities commissions. This is an odd arrangement, considering that the Fed is an important public institution dealing with an extremely important public good—money— that is supported by public debt. Moreover, monetary policy is directed by a secretive committee that works in nearly complete isolation from any institution of democratic government. There is no democratic structure in which people and communities can press their political will to influence Fed policy.

It has become clear since the beginning of the Greenspan Put era, that the central bank's policies have lost connection with the people and communities it was chartered to serve. It is a derelict institution, and as such its charter needs to be redrawn in ways that would restore the district banks to true-purpose banking and provide facilities that would serve RLBs as we have defined them. The 1912 Commission's report concludes with this passage,

> We were therefore obliged to originate a plan which would answer the exacting requirements of American conditions that would meet the needs of a progressive nation, with its hundred millions of energetic and enterprising people, whose development has been impeded by a defective and inefficient monetary system. The plan we propose is essentially an American system, scientific in its methods, and democratic in its control.[58]

In July 2011, at the behest of Bhutan, a resolution was passed unanimously by the 193 member states the United Nations to formally adopt a new economic paradigm. If such reforms as we are suggesting here were to take root in these countries, an alternative paradigm could begin to ascend as a priority among them nations and within the global community. The most significant change would be to move source funds away from greed-inspired speculation and toward projects that provided resources for long-term, genuine wellbeing. The process has already begun and all that is required now is the tenacity and patience to see it to completion. Of course, this will take a long time and will not be easy, but it will be far easier than trying to stage a revolution or continue swinging through ever -larger and ever more debilitating financial system instabilities. The RLB movement is a slow-cooked, bottom-up movement toward evolutionary transformation from greed to wellbeing. It is predicated on skillful means for social change garnered from a mindfulness practice.

SIX

Stepping out of the circle of pathology

Pulling ourselves out of the wreckage of financial instability with new business models is only part of the process of transforming greed into wellbeing. As we build models for new enterprises in socially engaged Buddhist economics, it remains important that we should continue to do both the inner work and the outer work. We cannot effectively do the outer work of changing society for the better so long as we remain individually afflicted by greed, aggression, and delusion. Much hard work of transforming entrenched habits remains to be done as we make the effort to stop treading on the hamster wheel, stop chasing illusions, and at the same time end our suffering that, paradoxically, stems from our desire for what we believe is the good life.

His Holiness the Dalai Lama comments on the paradox of material affluence and spiritual poverty is Western society: "It frequently happens that when I arrive in a new country, at first everything seems very pleasant, very beautiful. Everybody I meet is very friendly. There is nothing to complain about. But then, day by day as I listen, I hear people's problems, their concerns and worries. Below the surfaces, so many feel uneasy and dissatisfied with their lives. They experience feelings of isolation; then follows depression. The result is the troubled atmosphere which is such a feature of the developed world."[1]

From the Genuine Progress Indicator data, the money indicator is on the rise, while genuine wellbeing, using these qualitative indicators, is falling, as signaled by family breakdown, crime, toxic environments, and diminishing leisure time. According to psychologist Douglas Bier, what is considered financial "success" comes at a tremendous cost that would be hard to express in monetary terms—exhaustion, stress, and spiritual emptiness.[2] The sacrifices we are making for financial gains, material wealth, and property are depleting our lives of real quality, as people are overwhelmed, stressed out, depressed, and live in fear of job insecurity. This is compounded by economic problems of insecurity and unaffordability. Particularly after the financial crisis of 2008 and the job cuts that followed, businesses that scramble to find ways to cut costs are making their employees work longer hours just in order to keep their jobs. Uncertainty in financial markets creates a general condition of anxiety in society. And, given the structure of our institutions and technology, which is exacerbating these conditions, there seems to be no end in sight.

The number of people in the workforce who are satisfied with their jobs is on a steady decline. Families are experiencing record foreclosures because they lack the means to make their mortgage payments for no other reason than that the homes they try to live in are subject to wild financial market speculation. At the same time, there is a bitter sense of entitlement to a share of a growing pot of gold, which is increasingly rendered meaningless by an upward spiral in the cost of living. The striving for affluence does not correlate with wellbeing in a society in which not only are most people habitually unhappy, but they seem to be so regardless of how much money they make.[3] Abounding are the corrosive effects of hamster wheel society, in which people find themselves in a system of competitive individualism that has led to an economic war of all against all.[4] Incomes have become more polarized than at any other period since the Great Depression of the 1930s, leaving large sectors of the public suddenly feeling far behind the most affluent, whose wealth soars.

The brutal relentlessness of hamster wheel economics is accentuated by technology and consumer electronics. Throughout the years 1980 to 2005 there was a general assumption, as Greenspan repeatedly suggested, that technology was going to transform economic production in ways that would liberate us from scarcity and require fewer resources. Computers and the internet were supposed to make us efficient and help us to save on material resources, but the reality was the opposite. During that 25-year period, the consumption of materials in North America increased by 54 percent: from 6.6 to 10.1 billion metric tons. As the region's population increased by only 35 percent during those same years, it is clear that material consumption per person has steadily risen. Information technology increased the pace of globalization and economic expansion, such that consumers were able to use up the planet's resources in unusually large quantities. As we continue to do this, we have charged headlong into a condition that Richard Heinberg succinctly calls, "peak everything."[5] We drive ourselves and our planet to exhaustion and, rather than assess the viability or sustainability of this debt driven system, most of us choose to ignore these such limitations and hold on to a blind faith that technology will always solve problems of scarcity.

It seems as if we are being swallowed up and drowning in a sea of digital and financial noise that we have come to accept as progress. But the most significant character of the hamster wheel is that it leads nowhere. The nowhere-ness implies a direction that cannot lead to genuine wellbeing, whatever it is that we are frenetically pursuing as our financial goals.

The corporate dominated capitalist system created a consumer society because it needs market expansion. Ubiquitous messages to keep spending assail us all from every quarter of the media—radio, internet, pop-ups, television, billboards. In every possible place that touches our conscious minds, are the same bombarding messages to keep chasing, keep spending, there is never enough, you are never good enough, and you need more. It should come as no surprise that people respond accordingly, as it seems that there is no alternative. The nexus of rules, symbols, and artifacts that comprise our working and consuming society is powerful and real. They influence our thoughts about our surroundings and ourselves, which inform our actions. Our actions reinforce the institutional structures, which again influence our thoughts, which in turn inform our actions again. This is an ongoing, mutually reinforcing process —a circle of pathology—and we and our planet get sicker.

Stepping out and staying in

Stepping out of the circle of pathology, however, does not mean stepping off the grid. The idea of completely disengaging from the system has a certain allure, but to advocate would be to merely replace one kind of delusion with another. Unless any of us have inherited and are independently wealthy, we all need to earn money to pay for expensive housing, health care, and food. With money, we are contenders in the GDP world of markets, and if we are without money in this world, we are stranded on an island amid a sea of money-for-product exchanges. Without money, people cannot share in the consumer culture that has become the norm and are shut out of a chance of "the good life," and find it difficult to live with a sense of dignity or self respect. The Buddha tried to walk away from all of this, and this led him to abject poverty. Social change has to be part of our movement away from the hamster wheel life because simply walking away from it is not really possible.

In his book *The Man Who Quit Money* (2012), author Mark Sundeen tells the story of a man who has attempted drop off the grid and live without money entirely. The man, Daniel Suelo, tells that his philosophy is to use only what is freely given or discarded and what is already present and already running; and do so without money. In the early 1990s, Suelo decided that money was nothing but an illusion, that the rat wheel was ugly and destructive, and that he just wanted to get away from American consumerism, phoniness, and headaches. He decided to never take money for work, ride by hitchhiking, eat leftover food thrown out by restaurants, and access information from books and internet material freely available in public libraries.[6] Suelo's view was summarized by Sundeen: "The most important result, however, of Suelo's experiments ... was a deeper analysis of his long time spiritual hobgoblin: money. 'I'm realizing that anything motivated by money is tainted, containing the seeds of destruction ... there is no honest profession – that's the paradox. The oldest profession [prostitution] is the most honest for it exposes the bare bones of what civilization is all about. It's the root of all professions.'"[7]

Another version of this revulsion for money and markets is what is called "gift economics." Gifting is an ideological approach to economics based on a principle of non-market and non-barter exchange, and on the notion that healthy, traditional relationships have been eroded by the instruction of market forces and the introduction of money.[8] With gifting, goods are not exchanged as value equivalents such as money-for-commodity or commodity-for-commodity. Rather, gifting exchanges are non-barter, non-market and are held to be an expression of a pre-established social structure derived from a set of social relationships such as among members of a community, kinship, or between parent and child. Advocates of gift economics contend that market exchanges are derived from the commodification of society.

The idea that money is inherently tainted creates a false impression about what money is. It makes no more sense to pathologize money than it does to claim that a plow is inherently tainted because it was once used by slave labor. Commodification is the process of making sure that everything can be bought and sold in markets because it is through that process that capitalist profits can be realized—buy low, sell high. Employers buy labor and other resources as cheaply as they can in commodity markets to sell them as dearly as possible in product markets in order to maximize profits. If an independent producer or craftsman, for example, takes a product they produced with their own labor to sell for money, this type of exchange is not commodification, nor is it part of a capitalist structure—there is no commodification of labor, nor is there exploitation as the source of capitalist profits. Commodification comes not from money or markets, but from capitalistic institutions. Markets did no always exist as part of capitalistic systems and had existed long before capitalism emerged in the early modern period.[9]

Money is an instrument that existed for thousands of years before the ascent of capitalism and the market system. Cultures were not corrupted by markets any more than they were corrupted by the boats that carried goods in trade. The corrupting influence was the greed that followed money and trade like a shadow. It is not possible to have a modern, functioning economic system without money and credit. We know this from bearing witness to economic history. We know from a look at the historical record that economies and tremendous hardship follows the destabilization and failure of monetary institutions. However, it is possible to have a modern, functioning economic system without greed. Money does not necessarily have to be fraught with greed or, in Suelo's words, prostitution. What matters is what we, with our own free will, make of it institutionally. Suelo and gifters can claim to have quit money, but only in so far as everyone else does not.

The importance of mindfulness

Active social participation is part of the Buddhist way. According to the teachings of the Buddha, people should not escape from life, but relate and engage as thoroughly as possible. Such engagement is the practice of mindfulness. Cultivated over time, with practice, mindfulness allows us to be present in our minds and directly engaged in our daily tasks without delusion or attachment. But these tasks are not random, they are directed toward bringing about human and ecological wellbeing, and this will involve playing a role in institutional and systemic change. With appropriate mindfulness, people can begin the hard work of restructuring key economic institutions that direct economic activity onto a new course that leads to systemic change and healthier livelihoods.

Jon Kabat-Zinn, Professor of Medicine Emeritus and advocate of Mindfulness based Stress Reduction, suggests that we should dig deeper, particularly after the vulnerabilities revealed in the aftermath of the 2008 crisis. Kabat-Zinn emphasizes that "We need to create a different kind of confidence and a new kind of economics, one that's not about mindless spending but more about marshalling resources for the greater good, for one's own being, for society, and for the planet." The key aspect for Kabat-Zinn is mindfulness: "Mindfulness can help us open the door to that by helping us go beyond approaches that are based on conceptual thought alone and that are driven by unbounded and legally sanctioned greed."[10]

If we can shift away from the greed-is-good mentality, we can open channels of thought and communication that will help to facilitate the work of building new institutions. From the perspective of socially engaged Buddhist economics, this work begins with the transformation of our habits of thought and action, both individually and in a broader social sense, starting with the self. On this Paul Rogat-Loeb notes, "Again and again, I've heard active citizens say that what motivates them the most is the desire to respect what they see in the mirror." Active social change requires self-reflection as well as "seeing ourselves from the viewpoint of our communities, the earth, maybe even God." That is, looking inwardly and reflectively is the essence of a meditation practice for progressive change. Loeb concludes, "looking in the mirror lets us step back from the flux of our lives and hold ourselves accountable."[11]

Healthy change can be energized by looking deeply and compassionately to see not only the self in economic society, but everyone else in society. The wheel keeps spinning as each generation karmically inherits the momentum from the generations before. Delusive self-obsession and greed are socialized and supercharged by the institutions and cultures that characterize a defiled cultural situation. In the previous chapter we saw some suggestions for how new business models, particularly those that deal with money, can be developed, but these suggestions will not lead to real change without the inner work of changing our habits of mind. Ken Jones emphasizes this point: "we need to create different social conditions of a kind that nurture positive personality change; and out of compassion we need to create those conditions because the present ones give rise to so much gross physical and mental affliction."[12] If we work toward social transformation and at the same time undertake meditative training, or mindfulness, that cultivates inner awareness, we can contribute to our own eventual "inconceivable" liberation from the hamster wheel.

Mindfulness and meditation

Every spiritual practice has some meditative component in which practitioners contemplate deeply certain teachings, imagery, or iconography. The practice we are exploring here, however, is the work of cultivating awareness and mindfulness, which begins with settling and stilling the mind. The practice is not easy, but with diligence and time it can lead toward a profound personal transformation. In the context of socially engaged Buddhist economics the goal is not only to eventually transform ourselves, but to work toward purposive social transformation that literally begins with changing our minds. As the techniques for mindfulness based meditation have been taught over thousands of years there are a multitude of ways to approach it—far too many to cover completely here. For our purposes, we will focus only on the basics of the practice so that those who are inspired can get to work on the practice right away, but keeping in mind that there is a wealth of good literature available for those who seek to deepen their experience.

In virtually all forms of mindfulness, whether Buddhist or otherwise, the practice begins with just sitting, nothing more. In the Zen Buddhist tradition, "just sitting" is called zazen. Most teachers suggest that it is best to begin by selecting a place that is clean, quiet, and empty of clutter if possible. A secluded part of the home, perhaps, or a Zen center if there is one nearby. Sitting posture is important because activities of the mind and the quality of meditation are affected by physical movement. If the body is still, it is easier to still the mind. If the body is fidgeting, so will be the mind. Eventually, with enough practice, zazen meditation can be done in the midst of all kinds of activities, including walking, jogging, eating, and working. But in the beginning it is generally considered best to just sit and pay attention. As the saying goes in Buddhism, "don't just do something, sit there."

Although it sounds simple, just sitting and stilling the mind is quite challenging at first. A helpful technique for beginners is to try focusing the mind on one's breathing. This is nothing more than paying attention to our breathing in its light and natural state while remaining open and clear in mind. The connection between the breath and the mind is profound and is a central feature of virtually all forms of Yoga. Breathing is a unique body function because it unconsciously continues and keeps us alive, like our heartbeats, yet it can easily be controlled by the conscious mind. It joins the conscious and unconscious minds. This practice, therefore, is to sit, breathe in and out naturally, and hold our concentration on this one thing only. It is simple, but not easy at first. In fact it can seem maddeningly difficult as we experience monkey mind—chatter and a seemingly endless cascade of mental noise: what time is it? I need to pay bills, he said this, she said that, and so on as the mind jumps from one thought to the next. To help with monkey mind, it is often recommended to augment the breathing with simple counting: inhale, exhale, "one;" inhale, exhale, "two;" and so on up to ten. Once you reach ten counts, return to one and start over again from one. This is an excellent exercise that can be practiced every day and develops one's ability to stay focused and aware. In time, focus and awareness develop naturally without counting and one can stay wholly concentrated on light, natural breathing. Cultivating this ability over time is like learning to play a musical instrument. It always starts with some unpleasant noise, but develops into wonderful harmonies and melodies with practice. Stilling the mind in this way is a practice of simply allowing thoughts to come to the mind, then letting them float away like a cloud. It is when the noise chatter in the mind has been quieted and you realize a state of calm and concentration that you can observe all that comes and goes within your own mind and around you. Such power is the opposite of delusion.

Mindfulness is also a practice of "letting go." This involves being aware of monkey mind and actively releasing whatever comes to the surface of consciousness. This can be particularly helpful for those of us who tend to dwell on things excessively, like when a piece of music gets stuck in an endless loop of mental replaying. Letting go is the conscious process of merely unclenching whatever captures our mental energy. It is important, however, to understand the difference between letting go and pushing away. If one starts ruminating about something and becomes unsettled, it is not helpful to mentally force it away. Aversion is another form of mental grasping, like a grasping hand that wants to yank, push, and pull. Grasping and aversion are both attachments and the purpose of letting go is nonattachment. When we make our meditation practice centered on just sitting, paying attention to breathing, we become more adept and skillful at detaching ourselves from the myriad of things that grip our conscious minds.

The Buddha understood that so much suffering arises from greed, aggression, and delusion, yet these afflictions are the manifestations of the deeper condition of craving and attachment. Throughout Buddhist literature much is written about nonattachment as a way to work through the problems associated with avaricious society. Cravings and attachments are the taproot of all forms suffering, and a mindfulness practice is the tool with which we can unlock ourselves from them. And when we unlock ourselves, we also emancipate ourselves from the Sisyphean slog on the hamster wheel.

Craving and covetousness are the primary conditions of the consumerist impulse and financial greed. Capitalism, if it is about anything at all, is about institutionalizing craving. Craving for profits drives production and marketing so as to stimulate cravings for consumption among the general population. Consumer culture feeds on attachment as people everywhere are flooded with media messages crafted specifically to create a sense that we continually cling to clothes, cars, accessories, and to accumulate more as a kind of shelter for the vulnerable ego. Ego-centrism is characterized by an obsessive attachment to the self—to the I-me-mine. But this is a trap. As we form attachments and obsessions, we also cling to the desire to make everything permanent. Nothing is permanent, and, accordingly, the contradiction between the desire to have things made permanent and the reality of impermanence creates more existential anxiety, leading to more clinging, more anxiety, and so on in a vicious circle. The circle of pathology becomes clear to see as it eventually leads to addiction. Addiction, craving, and attachment are all on the same continuum. The I-me-mine ego structure is essentially a dreamlike thing; yet so many of us are so deeply attached to the thing that we are willing to lie, cheat, steal, and even self-destruct, as our powers of rational thought have been captured by the addictive voice that keeps telling us that "more is better" and "greed is good." The one most salient characteristic of addiction is destructive lack of control. Margaret M. Stevens relates a story that gives insight into this dilemma.

> [There was] a man who died and found himself in
> a beautiful place, surrounded by every conceivable

comfort. A white jacketed man came to him and said, 'You may have anything you choose: any food, any pleasure, and any kind of entertainment.' The man was delighted, and for days he sampled all the delicacies and experiences of which he had dreamed on Earth. But one day he grew bored with all of it, and calling the attendant to him he said, 'I'm tired of all this, I need something to do. What kind of work can you give me?' The attendant sadly shook his head and replied, 'I'm sorry, sir. That's the one thing we can't do you for you. There is not work here for you.' To which the man answered, 'That's a fine thing. I might as well be in hell. The attendant said softly, 'Where do you think you are?'"[13]

If our minds are troubled and poisoned with discontent, then our actions will reflect that trouble, and those actions will affect others. Through habituation and influence, this gives troubling characteristics to our social structures. If the discontent is the feeling that we need to aggressively outdo our peers by using debt to finance the purchase of bigger, better, faster new toys to race on the hamster wheel, this will succeed only in hastening conditions of human and environmental ruin all around us. Nonetheless, the all-important GDP numbers will rise in a cheerful delusion of wellbeing. And our actions, like all addictive behavior, are packaged in the baggage of denial.

Mindfulness is a way to transform delusion and denial with clarity and understanding. Mindfulness meditation is a means by which we can become more self-aware, more mindful of our motivations, and, as such, is a means to recovery and to wellbeing. With time and practice we can step out of the circle of pathology and actually reverse the vicious circle. With that positivity as a foundation, according to Paramananda, "we can then act in the world creatively in ways that will help both ourselves and others."[14] The daily meditation practice of mindfulness literally opens the mind. Mindfulness meditation is a tool by which we develop awareness and slowly chip away at the wall of delusion that blocks the living light of reality.

Depending on the extent of one's practice, mindfulness can lead to a spectrum of benefits, ranging from a simple ability to relax to a deep spiritual enlightenment as was experienced by the Buddha. The Zen and Vipassana traditions within Buddhism place much emphasis on meditation and mindfulness, but not so much in a religious sense as we understand the meaning of the terms in Western cultures. These are more like training programs for the mind. Some, particularly in the US, have taken an entirely secular approach to meditation practice. The practice can be powerfully inspiring, causing some imbue their practice with a kind of religiosity. What direction the practice takes is up to each individual. Buddhism has had a profound influence in Asian cultures for two and a half millennia; and over a shorter period in the West. During this time, art, rituals, poetry, music, and food have taken on Buddhist influence, although always rooted in local customs, traditions, and language. Naturally, specific cultures will have their own interpretations of the meaning of mindfulness meditation. I encourage readers to explore how people have found many different ways to express inspiration and experience they gain from their practice. The focus here, however, is on practical daily living and a lifelong commitment to finding peace and liberation from greed, aggression, and delusion for our society and ourselves.

Recall that for the Buddha, right mindfulness originated as part of the four noble truths of suffering. It is a way of developing the skillful means of dealing with difficulties that arise both from within ourselves and from our social surroundings. With a mindfulness practice, people can begin to gain clearer insights into who they really are by gradually allowing the fog of delusion to clear away. Just as a blurry photo image gradually comes into focus, we can see things as they truly are, and from this insight a more compelling sense of interbeing develops naturally, along with compassion, and people may find themselves a more comfortable place in society alongside their fellow human beings. Regardless of whether one approaches mindfulness from a religious or secular viewpoint, mindful cultivation through meditation is the crucial first and most challenging step toward liberation.

Mindfulness is a level of awareness that is always focused on being in the present moment. Done correctly, it acts as a kind of mirror of our own thoughts, reflecting precisely what is happening and exactly the way it is happening.[15] It is a state of noticing the flow of all things which allows us to be attentive to what is happening in the moment, and to the origins of our motivations—particularly those that sprout from the seeds of greed, aggression, and delusion that exist within us all.

Mindfulness and social engagement

From the socially engaged Buddhist perspective there is a social aspect that needs to be addressed as much as the inner motivation. Buddhist teacher Gregory Kramer informs us that "A great deal of our suffering in life is in relationship to other people. We cannot reasonably expect individualistic philosophies and solitary practices to directly address the pain that arises between two people or in society at large."[16] When we give the meditation practice a social dimension, it becomes a dual process that begins by looking deeply into ourselves and extending outward into the stream of living society. Mindfulness meditation, therefore, is also a social practice in the sense of opening up and becoming aware of our surroundings and our institutions. The more we become self-aware of pathological motivations and addictions, the more we become socially aware of the same things as they are reified in our social structures. At the same time, as we still our minds individually, we become more aware of the misery that others experience, and of the misery we can bring to others by our actions. With mindfulness, we become increasingly aware of how we habitually fabricate many of our own problems. With this awareness we begin to see how we fabricate problems not only for ourselves but for others as well. With better awareness, we can also see that everyone shares similar stresses, peeves, doubts, fears, and joys. We are not alone in our misery, nor are we alone in our wellbeing. With mindfulness we enter into a state of being in which we are no longer socially or karmically oblivious, and from this wisdom flows compassion. The broader social meaning of mindfulness is explained by David Loy: "Buddhism encourages mindfulness and awareness, and especially today it's necessary for that awareness to extend beyond our seating cushions and dharma practice halls, to embrace a broader understanding of what is happening in our world, to our world—a world that cries out in pain."[17] There is no distinction between a personal practice and the world around us because true mindfulness is to cultivate an awareness of everything which has any relation to our individual selves.

On the basis of this self and social awareness, socially engaged Buddhist economics can begin to take steps toward positive social change. The circle turns in a different direction, away from pathology and toward wellbeing, as clarity and kindness lead to positive actions in the world, which in turn give rise to further positive mental states. The vicious circle transforms into the compassionate circle.[18]

Mindfulness meditation is thus an empowering tool for social change. As we change ourselves and become more aware of the impact we have on each other and on our environment, we come to see that in a multitude of ways we are not hopelessly trapped by greed, aggression, and delusion. Even if it takes years to liberate ourselves and many years more to liberate our social structures from defilement, there is great hope and joy in knowing that we have started out on the path of transformation. As the wheels of karmic volition turn in a different direction, no matter how imperceptible this may be, we can take comfort in knowing that we are moving in a different direction. Much hard work remains ahead and we need not dwell on the results of this work, as long as we stay on the rails through true mindfulness. However, concerns are being raised that mindfulness is getting pulled in a different and potentially destructive direction.

Avoiding McMindfulness

Depending on the extent of our practice, mindfulness can lead to a spectrum of benefits ranging from an enhanced ability to deal with stress to a deep spiritual enlightenment as experienced by the Buddha. As people become more aware of the many benefits of mindfulness, it has become enormously popular, particularly in the UK and the US. According to Willem Kuyken, director of Oxford Mindfulness Centre, mindfulness is fast growing in popularity as it is helping fill a need in society in which people everywhere are seeking for ways to cope with the constant stimulus of economic life. He notes that, "If distraction is the pre-eminent condition or our age, then mindfulness in the eyes of its enthusiasts is its most logical response." In other words, it is helping people to cope with the pressures of life on the hamster wheel. Understanding and transforming our minds helps us to make better choices. We become wise, rather than slaves to our delusions.

In the light of the transformative powers of a true mindfulness practice, there has been a rush of books and articles since the mid-2000s on topics ranging from eating habits to dealing with workplace stress to cognitive therapy techniques. Mindfulness helps suffering, and thus is increasingly seen as a positive force in alleviating this suffering. As such, different approaches to mindfulness have developed. Among the most popular approaches are those that have severed mindfulness completely from its Buddhist roots.

The most notable advocate of non-Buddhist mindfulness is Jon Kabat-Zinn at the University of Massachusetts Medical Center. We practice mindfulness, Kabat-Zinn contends, to be empowered "by a connection to something deeper within ourselves, a discerning wisdom that helps to penetrate and transcend the fear and the pain, and to discover some peace and hope within our situation as it is."[19] Kabat-Zinn is emphasizing the use of mindfulness as a way of coping with the hamster wheel "situation as it is." Notwithstanding the positive benefits of this work, it is of concern that so much of the popular literature on mindfulness has to do with the cooption of mindfulness by the corporate agenda. As this happens, mindfulness becomes blurry and faddish and misses the most important aspect of the Buddhist tradition—transformation. The key difference between the Buddhist approach and the secular, corporatized approaches to mindfulness is the notion of change. The whole point of mindfulness in the Buddhist way is not to merely cope with pathological conditions that create suffering, but to change them. And for socially engaged Buddhist economics this includes the radical notion of transforming our economic and financial institutions away from the grasping and clawing environment of the corporate world and toward alternatives devoted to genuine liberation from all that, and toward wellbeing. Corporate mindfulness, also derisively referred to as McMindfulness, is a trend that seeks to make mindfulness into a profitable commodity. In so doing, it reverses the transformation of greed to wellbeing back to greed again. Before we look at the criticisms of corporate mindfulness, however, it is important to acknowledge that those who advocate integrating mindfulness into the corporate workplace do make some valid points which should not be overlooked.

The prototype formula for mindfulness, reducing workplace stress, and enhancing performance was a program developed by Kabat-Zinn called Mindfulness Based Stress Reduction (MBSR). He describes MBSR as "based on rigorous and systematic training in mindfulness, a form of meditation. ... It is a systematic approach to developing new kinds of agency, control, and wisdom in our lives, based on our inner capacity for paying attention and on the awareness, insight and compassion that naturally arise from paying attention in specific ways." Drawing on this practice, Kabat-Zinn developed a clinic to help people deal with stress: "the MBSR program is a vehicle for active learning, in which people can build on the strengths that they already have and, as we noted, come to do something for themselves to improve their own health and well-being."[20]

Inspired by the MBSR program, journalist and author of *Mindful Work* (2015), David Gelles, tells numerous stories of how large companies are incorporating mindfulness into management strategies because it helps to build the bottom-line profits. Gelles relates a case study in which the MBSR program was administered to the employees of a biotech company in Wisconsin. The company, Promega, is fast paced and places much stress on its employees to perform. After completing the course, the workers who participated in it reported that they "were less stressed, felt less anxiety, and had more energy at work." Moreover, the mindfulness program had improved their immune systems and personal confidence. Accordingly, in classic win-win optimism, workers feel better, perform better, and the business reaps rewards. Improved immune systems, more energy, and workplace happiness are all positive things that contribute to wellbeing.

Sharon Salzberg, in her book, *Real Happiness at Work* (2014), acknowledges that meditation and mindfulness are techniques available to us for becoming more productive, satisfied, and peaceful at work. "Through meditation," she writes, "we can come to understand work problems as a potential source of achieving greater clarity." Salzberg adds that with a meditation practice, "it is possible to be competitive without being cruel—and committed without being consumed. Even in a job climate where being fired is a real and present danger, we have the power to improve our work lives immeasurably through awareness, compassion, patience, and ingenuity."[21] In these ways, mindfulness is seen as a source of company value, and management consultants have jumped on the mindfulness training bandwagon in droves.[22] This is where corporate mindfulness becomes problematic.

The corporate and financial institutions that dominate the global economy are powerful structures that have been formed in a crucible of habitualized greed; that is, the embodiment of institutionalized greed. To work on ourselves yet ignore the need to change our institutions is a contradiction. We have become what we are in part because we are conditioned to our social milieu. In the circle of pathology, our individual habits of thought and action are inseparable from the habits of thought and action embodied in our economic institutions. True change from greed to wellbeing has to involve the transformation of both.

In his book, *The Power of Habit: Why We Do What We Do in Life and Business* (2014), Charles Duhigg describes what he calls the habit loop. His work stems from research at the Brain and Cognitive Sciences Department at MIT on habit formation. What the MIT scientists discovered is that habits occur so that we humans do not have to relearn how to behave each day. "Habits, the scientists say, emerge because the brain is constantly looking for ways to save effort. Left to its own devices, the brain will try to make almost any routine a habit."[23] In other words, because of the brain's habituation capability, we do not have to be constantly preoccupied with things like walking, chewing food, brushing our teeth. As habits, they come automatically, which then frees the mind to be thinking about other things. The habit loop is a fairly mechanical process of responding to a cue of some kind, receiving a reward for the cue, and making the response routine so as to keep receiving the rewards. "Over time, the loop – cue, routine, reward; cue, routine, reward; becomes automatic."

The importance of understanding this loop lies in awareness. Habits of thought and action are, by definition, things people think and do automatically, without conscious awareness. But the more we understand how habits work with mindfulness, the easier it will be to bring them under control.

When we talk about institutionalization, we are adding another layer to this process. We are talking about not only individual habits, but those which condition our individual habits through institutional forces, namely the things that define corporate culture, whether the habits, individual or institutional, actually lead to wellbeing. If greed, aggression, and delusion are part of a corporate culture, then the project of mindfulness within these institutions will be fraught with contradictions. People have to stay scrambling on the hamster wheel because that is what is required to keep the system spinning, and that scramble is habituated by all the cues, messages, rewards, and routines that Duhigg and MIT researchers have observed. These habits are powerful. "They shape our lives far more than we realize," says Duhigg, "they are so strong, in fact, that they cause our brains to cling to them at the exclusion of all else, including common sense."[24] Changing our institutionalized habits is as important as changing our individual habits. The economic and financial institutions that govern the economies of the world need to be transformed or replaced entirely, not merely coped with. At center of the critique of corporate mindfulness is that it ignores this need for radical transformation and social engagement. Rather, it presupposes a condition in which we shall all remain trapped on the hamster wheel economy, and simply provides ways to cope with the stress that arises accordingly.

In an article for *Salon* titled "Corporate Mindfulness is Bullsh*t," Ronald Purser, a business professor at San Francisco State University, and Edwin Ng challenge the credibility of mindfulness as it has gone mainstream. They challenge Gelles and others to address the broader corporate structure and consumer culture that imposes such stressful conditions in the first place: "those celebrating the mindfulness boom have avoided any serious consideration of why stress is so pervasive in corporations and society."[25]

The authors mention Amazon as a case in point as it was succinctly profiled in a recent *New York Times* article, "Jeff Bezos and the Amazon Way," by Joe Nocera. In order to satisfy Wall Street's demand for greater profits, Amazon workers "were pushed harder and harder to work faster and faster until they were terminated, they quit, or they got injured." Nocera and other who similarly describe Amazon's corporate culture provide exemplary descriptions of life on the hamster wheel. Nocera adds, "Amazon – and to be sure, any number of other companies as well – has taken this idea to its logical extreme: bring people in, shape them in the Amazon style of confrontation and workaholism, and cast them aside when they have outlived their usefulness."[26]

The authors of the *Salon* piece challenge Gelles: "Would Gelles offer his advice with a straight face to these employees of Amazon, telling them that they have imposed stress on themselves ...?" Even so, Amazon works for its shareholders and conforms to the expectations of Wall Street and consumers who demand low prices and fast service. In socially engaged Buddhist economics, these are all institutional and cultural problems. And in the spirit of interbeing, when we look at Amazon, Walmart, Microsoft, Goldman Sachs, Northern Rock, and Wall Street we are looking in the mirror.

Amazon is a pressure cooker corporate institution because Wall Street demanded so when it was taking shape in the 1990s. Wall Street is there to maximize shareholder equity in a large part because fund managers—those who look after nest-eggs —demand it so. And the population of people who have their retirement money invested in these nest-eggs demand it as well. There is no Us vs. Them.

Purser and Ng cite a Stanford–Harvard study that emphasizes that employee stress is related to the hamster wheel characteristics of contemporary businesses and corporations, "lack of health insurance, threats of constant layoffs and job security, lack of discretion and autonomy in decision-making, long work hours, low organization justice, and unrealistic job demands." They challenge that, rather than cultivating awareness of the conditions that cause suffering and removing those conditions, "corporate mindfulness goes no further than encouraging individuals to manage stress so as to optimize performance." Gelles, in his defense, said in an interview that "We live in a capitalist economy, mindfulness can't change that."[27]

It is in this comment that I believe Gelles is wrong. I cannot imagine a more important reason to practice mindfulness than to develop awareness of the troubling economic conditions in which we live—particularly the greed, aggression, and delusion that go so intimately with capitalism—and to change those conditions. I submit further that a sincere mindfulness practice may be the *only* way people will be able to extricate themselves from the hamster wheel economics of capitalism.

David Loy teamed up with Ron Purser for another article challenging corporate mindfulness. Coining the term "McMindfulness," the authors raise warning flags about the corporate mindfulness movement as becoming a packaged commodity. "The booming popularity of the mindfulness movement," the authors write, "has also turned it into a cottage industry." It has become a product that management consultants have been marketing to corporate executives with the promise of bottom-line improvements derived from better efficiency, less absenteeism, and improved management skills. In an attempt to "brand" mindfulness as non-ideological (presumably not to step on religious toes), corporate mindfulness has relinquished all ties and affiliations to its Buddhist origins. Gelles takes it further by describing mindfulness as it is packaged by MBSR as a consumer product: "as an introduction to mindfulness, MBSR shares the qualities of the best consumer products on the markets: high quality, deeply reliable, and well worth the investment."[28]

In Kabat-Zinn's 650-page tome, *Full Catastrophe Living*, references to Buddhism appear briefly in the introduction and then not again until page 473, when he makes a distant reference to the Buddhist origin of mindfulness, which he simply dismisses as "a very unusual religion."[29] Loy and Purser contend that this exclusion is a matter of marketing expediency, "uncoupling mindfulness from its ethical and religious Buddhist context is understandable as an expedient move to make such training a viable product on the open market."

Loy and Purser show that mindfulness is a piece of a broader liberative and transformative practice involving all eight domains of the noble path. They criticize the individual self fulfillment message of corporate mindfulness in society: "Such an individualistic and consumer orientation to the practice of mindfulness is essentially impotent for mitigating the causes of collective and organizational distress. Mindfulness training has wide appeal because it has become a trendy method for subduing employee unrest, promoting tacit acceptance of the status quo, and as an instrumental tool for keeping attention focused on institutional goals." The goals here being shareholder equity. The authors quote Bhikkhu Bodhi, an outspoken Western Buddhist monk: "Buddhist practices could be easily used to justify and stabilize the status quo, becoming a reinforcement of consumer capitalism."[30]

Consumer capitalism, corporate goals, and corporate mindfulness are all part of the hustle and noise of hamster wheel economics. Mindfulness is also an element situated within a broader body of Buddhist thought. But Nhat Hanh teaches us that it is not only a part of Buddhist thought, "it is at the heart of the Buddha's teachings."[31] We can say that mindfulness is to Buddhism what greed is to capitalism, and there is no juncture where these can be considered compatible. If we try to surgically remove mindfulness from Buddhism to make it a product, we are taking the heart from the body, and by so doing we destroy it.

The fallacy of corporate mindfulness is that it presumes that corporate institutions can be made more humane and sustainable by training their personnel in how to meditate while leaving the institutions exactly unchanged. It makes one wonder whether, if corporate mindfulness gurus had lived in mid-19th-century America, they would have been hired by slaveowners to teach slaves how to meditate and thereby be more productive and less stressed. But slavery was not an individually conceived business model, it was (is) an institution.

When we talk of fund managers pressuring businesses to improve their bottom lines, these are the institutional investors. Institutional investors have a fiduciary responsibility to future retirees, endowments, and foundations, which are institutions that represent people and community interests everywhere. All of these people with their responsibilities and these institutions comprise the nuts and bolts and raw material of the hamster wheel.

This hamster wheel, in other words, is of our own making. We have collectively inherited the karmic delusion that this is the only way to happiness. To change this, it will be up to us, collectively, to deconstruct the delusion and move in a different direction. Mindfulness is a simple and direct way to approach the process of deconstructing the mental habits, compulsions, addictions, and delusions that keep us on the wheel.

Mindfulness is a cultivation of true awareness of the state of ourselves, our thoughts, our actions, our habits, our social world, and the state of the rat wheel. As Glassman and so many others have argued, once we do the hard inner work of fostering awareness and breaking the habit loops, we can turn our attention to creating new institutional structures for ourselves. Nhat Hanh writes, "we spend a lot of time looking for happiness when the world right around us is full of wonder."[32] The rat wheel is full of hustle and noise and so we are unable to hear "the call of beauty … mindfulness is the practice that quiets the noise inside us…. In order to really *be*, you have to be free from the thinking, free from anxieties, free from fear, free from longing."[33]

The steepest part of the climb out of suffering is that which involves being engaged in the world. We cannot know for sure what will be the most defining aspects of economic society for future generations, but we can be sure that whatever they are they will be those that we have a chance to shape for the better today. This sense of karmic responsibility—like leaving water in the jug for those who are coming later and will be thirsty—is the most profound dimension of socially engaged Buddhist economics. In this karmic sense, we can build alternative monetary institutions that future generations will inherit and build upon as an ongoing project of evolution.

As we have seen, money and financial systems are centrally important. Entire economic systems can fail catastrophically if these institutions become unstable. People everywhere need money because we live in a world of markets. Money is ultimately just an instrument, just as are stocks, bonds, and deeds to property. The troubles begin with the attitudes we attach to them and the motivations for what and how we use these instruments, and the social structures that solidify as a result of these motivations. With this thought, we will give Nhat Hanh the last word on mindfulness.

> Mindfulness gives you the inner space and quietness that allow you to look deeply, to find out who you are and what you want to do with your life. You won't feel the need to make yourself run after meaningless pursuits anymore. You've been running … you push yourself to achieve this and that condition so you can be happy. You believe you don't have enough conditions to be happy right now, and so you develop the habit many people have of constantly running after one thing or another. … [But] all the wonders of life are already here. They're calling you. If you can listen to them, you will be able to stop running. What you need, what we *all* need, is silence. Stop the noise in your mind in order for the wondrous sounds of life to be heard. Then you can begin to live your life authentically and deeply.[34]

SEVEN

Accepting impermanence

A central theme in Buddhist thought is the notion of impermanence. It is often referred to as "anicca" in traditional Buddhist literature, meaning that everything formed in this universe is ceaselessly changing. Nothing endures forever. There is only process, flux, and time. The 13th-century Zen master, Dogen, calls it "being-time," indicating that because everything is changing, everything is time. He pointed to a 16-foot golden figure, a seemingly very solid and unchanging object, and said this is time.[1] In the Buddhist view, everything—a golden statue, the sun, the mountains—is temporal and flowing along the one-directional arrow of time.

This realization of the temporality and flux of physical reality was understood intuitively by Buddhists, and, centuries later, Western philosophers and scientists drew the same conclusions as they observed that all things that have form combine the stability of structure with the fluidity of change. Like a whirlpool, everything is both a structure and a process, and everything is contingent as it arises and passes away while being dependent on other things that also arise and pass away. The Taoist sage Zhuang Tzu observed over two thousand years ago, "How Heaven revolves! Do the Sun and the Moon contend about their respective places? Is there someone presiding over and directing those things? Or is there perhaps some secret mechanism in consequence of which they cannot but be as they are?"[2] In similar deep reflection, theologian and philosopher Teilhard de Chardin writes, "By standards of our human existence, the mountains and stars are a model of majestic changelessness. Now we discover that observed over a sufficiently great duration of time, the earth's crust changes ceaselessly under our feet, while the heavens sweep us along in a cyclone of stars."[3]

In the 1970s, Nobel prize-winning chemist Ilya Prigogine began to form an entirely new approach to physical science that he called "dissipative structures." He observed that all living things in their natural state are both structure and process and that contradictory tendencies coexist in all living systems: simultaneous stillness and motion. Old-paradigm science based on the Newtonian mechanistic framework, which was criticized by Schumacher and the institutionalist economists, failed to come to terms with the inherent nature of this simultaneous existence of structure and change. The machine metaphors that are still used by economists today are obsolete. Prigogine writes, "For classic science it was the clock; for nineteenth-century science, the period of the Industrial Revolution, it was an engine running down." Running down in this case refers to the second law of thermodynamics, or the law of entropy, which tells us that useable energy is disappearing. The law of entropy is an expression of being-time—an arrow of time that always points from hot to cold.[4]

Prigogine asserts that science needs a new metaphor as new scientific discoveries are fundamentally not compatible with Newtonian, mechanistic imagery. He compels us to ask the question, "What will be the symbol for us?" and, like Dogen, refers to sculpture: "What we have in mind may perhaps be expressed best by reference to sculpture ... In some of the most beautiful manifestations of sculpture, be it in the dancing Shiva or in the miniature temples of Guerrero, there appears very clearly the search for a junction between stillness and motion, time arrested and time passing. We believe that this confrontation will give our period its uniqueness."[5]

Entropy itself has been invoked to interpret the nature of biological and social evolution in ways that characterize life as the process of survival by means of harnessing useable energy (negative entropy) from the surrounding environment and turning it to ash. As living systems draw useable energy from their environments, they are able to arrest the process of entropic degradation within their own biological system, but at the same time accelerate the process of degradation in their habitat. On this, anthropologist, Leslie White writes, "Maintenance of life is achieved by offsetting the entropy produced by the very process of living with negative entropy obtained from the environment 'by sucking orderliness from the environment.' By obtaining more negative entropy from the environment than the positive entropy produced by the process of living, i.e., by utilizing increasing amounts of energy as it flows through living systems to build more complicated structures."[6] The hamster wheel can keep spinning and grow for as long as it can suck increasingly large amounts of energy out of the surrounding world. White concludes that "it follows that this must be the basic function of culture also: the harnessing of energy and putting it to work in the service of man."[7] To that end, we humans have performed exceptionally well. But this performance will necessarily give way to something else because of the basic fact that it is running out of fuel.

Inevitable change and impermanence

When we look at the historical record of cultural evolution, we can see that major changes in societies usually occur when the economic foundation is disrupted. The Roman Empire crumbled when its Mediterranean network of trade and slavery was thrown into chaos by invasions. Similarly, the feudal agrarian systems dissipated when plague epidemics destroyed the farming population. Germany's Weimar Republic fell to pieces with the collapse of its currency. Today, something similar is happening in the global economy as resource limitation, particularly of oil, and global warming are beginning to shake the foundation of our entire way of life and rendering the growth-driven system obsolete. No amount of technological innovation or central bank alchemy can change this basic fact.

On this point, Richard Heinberg warns that "the conventional wisdom on the state of the economy – that the financial crisis that started in 2008 was caused by bad real estate loans and that eventually, when the kinks are worked out, the nation will be back to business as usual – is tragically wrong."[8] When he talks of working out kinks, Heinberg is alluding to central bank policies formed around the doctrinaire Greenspan Put.

The world of central banking systems is now built on a foundation of debt and stock market speculation and a presumption that as long as these continue, the global economy will be healthy and strong. As of this writing, there has been no apparent change in this presumption. The Fed kept target interest rates close to zero through the Bernanke years and continues to do so under the leadership of Janet Yellen. Over most of the summer of 2015, the Fed prepared the public for a policy shift to begin pulling some of the speculative liquidity out of the banking system and start raising interest rates. But no sooner had it started this than a crash in the markets sent shock waves through Wall Street. The *New York Times* reported, "It's clear that the Fed officials think that the economy is well on the path toward healing ...,"[9] and healing here is interpreted as steady growth in GDP. The turbulence caused by speculators' collective panic over the possibility that higher rates would cause higher costs of leveraged trading gave the Fed pause for thought.

Yellen announced in a news conference that "The Fed should not be responding to the ups and downs of markets ... but when there are significant financial developments, it's incumbent upon us to ask ourselves, 'What is causing them?' What we can't know for sure is how much concerns about the global economic outlook are drivers of those developments."[10] "Concerns about global economic outlook" means concerns about continuing growth in GDP. In their desperate attempts to sustain this, central banks everywhere, like the Fed, are doing what they know they should not do—keeping market bubbles inflated and caving in to the whims of greed-inspired speculation. The Fed justifies its policies with the contention that speculative greed ultimately keeps the hamster wheel spinning and, as long as it does, we all will experience wellbeing. In that respect, Yellen has already answered her own question. Debt, the greed-infected cloud of hot money, and market bubbles are the drivers. But the question she and other central bankers are not asking is to where we are all being driven.

Heinberg pulls the view of all this back down to earth: "as we back up to take a wider view, we notice larger and longer-term trends that have played even more important roles. One key factor was the severance of money from its moorings."[11] By moorings, he is referring to the gold standard and precious metals that once backed currency. But the same idea applies when we anchor money to the one thing that is most important in relation to it—what you can buy with it. As long as we continue to expect, as do the Fed and all of its constituents, that financialized instruments should always grow, then our expectations of what we can buy with money should always grow proportionally. This takes us back to the law of entropy and our inability to deal with it. Endless growth is predicated on the notion that there will always be an infinite supply of useable energy from which our economic systems can draw fuel, but this is a stark disregard of the law of physics.

The central message of the Greenspan Put as perpetuated by Yellen is that what drives Wall Street is what drives the rest of the economic system. This is only part of the story of economic growth. The financial sector may be the driver, but economies are pushed to grow because that is what people everywhere expect from their financial investments. It is perfectly natural for everyone now to expect continuously compounding financial returns without giving things a second thought. Even if the markets crash, the general assumption is that they will bounce back and continue appreciating. If we look at the last 200 years of stock market history, that certainly seems to be the case—a long-term trend showing a 7 percent rate of return after factoring out price inflation. It is no surprise, then, that people see this as a normal aspect of our economy.

Popular assumptions, however, are not always grounded in scientific reality. Most of us want to believe in them because the endless accumulation of money is a very alluring idea. People pour trillions into various funds for speculation in the markets because they have come to expect that these investments will continuously appreciate in value. The money value gained from this is anticipated to be used to provide for our needs in retirement, or to pay for our children's education. People say that money doesn't grow on trees. Rather, it grows in the financial system, toward an infinite horizon. For all this growth in money and financial wealth to be meaningful, people, the amount of stuff you can buy with it—the stuff of GDP—must also grow. After all, what good is it to become a millionaire if you can't buy a million dollars' worth of stuff with the money?

The hamster wheel has us trapped. If the financial side of the economy stops growing, businesses will not generate profits and they will fail. Capital for further investment will dry up, businesses will shut down, and people will lose their jobs. As joblessness rises, consumer spending falls, and the financial side collapses further. To prevent this, we stay the course and hold on to the delusion that our financial wealth will continue to accumulate, consumers will continue to spend, profits will continue to rise—and the wheel keeps turning. Economic growth is driven by its own self-reinforcing momentum that can be changed only by either deliberately building a different system or crashing into the wall of physical limitations. The denial of the reality of physical limitations—in particular, the finite nature of fossil fuels and the horrific damage wrought by their continued use—is what Heinberg says is so tragically wrong.

For some time now, growth addiction has been enabled by technology addiction, although this is merely prolonging the inevitable. It seems that whenever someone raises the issue of limits to growth, the general response is often angry and overwhelming backlash. Most do not want to hear this because it implies changing our habituated ways. The "technology will always save us" belief is a powerful and compelling opiate, and those addicted to it are willing to believe in any kind of magic rather than withdraw from their habits. Heinberg's sober voice presents us with two concise and equally true statements about our deeply habituated need to stay attached to the fossil fuel, hydrocarbon production system:

- Hydrocarbons are so abundant that, if we burn a substantial portion of them, we risk a climate catastrophe beyond imagining.
- There aren't enough economically accessible, high-quality hydrocarbons to maintain world economic growth for much longer.[12]

If climate change is a sign of anything, it is an indication that our economic system cannot be sustained. It's impermanence is real, and this can be very unsettling to minds that habitually cling—which is those of most of the human population. In our minds we try to make the impermanent permanent by imagining enduring structures that do not exist. Buddhist environmentalist Lily de Silva explains, "Though we use a noun called 'rain' which appears to denote a 'thing,' rain is nothing but the process of drops of water falling from the skies. Apart from this process, the activity of raining, there is no rain as such which could be expressed by a seemingly static nominal concept."[13] But grasping at figments or notions is delusion, and delusion causes suffering because it is inevitably shattered by reality.

Accepting impermanence is as difficult as accepting mortality. But as we do so, we become liberated and no longer paralyzed by our attachments. Robert Reich said that if we took the greed (and we might as well add delusion and aggression) out of Wall Street, we would have nothing left but pavement. This would be a fabulous opportunity, as the field would become wide open for possibilities for real and lasting change. It is easy to get overwhelmed by the prospect of change, but to struggle against it leads only to hopelessness and despair. Such despair is a human emotion that stems from a blindness to the opportunities for real and positive change that are now presenting themselves. From our perspective of socially engaged Buddhist economics, rather than surrendering to powerlessness, we should become engaged in our own communities and welcome new approaches to meeting our needs. If we accept the impermanence of the hamster wheel way of life, we will be forever liberated from it. But, as I have been arguing throughout, this requires both the inner work of changing our minds and the outer work of changing our institutions.

The institutions that reign over the global economy are giant corporations that together form an oligarchy. In many ways, particularly in the US, these companies are treated with awe—a kind of fearful worship—by political leaders as well as by the general public, even by many of those who are striving for a better system. Woody Tasch, in his book, *Slow Money: Investing as if Food , Farms, and Fertility Mattered* (2008), writes that "We must be critical but not too critical ... of mature corporations." In other words, corporations have a fiduciary responsibility to shareholders and fund managers and, in the spirit of market populism, that responsibility is sacrosanct.[14]

This sensibility seems oddly contradictory for a country like the United States that regards itself as the unparalleled vanguard of all democratic movements. Nobel laureate and institutionalist economist Gunnar Myrdal wrote in *Rich Lands and Poor* that in countries like the US there exists a "moral discord" between the common adherence to egalitarian principles of governance such as the basic political rights and enfranchisement of all persons and the starkly repressive conditions of real life in a plutocracy where money rules. Echoing Tasch's sentiments, it would seem that Americans want justice, but not too much justice; they want to place Wall Street under scrutiny, but not too much scrutiny, for fear that such action might impede capital gains. It would appear that it is easier for an entire population to live with this moral discord and denial than to face the deeper problem of institutionalized greed and how it grinds us down. The discord is softened by bogus economic theory built on an assumption that greed is a good thing. On this Myrdal writes, "Economic theory is only a segment of total culture. It becomes modulated to serve opportunistic rationalization needs. In order to live as comfortably as possible with the moral discord in their hearts, people need an economic theory that diverts attention from this moral discord."[15]

Such diversion is found in the assertion in mainstream economics that the vice of self-indulgence and greed will ultimately lead to the virtue of prosperity for all. This is the ultimate rationalization for neoliberalism. For people raised on a diet of liberalist ideology, political democracy has been twisted away from its original meaning of establishing a commonwealth for the good of the majority. Rather, it has come to mean an open playing field in which each individual is free to chase on the hamster wheel after the spoils of capitalism, with a kind of righteous conviction. One of the standard American shibboleths is that capitalism and political democracy are the same extensions of freedom—economic freedom and political freedom. But this is a misconception. Democracy is an extension of political franchise to a broad segment of the population. Capitalism retains economic franchise for only a small segment of the population that profits from the ownership of capital.

Morris Berman contends that Americans have never been able, nor have ever even tried, to reconcile the deeply rooted moral discord between political and economic conditions. He writes, "material acquisition and technological innovation were druglike substitutes for a commonwealth, a truly human way of life, that Americans had largely rejected from early on." In its earliest years America was torn between being a land destined for the unrepentant acquisitiveness of the hustlers on the one hand, and on the other hand being a nobler commonwealth for the collective good. Samuel Adams, one of America's Founding Fathers, saw that the former was gaining traction and grieved that the United States was on its way to becoming "more avaricious than any other nation that ever existed." In the struggle for America's soul, the hustlers—a kind of caricature of greed, aggression, and delusion—won out, but not without criticism.[16]

Thorstein Veblen launched a scathing critique of the hustler society that America had become. He lampooned the wealthy segments of the population as they displayed their affluence by flaunting their ownership expensive consumer goods. The various accoutrements of the so-called good life signified the winners in the hustlers' game, like trophies. Following Veblen have been generations of dissident American intellectuals who lament how their country has become a soulless swamp of corporate commercialism. People seeking to live with a sense of dignity in the US find that there are few choices left to them that have not been consumed by corporate interests. American life, according to dissident Randolph Bourne, has become rudimentary and uninspired. Rephrasing Marx and Engels, he writes, "The world has nothing to lose but its chains – and its own soul to gain."[17]

The American Dream is a delusive construct that perpetuates institutionalized and acculturated greed. It also keeps the population perpetually enslaved to the ever changing fads of consumerism, or, in Berman's terms, enslaved to the hustler's life. In *The Power Elite* (1956), sociologist C. Wright Mills chronicles the troubling phenomenon of a feverish striving among the population to clone themselves after those in already established structures of power within their political, military, and economic institutions. Mills and others warned about the social pathology that would result from widespread covetousness becoming a cultural norm—a nation of hungry ghosts becoming violent. Yet, like so many other warnings, those of Mills and others were largely and consistently ignored, and in fact were coopted in such a way as to generate consumer fads and even more acquisitive impulses—the ultimate hustler's coup.

Why is it so difficult to change? One reason is that it would require people to question the values of their culture in significant numbers. Another is what Samuel Adams saw as the Americans' peculiar habit of always running headlong into the mad grab for riches, and this habit has long become ingrained and normalized. It is an addiction, and it is very hard for addicts to imagine themselves free from their addictions—particularly ones that have been around for over two centuries. Of this, Berman writes, "if the American Dream is really about unlimited abundance, and if we are addicted to that as a goal, then alternatives to that way of life are simply too scary to contemplate. Try telling a full-blown alcoholic to put down that glass of Scotch ... addiction has a certain 'systemic' pattern to it that is typically not self-corrective. Both capitalism and alcoholism are characterized by cycles of increasing dysfunction, 'runaway,' and breakdown, and the system can do this for a fairly long time."[18] That is, until the physical constraints of the planet pull the plug.

It is no doubt bitter medicine for Americans and others who suffer from these same afflictions to see their consumerist lifestyles in this way. But if we could, we would see that our addiction, like all addictions, is taking us down a path toward self-destruction. Ken Jones sees this through a Buddhist-institutionalist lens,

> As it is with individual lives, so it is with institutions, societies, and cultures: They may be swept into ruin by karmic and other tangled conditionality even though they have the objective means to avert their fate and more than enough warning of it. The actors are driven by addictive behavior and a kind

of tunnel vision that is ultimately self-destructive. And when the majority is locked into mutually affirming karma it may be particularly difficult for even a well-informed minority to achieve a change of direction."[19]

In a perfect circle of pathology, the mad grab for money on the hamster wheel leaves us without a moral center and socially and spiritually malnourished, and so, in a vain attempt to fill that emptiness we turn to consumer goods, the means to which, of course, is money. The more we grab for money, the more we feel the need to have things to show for the effort, which leads to more grabbing and more greed.

There is no convincing reason why all of us should not be compelled to take a hard, critical look at ourselves, along with our values, mythology, and shibboleths. But we are unlikely to do this as long as we can continue to be lulled into a state of somnambulant apathy by the financial market bubbles and technological gadgetry that hustle up a collective delusion of progress. Such apathy is hinged to a notion of birthright and entitlement—a Faustian deal, perhaps, made with the promise that we will forever and ever be riding that elevator of prosperity that is rigged to always go in the upward direction and that is powered by an oligarchy of corporate institutions.

If it were possible to free the mindset and expectations associated with this doomed system, it would become much easier for us to imagine ourselves evolving into an economically and ecologically healthier society. When we are no longer burdened by the cultural baggage associated with a system that is psychotically trying to achieve infinite growth on a finite planet, we will be able to more effectively explore the possibilities for consciously evolving toward new and healthier ways of living. As Schumacher taught us, this developmental process cannot happen without insight and wisdom, without which we are certain to remain trapped in a destructive society that is fraught with cynical, self-aggrandizing habits of consumption, greed, and, ultimately, violence and despair. The crises we face stem not only from how we act in the world, but also from how we perceive the world. Bringing this vision to action and real change is no small matter and will be a process that will take time and enormous effort. And although it may even appear impossible from where we are standing now, I would venture to say that it is not nearly as impossible as trying to survive another few decades in the economy of business as usual.

APPENDIX

Five elements of a Buddhist approach to economics

The first element of this approach is to recognize that the greatest challenges in dealing with climate change, energy depletion, and financial system instability are institutional, not technological. Technology will obviously play an important role in helping communities deal with the twin crises of climate change and energy descent. But as we become too dependent on technology, particularly here in North America, we tend to ignore the underlying institutional forces that drive global economic growth and unsustainable debt. Our dominant financial and corporate institutions are largely driven by an expectation that financial markets should always pay off with high returns; that is, money invested is always expected to grow. The transnational corporations and partners in governments are the taskmasters that push economic growth in every corner of the world. Technology, no matter how sophisticated, cannot change the immutable laws of physics that have placed real limits to such growth, and we have already begun to bump against to these limits. If we are serious about facing limits to growth, the assumptions of endless growth in production, consumption, and stock values will have to change.

The second element is that once we recognize that the continuous growth is institutionally driven, we must also recognize that institutional transformation must be part of the solution. A genuine long-term solution will require that we reverse the current relationship between technology and institutions. Rather than clinging to the hope that technology will allow us to continue with business as usual, we must first transform our economic institutions, which will allow appropriate forms of technology to naturally follow. Part of this technological mix is creating new economic indicators. Crafting new economic institutions entails building alternative business models, forward-looking government agencies and programs, and other structures that are governed by new sets of rules. These institutional rules can range from formal laws that have strict "or else" consequences to informal shared strategies. But as we are creating an economic paradigm for social and environmental wellbeing, these rules must be anchored to a solid foundation of certain core ethical principles.

The third element is to recognize that new institutions must be based on a different set of ethical principles. Insofar as we will be creating new structures for social and environmental well-being, our institutional rules must also be anchored to a solid foundation of core ethical principles. What we finally draft for this set of principles will have to be worked out by a broader United Nations consensus. But perhaps we can begin with these basic statements: (1) our economic activity meets the needs of people in ways that are wholesome and genuine that are free from the defilements of greed, aggression, and delusion; (2) in ways that are stable and equitable; and (3) in ways that do not systematically damage the carrying capacity of our planet for all variations of life and future generations. Once we arrive at a consensus on our core set of ethical principles, these principles can then be drafted into the formal and informal rules that govern our economic institutions.

The fourth element is to recognize that economic relocalization is inevitable and accordingly so should be our efforts for institutional change. As oil becomes increasingly scarce and expensive, it will become much more difficult to rely on the global division of labor as so many of us do now. In the coming decades, economies and communities will have to relocalize in order to become more self reliant in the face of mounting scarcities. In the spirit of E.F. Schumacher, if smaller scale economic systems are inevitable, it will be up to all of us to make them beautiful. That is, to evolve community based commonwealths centered on principles of wellbeing. At the same time, however, relocalization must be done with a broader sense of humanity. If we cannot make real changes for wellbeing in our own local communities, a global strategy is unlikely to materialize. Though we may not see it directly, the good work we do in our communities will have a global impact as everything is connected to everything else.

The fifth element is to recognize that we can build on the momentum for change that has already begun. There are practical examples of business models and government initiatives all around us that are directed toward wellbeing: banks that are chartered for stability and rooted in sound ethical principles and not the idolatry of money, business models that place social and environmental betterment above profit maximization, cooperatives that are directed toward shifting resources and ownership into underserved populations, national legislation with provisions to set aside funds for developing local alternative institutions, and many more. Currently these initiatives exist only on the margins of the global economy, but they also represent the beginnings of the change we seek. It is crucial for us to expand on these initiatives in significant ways, and to bring them out of the margins and directly into the political and economic forefront. It is increasingly apparent that people everywhere are looking for ways to do things differently, but are finding it difficult because our conventional institutions are not providing them with the opportunities to do so. This energy needs constructive expression otherwise it will collapse into lethargy. Our task, therefore, is to create many more and new relocalized, valuesbased institutions that can absorb this energy and direct it toward true social and environmental wellbeing.

Notes

Introduction

1   PSAC, 1965, Restoring the Quality of Our Environment, http://dge.
    stanford.edu/labs/caldeiralab/Caldeira%20downloads/PSAC,%20
    1965,%20Restoring%20the%20Quality%20of%20Our%20Environment.
    pdf.

2   Although the idea of "The Three Fires" goes back to the original teachings
    of the Buddha, contemporary scholar, David Loy, is credited for developing
    this as a sociological phenomenon.

Chapter One

1   Robert Reich, "If You Took the Greed Out of Wall Street, All You'd Have
    Left Is Pavement: Why Greg Smith's Critique is Way Too Narrow," March
    16, 2012. http://robertreich.org/post/19402713930; Greg Smith, *The New
    York Times*, Op Ed., "Why I Am Leaving Goldman Sachs," March 14, 2012.

2   R.H. Tawney, *Religion and the Rise of Capitalism* (NY: Harcourt Brace
    Jovanovich, 1954 [1926]), p. 235.

3   David Loy, *Money, Sex, War, Karma: Notes for a Buddhist Revolution* (Boston:
    Wisdom Publications, 2008), p. 89.

4   Joel Bakan, *The Corporation: The Pathological Pursuit of Profit and Power* (NY:
    Free Press, 2004), p. 5.

5   Ibid.

6   Dirk Philipsen, *The Little Big Number: How GDP Came To Rule the World
    and What To Do About It* (Princeton University Press, 2015), p. 44.

7   Bakan, *The Corporation*, p. 5.

8   https://projectintegrity.files.wordpress.com/2014/12/bernard-mandeville-
    the-fable-of-the-bees-1712.pdf.

9   Adam Smith, *An Inquiry into the Nature and Causes of The Wealth of Nations*
    [1776] (The University of Chicago Press, 1976), Book I, Chapter II, p. 18.

10 This has come to be known as "neoclassical" economics.

11 See the "marginal analysis" sections on consumer and business theory in
    any standard neoclassical economics textbook.

12 Ayn Rand, *The Virtue of Selfishness: A New Concept of Egoism* (NY: The New
    American Library, 1961), pp. 13–18.

[13] Interview September 23, 1987, as quoted by Douglas Keay in the magazine *Woman's Own*, October 31,1987, pp. 8–10.

[14] John M. Keynes, *Collected Writings*, Donald E. Moggridge, ed. (London: Macmillan, 1971),Vol. IX, pp. 329, 331.

[15] Philipsen, *The Little Big Number*, p. 47.

[16] Thich Nhat Hanh, *Silence: The Power of Quiet in a World Full of Noise* (NY: Harper Collins, 2015), p. 71.

[17] Gabor Maté, *In the Realm of Hungry Ghosts: Close Encounters with Addiction* (Berkeley, CA: North Atlantic Books, 2008), pp. 1–3.

[18] Ibid.

[19] Sulak Sivarksa, *The Wisdom of Sustainability: Buddhist Economics for the 21st Century* (Kihei, Hawaii: Koa Books), p. 14.

[20] Ken Jones, *The New Social Face of Buddhism: An Alternative Sociopolitical Perspective* (Boston: Wisdom Publications, 2003), p. 38.

[21] E.F. Schumacher, *Small Is Beautiful: Economics as if People Mattered* (NY: Harper and Row, 1973), p. 15.

[22] Ibid, pp. 31–33.

[23] Harvard Alumni Bulletin, http://www.alumni.hbs.edu/bulletin/1997/december/theory.html.

[24] E.K. Hunt, *Property and Prophets: The Evolution of Economic Institutions and Ideologies* (NY: M.E. Sharpe, 2003), p. 126.

[25] David Korten, *When Corporations Rule the World* (San Francisco: Berrett-Koehler, 2002), pp. 75–76.

[26] Schumacher, *Small Is Beautiful*, p. 94.

[27] Ibid, p. 90.

[28] Ibid, p. 145.

[29] Ibid, p. 52.

[30] Ibid, p. 53.

[31] The teachings of the Buddha are often referred to as the law of enlightenment, or dharma. The spelling changes depending whether it is derived from Sanskrit or Pali. Out of habit I use the Sanskrit version "dharma" as opposed to the Pali version "dhamma."

[32] Thich Thien An, *Zen Philosophy Zen Practice* (Berkeley, CA: Dharma Publishing, 1975), p. 3.

[33] *Majihima Nikaya*, translated as *The Middle Length Discourses of the Buddha*, by Bhikku Nanamoli (Boston: Wisdom Publications, 2nd ed., 2001), p. 335.

[34] Ibid.

[35] Ibid, pp. 175 and 329.

[36] Paramananda, *Change Your Mind: A Practical Guide to Buddhist Meditation* (Birmingham, UK: Windhorse Publications, 1996), p. 1.

[37] In Bodhgaya today there is a shrine at the Mahabodhi temple built around a pipal tree that is believed to be a descendant, through a succession of replantings, from the original tree under which Siddhartha experienced his enlightenment.

[38] Thien An, *Zen Philosophy Zen Practice*, pp. 3–11.

[39] Thich Nhat Hanh, *The Heart of the Buddha's Teaching: Transforming Suffering into Peace, Joy, and Liberation* (NY: Broadway Books, 1998), p. 7

[40] *Samyutta Nikaya*, translated as *The Connected Discourses of the Buddha*, by Bhikku Bodhi (Boston: Wisdom Publications, 2000), p. 1843.

[41] Nhat Hanh, *The Heart of the Buddha's Teaching*, p. 257.

[42] Jones, *The New Social Face of Buddhism*, p. 3.

[43] Walpola Rahula, *What The Buddha Taught* (NY: Grove Press, 1959, revised 1974), p. 16.

[44] Ibid, p. 32.

[45] Deborah Gregory, *Unmasking Financial Psychopaths* (NY: Palgrave Macmillan, 2014), p. 40.

[46] Gregory Kramer, *Insight Dialogue: The Interpersonal Path to Freedom* (Boston: Shambhala, 2007), p. 77.

[47] Nanamoli, *The Middle Length Discourses of the Buddha*, p. 117.

[48] Nhat Hanh, *The Heart of the Buddha's Teaching*, p. 64.

[49] See Bhikku Bodhi, http://www.urbandharma.org/udharma10/bbodhi10.html.

[50] Phra Prayudh Payutto, *Buddhadhamma* (NY: SUNY Press, 1995), pp. 159–60.

[51] Loy, *Money, Sex, War, Karma*, p. 3.

[52] Apichai Puntasen, *Buddhist Economics: Evolution, Theories and Its Application to Various Economic Subjects.* (A translated version of selected chapters from his book in Thai (3rd Edition) Bangkok, Amarin Press, 2004), p. 38.

[53] Phra Prayudh Payutto, "Buddhist Economics: A Middle Way for the Market Place," http://www.urbandharma.org/udharma2/becono.html, translated by Dhammavijaya and Bruce Evans (1992), p. 5.

[54] Puntasen, *Buddhist Economics*, pp. 15–17.

[55] Thich Nhat Hanh, "The Sun My Heart," in Stephanie Kaza and Kenneth Kraft, eds., *Dharma Rain: Sources of Buddhist Environmentalism* (Boston: Shambala, 2000), p. 85.

[56] Puntasen, *Buddhist Economics*, p. 20.

[57] Puntasen, *Buddhist Economics*, pp. 18–19.

[58] Collin Ash, "Do Our Economic Choices Make Us Happy?" in Laszlo Zsolnai, ed., *Ethical Principles and Economic Transformation – A Buddhist Approach*, 2011, p. 116.

[59] Ibid, pp. 119–120.

[60] Quoted Sivarksa, *The Wisdom of Sustainability*, p. 19.

[61] John B. Cobb, "A Buddhist-Christian Critique of Neo-Liberal Economics," *Hsi Lai Journal of Humanistic Buddhism*, Vol. 7, 2006, p. 84.

[62] Gregory, *Unmasking Financial Psychopaths*, p. 31.

Chapter Two

[1] David Loy, *Money, Sex, War, Karma: Notes for a Buddhist Revolution* (Boston: Wisdom Publications, 2008, p. 63.

[2] R.D. Hare, *Without Conscience: The Disturbing World of the Psychopaths Among Us* (NY: Pocket Books, 1993), p. 177

3   Philip Kapleau, "Responsibility and Social Action," in Stephanie Kaza and Kenneth Kraft, eds., *Dharma Rain: Sources of Buddhist Environmentalism*, (Boston: Shambala, 2000), p. 244.

4   Sulak Sivaraksa, *The Wisdom of Sustainability: Buddhist Economics for the 21st Century* (Kihei, Hawaii: Koa Books), p. 15.

5   Loy, *Money, Sex, War, Karma*, p. 89.

6   Sivaraksa, *The Wisdom of Sustainability*, p. 19.

7   Howard Zinn, *You Can't Be Neutral on a Moving Train: A Personal History of Our Times* (Boston: Beacon Press, 2002)

8   Ibid, p. 243.

9   Stephanie Kaza, "Overcoming the Grip of Consumerism," in Sulak Sivaraksa, Pipob Udomittipong, and Chris Walker, eds., *Socially Engaged Buddhism for the New Millennium* (Bangkok, Thailand: The Sathirakoses-Nagapradipa Foundation), p. 60.

10   Ibid, p. 65.

11   Ibid, p. 68.

12   Ibid.

13   William Leach, *Land of Desire: Merchants, Power and the Rise of a New American Culture* (NY: Random House, 1993), p. 15.

14   Thich Nhat Hanh, "The Sun My Heart," in Stephanie Kaza and Kenneth Kraft, eds., *Dharma Rain: Sources of Buddhist Environmentalism* (Boston: Shambala, 2000), p. 86.

15   Quoted in "The Madhupindika Sutta and the Reality of Conflict," in Sulak Sivaraksa, Pipob Udomittipong, and Chris Walker, eds., *Socially Engaged Buddhism for the New Millennium* (Bangkok, Thailand: The Sathirakoses-Nagapradipa Foundation), p. 324.

16   Christopher Queen, "Introduction: A New Buddhism," in Christopher Queen, ed., *Engaged Buddhism in the West*, (Boston: Wisdom Publications, 2000), p. 1.

17   Ibid, p. 5.

18   Graeme MacQueen, "Engaged Nonviolence," in [editors,] *Socially Engaged Buddhism for the New Millennium* (Bangkok, Thailand: The Sathirakoses-Nagapradipa Foundation), pp. 260–261.

19   John McConnell, "The Realism of Applying Damma to Situations of Conflict," in Sulak Sivaraksa, Pipob Udomittipong, and Chris Walker, eds., *Socially Engaged Buddhism for the New Millennium* (Bangkok, Thailand: The Sathirakoses-Nagapradipa Foundation), p. 315.

20   Helena Norberg-Hodge, "Buddhist Engagement in the Global Economy," in Sulak Sivaraksa, Pipob Udomittipong, and Chris Walker, eds., *Socially Engaged Buddhism for the New Millennium* (Bangkok, Thailand: The Sathirakoses-Nagapradipa Foundation), pp. 34–36.

21   Ibid, p. 41.

22   Queen, "Introduction: A New Buddhism," p. 2.

23   Patricia Hunt-Perry and Lyn Fine, "All Buddhism Is Engaged: Thich Nhat Hanh and the Order of Interbeing," in Christopher Queen, ed., *Engaged Buddhism in the West* (Boston: Wisdom Publications, 2000), p. 47.

[24] Ibid, p. 46.

[25] Rebecca Solnit, *A Paradise Built in Hell* (NY: Penguin Books, 2009) and *The New York Times* review, "Delighted By the Joy of Bad Things," August 20, 2009.

[26] Matt Taibbi, *Griftopia* (NY: Spiegel & Grau, 2011), p. 35.

[27] Thich Nhat Hanh, *The Stone Boy and Other Stories* (Berkeley: Parallax Press, 1996), p. 63.

[28] Thich Nhat Hanh, *Zen Keys: A Guide to Zen Practice* (NY: Doubleday, 1995 [1974]), pp. 42–43.

[29] Bernard Glassman and Rick Fields, *Instructions to the Cook: A Zen Master's Lessons in Living a Life That Matters* (NY: Bell Tower, 1996), p. 88.

[30] Christopher Queen, "Glassman Roshi and the Peacemaker Order: Three Encounters," in Christopher Queen, ed., *Engaged Buddhism in the West* (Boston: Wisdom Publications, 2000), p. 100.

[31] Thich Thien An, *Zen Philosophy, Zen Practice* (Berkeley, CA: Dharma Publishing, 1975), p. 109.

[32] Glassman and Fields, *Instructions to the Cook*, pp. 59–60.

[33] See http://greyston.com/about-greyston, see also, Joel Magnuson, *The Approaching Great Transformation: Toward a Livable Post Carbon Economy* (NY: Seven Stories Press, 2013) on B Corporations.

[34] See http://greyston.com/about-greyston.

[35] Ibid.

[36] http://zenpeacemakers.org/zpo-mission-vision-and-core-values/.

[37] Christopher Titmuss, "Practicing with Passion," in Stephanie Kaza and Kenneth Kraft, eds., *Dharma Rain: Sources of Buddhist Environmentalism* (Boston: Shambala, 2000), p. 257.

[38] Joseph Goldstein, "Three Means to Peace," in Melvin McLeod, ed., *Mindful Politics: A Buddhist Guide to Making the World a Better Place* (Boston: Wisdom, 2006), p. 121.

[39] Glassman and Fields, *Instructions to the Cook*, p. 19.

[40] Elinor Ostrom, *Understanding Institutional Diversity* (Princeton University Press, 2005), p. 186.

[41] Walton Hamilton, "Institutions," *Encyclopedia of the Sciences* (NY: Macmillan, 1932), p. 84.

[42] William M. Dugger, *An Alternative to Economic Retrenchment* (NY: Petrocelli Books, 1984), p. 57.

[43] David Hamilton, *Evolutionary Economics: A Study of Change in Economic Thought* (Albuquerque, NM: University of New Mexico Press), p. 6.

[44] Thorstein Veblen, *The Theory of the Leisure Class* (NY: Penguin Books, 1979 [1899]).

[45] Thorstein Veblen, *The Instinct of Workmanship and the State of Industrial Arts* (NY: B.W. Huebsh, 1922), pp. 38, 103–137, and 146–170.

[46] Hamilton, *Evolutionary Economics*, pp. 55–56.

[47] See the collection of essays titled, "Eighteen Brumaire of Louis Bonaparte," prepared for the Internet by David J. Romagnolo, http://www.marx2mao.com/M&E/EBLB52.html.

[48] Alfred Schutz, *On Phenomenology and Social Relations* (University of Chicago Press, 1970), p. 80.

[49] Veblen, *The Theory of the Leisure Class*, p. 68.

[50] Ibid, p. 75.

[51] Ken Jones, *The New Social Face of Buddhism: An Alternative Sociopolitical Perspective* (Boston: Wisdom Publications, 2003), p.17.

[52] E.F. Schumacher, *Small Is Beautiful: Economics as if People Mattered* (NY: Harper and Row, 1973), pp. 191 and 204.

[53] Allan Gruchy, *Modern Economic Thought: The American Contribution* (NY: Prentice-Hall, 1947) pp. 560–565.

[54] Ibid, pp. 112–113.

[55] Hamilton, *Evolutionary Economics*, p. 91.

[56] Joseph Schumpeter, *History of Economic Analysis* (Oxford University Press, 1954), pp. 125–126.

[57] Russell Dixon, *Economic Institutions and Cultural Change* (NY: McGraw-Hill, 1941), p. 5.

Chapter Three

[1] Dirk Philipsen, *The Little Big Number: How GDP Came To Rule the World and What To Do About It* (Princeton University Press, 2015), pp. 40–42.

[2] Ibid, pp. 44–46.

[3] Quoted in Alehandro Adler Braun, "Gross National Happiness in Bhutan: A Living Example of an Alternative Approach," *The Wharton Asia Economic Review*, Spring, 2011, Vol. 2, No. 2, p. 1.

[4] Simon Kuznets, "National Income, 1929–1932," *National Bureau of Economic Research*, Bulletin 49, January 26, 1934.

[5] Robert Heilbroner, *The Worldly Philosophers: The Live[s], Times, and Ideas of the Great Economic Thinkers*, 7th ed. (NY: Touchstone, 1995), p. 266.

[6] Yuval P. Yonay, *The Struggle Over the Soul of Economics: Institutional and Neoclassical Economists in America between the Wars* (Princeton New Jersey: Princeton University Press, 1998), p. 51.

[7] Philipsen, *The Little Big Number*, pp. 94, 98.

[8] Ibid, p. 87.

[9] John P. Lewis and Robert C. Turner, *Business Conditions Analysis*, 2nd ed. (NY: McGraw-Hill, 1967 [1959]), p. 15.

[10] Kuznets, "National Income, 1929–1932," pp. 7–10.

[11] Quoted in Philipsen, *The Little Big Number*, p. 105.

[12] Kuznets, "National Income, 1929–1932," p. 1.

[13] Ibid, p. 3.

[14] Paul Kennedy, *The Rise and Fall of the Great Powers* (NY: Vintage Books, 1987), p. xv.

[15] Philipsen, *The Little Big Number*, pp. 178–183.

[16] *Washington Post*, editorial, August 3, 2012.

[17] See http://www.neweconomics.org.

[18] See http://b.3cdn.net/nefoundation/d8879619b64bae461f_opm6ixqee. pdf, p. 3.

[19] Ibid, p. 14.

[20] W.D. Nordhaus and J. Tobin, "Economic Growth," National Bureau of Economic Research, 1972, No. 96, p. 1.

[21] Herman Day and John B. Cobb, For *The Common Good: Redirecting the Economy toward Community, the Environment, and a Sustainable Future*, 2nd ed. (Boston: Beacon Press, 1994 [1989]), pp. 401–455.

[22] See http://rprogress.org/publications/2007/GPI%202006.pdf, pp. 8–18.

[23] Ibid, pp. 19–20.

[24] Karma Ura, Sabina Alkire and Tshoki Zangmo, "Gross National Happiness and the GNH Index," in John Helliwell, Richard Layard, and Jeffrey Sachs, eds., *World Happiness Report* (NY: Columbia University, 2012), p. 109.

[25] Ibid.

[26] Alejandro Adler Braun, "Gross National Happiness in Bhutan: A Living Example of an Alternative Approach," *The Wharton Asia Review*, Spring, 2011, Vol. 2, No. 2.

[27] Ura, Alkire and Zangmo, "Gross National Happiness and the GNH Index," p. 109.

[28] Dasho Karma Ura, "GNH as a Buddhist Social Contract," in *Dharma World*, http://www.kosei-shuppan.co.jp/english/text/mag/2007/07_101112_10. html.

[29] Ibid.

[30] Ibid.

[31] Ibid.

[32] "Gross National Happiness in Bhutan: The Big Idea from a Tiny State That Could Change the World," *The Guardian*, December 1, 2012.

[33] All of the following elements are summarized in *World Happiness Report*, p. 110–120.

[34] Braun, "Gross National Happiness in Bhutan," 2011.

[35] Ibid.

[36] "Sarkozy Attacks Focus on Economic Growth," *Guardian*, September 14, 2009.

[37] Ibid.

[38] Prime Minister Jigme Thinley's speech at the UN conference, April, 2012.

[39] This was part of the documents the participants received as part of the preliminary reading materials.

[40] http://www.un.org/millenniumgoals/2015_MDG_Report/pdf/ MDG%202015%20rev%20(July%201).pdf.

[41] *Monthly Review*, 2006, Vol. 7, Issue 10.

[42] See *The Future We Want*, Section C No. 19, https://sustainabledevelopment. un.org/futurewewant.html.

[43] Sunita Narain, "Rio+20: Why It Failed?" *Huffington Post*, July 4, 2012.

[44] Philipsen, *The Little Big Number*, p. 50.

Chapter Four

[1] Thomas Frank, "The Rise of Market Populism," *The Nation*, October 30, 2000.

[2] Margrit Kennedy, *Occupy Money: Creating an Economy Where Everybody Wins* (Vancouver, Canada: New Society Publishers, 2012), p. 9.

[3] Ibid, p. 29.

[4] Robert Shiller, "Why Smart Money Can't Stop a Housing Market Bubble," *New York Times*, July 26, 2015.

[5] David A. Stockman, *The Great Deformation: The Corruption of Capitalism in America* (NY: Public Affairs, 2013), p. 289.

[6] Doug Henwood, *Wall Street* (NY: Verso, 1997), p. 175.

[7] Ibid, pp. 176–178.

[8] Frederich Nietzsche, *Beyond Good and Evil: Prelude to a Philosophy of the Future* (Cambridge University Press, 2002 [1886]), p. 156.

[9] George Soros, *The Crisis of Global Capitalism: Open Society Endangered* (NY: Public Affairs, 1998), pp. xx–xxii.

[10] John W. Barnum, "What Prompted Airline Deregulation 20 Years Ago?" Presentation to the Aeronautical Law Committee of the Business Law Section of the International Bar Association, September 15, 1998.

[11] Jonathan Lewinsohn, "Bailing Out Congress: An Assessment and Defense of the Air Transportation Safety and System Stabilization Act of 2001," 115 *Yale Law Journal* 438 (2005).

[12] See the public law documentation at http://www.gpo.gov/fdsys/pkg/STATUTE-93/pdf/STATUTE-93-Pg1324.pdf.

[13] Nomi Prins, *All the President's Bankers: The Hidden Alliances That Drive American Power* (NY: Nation Book, 2014), p. 340.

[14] Frederick Sheehan, *Panderer to Power: The Untold Story of How Alan Greenspan Enriched Wall Street and Left a Legacy of Recession* (NY: McGraw-Hill, 2010), p. 88.

[15] Martin Mayer, *The Greatest-Ever Bank Robbery: The Collapse of the Savings and Loan Industry* (NY: Scribner's and Sons, 1990).

[16] Sheehan, *Panderer to Power*, p. 89.

[17] T. Curry and L. Shibut, "The Cost of the Saving and Loan Crisis," *FDIC Banking Review*, 2000, pp. 26–35.

[18] Ibid.

[19] Ibid, p. 341.

[20] Sheehan, *Panderer to Power*, p. 92.

[21] Ibid.

[22] Stockman, *The Great Deformation*, p. 317.

[23] Portfolio insurance was a derivative that was structured around stock index futures and options. If stock prices started to seem unreasonably high, the instrument would allow an option to cash out without directly impacting the market. If prices fell, the instrument would allow the option of short selling that would offset losses from the fall in price. In this way, large numbers of owners of derivatives could put downward pressure on stock

prices even though the stocks themselves had not been traded. This is what happened in 1987.

[24] "Stocks Plunge 508 Points, A Drop of 22.6%; 604 Million Volume Nearly Doubles Record," *New York Times*, October 20, 1987.

[25] Justin Martin, *Greenspan: The Man Behind the Money* (Cambridge, MA: Perseus, 2000), pp. 173–174.

[26] Sheehan, *Panderer to Power*, p. 113.

[27] Stockman, *The Great Deformation* , p. 318.

[28] The term Washington Consensus was coined in 1989 by English economist John Williamson.

[29] For more on the Washington Consensus and its mission, see David Korten, *When Corporations Rule the World* (San Francisco, CA: Berrett-Koehler and Kumarian Press, 2002, 2nd ed.) and Joseph Stiglitz, *Globalization and Its Discontents* (NY: W.W. Norton, 2002).

[30] Jorge G. Castaneda, *The Mexican Shock: Its Meaning for the US* (NY: The New Press, 1995), pp. 177–187.

[31] Newt Gingrich, "Vindication of the Mexican Bailout," *New York Times*, editorial, January 18, 1997.

[32] Benjamin Friedman, "Globalization: Stiglitz Case," *New York Review of Books*, August 15, 2002, Vol. 49, Issue 13, pp. 89–90.

[33] See http://en.wikipedia.org/wiki/Asian_financial_crisis#Thailand.

[34] Stiglitz, *Globalization and Its Discontents*, p. 97.

[35] Ibid, p. 99.

[36] From an interview for PBS, Frontline: Season 17, Episode 11, "The Crash," June 29, 1999.

[37] See transcripts from the PBS documentary "Commanding Heights." http://www.pbs.org/wgbh/commandingheights/

[38] James K. Glassman and Kevin A. Hassett, *DOW 36,000: The New Strategy for Profiting from the Coming Rise in the Stock Market* (NY: Times Books, 1999), p. 22.

[39] John K. Galbraith, *A Short History of Financial Euphoria* (NY: Penguin Books, 1990), p. 4.

[40] Kathryn J. Byun, "The U.S. Housing Bubble and Bust: Impacts on Employment," *Bureau of Labor Statistics Monthly Labor Review*, December 2010, p. 3.

[41] Dan Wilchins, "Lehman Files for Bankruptcy, Plans to Sell Units," *Reuters*, September 15, 2008.

[42] *Business Week*, July 11, 2008, p. 66.

[43] See the Bureau of Labor Statistics historical employment data at http://data.bls.gov/timeseries/CES0000000001?output_view=net_1mth; see also Byun, "The U.S. Housing Bubble and Bust," pp. 10–16.

[44] "Too Big Not to Fail," *The Economist*, February 18, 2012.

[45] Deborah Gregory, *Unmasking Financial Psychopaths* (NY: Palgrave Macmillan, 2014), p. 74.

[46] William A. Fleckenstein, *Greenspan's Bubbles: The Age of Ignorance at the Federal Reserve* (NY: McGraw-Hill, 2008), p. 27.

47 Ibid, p.18.
48 Steven Greenhouse, "For Clinton, A Place on the Bottom Line," *New York Times*, October 24, 1993.
49 Sheehan, *Panderer to Power*, p. 215.
50 See FOMC meeting transcript, February 3–4, 1994, pp. 20–21. http://www.federalreserve.gov/monetarypolicy/files/FOMC19940204meeting.pdf.
51 See FOMC meeting transcript, September 24, 1996; p. 33 and pp. 20–21. http://www.federalreserve.gov/monetarypolicy/files/FOMC19940204meeting.pdf.
52 Sheehan, *Panderer to Power*, p. 260.
53 Ibid, p. 155.

Chapter Five

1 Herbert Marcuse, *One-Dimensional Man* (Boston: Beacon Press, 1964), p. 23.
2 Andrew Jackson, "The Rich and Powerful Bend Government to Selfish Purposes," in Edward Pessen, ed., *Jacksonian Panorama* (Indianapolis: Bobbs Merrill, 1976), p. 275.
3 Harry N. Scheiber, "The Pet Banks in Jacksonian Politics and Finance, 1833–1841," *Journal of Economic History* 33, 1963, pp. 196–214.
4 Quoted in Jenny B. Wahl, "He Broke the Bank, but Did Andrew Jackson also Father the Fed?" in Paul Finkelman and Donald R. Kennon, eds., *Congress and the Emergence of Sectionalism from the Missouri Compromise to the Age of Jackson* (Ohio University Press, 2008), p. 188.
5 Joel Magnuson, *Mindful Economics: How the US Economy Works, Why It Matters, and How It Could Be Different* (NY: Seven Stories Press, 2008), pp. 146–147.
6 Gary M. Walton and Hugh Rockoff, *History of the American Economy*, 6th ed. (NY: Harcourt Brace Jovanovich, 1990) pp. 412–413.
7 Magnuson, *Mindful Economics*, p. 149.
8 See the "National Monetary Commission Letter From Secretary of the National Monetary Commission Transmitting, Pursuant to Law, The Report of the Commission," January 9, 1912 ["Report of the Monetary Commission"], at this website: http://www.federalreservehistory.org/Media/Material/Period/9-238, pp. 7–8.
9 Ibid, p. 9.
10 Ibid, pp. 9, 28–29.
11 http://www.federalreserve.gov/aboutthefed/mission.htm.
12 wiki https://en.wikipedia.org/wiki/2008_United_Kingdom_bank_rescue_package.
13 "Central Banks Can't Save the Markets from a Crash. They Shouldn't Even Try," *Guardian*, August 30, 2015.
14 William A. Fleckenstein, *Greenspan's Bubbles: The Age of Ignorance at the Federal Reserve* (NY: McGraw-Hill, 2008), p. 19.
15 Frederick Sheehan, *Panderer to Power: The Untold Story of How Alan Greenspan Enriched Wall Street and Left a Legacy of Recession* (NY: McGraw-Hill, 2010), p. 79.

[16] Fleckenstein, *Greenspan's Bubbles*, pp. 42–45.

[17] Ibid, pp. 44–45.

[18] Ibid, p. 54.

[19] See http://articles.baltimoresun.com/1999–07–03/business/9907030134_1_composite-index-york-stock-exchange-stocks-rose.

[20] Justin Martin, *Greenspan: The Man Behind the Money* (Cambridge, MA: Perseus, 2000),, p. 219.

[21] Quoted in Matt Taibbi, *Griftopia* (NY: Spiegel & Grau, 2011), p. 63.

[22] House Committee on the Budget, "Economic and Budgetary Outlook," October 8, 1997.

[23] House Subcommittee on Domestic and International Monetary Policy of the Committee on Banking and Financial Services, The Federal Reserve's Semiannual Monetary Policy Report, February 24, 1998.

[24] Sheehan, *Panderer to Power*, p. 169.

[25] Hearing of the Senate and House Committees on the Budget, January 10, 1995.

[26] FOMC meeting transcript, December 16, 1997, pp. 57–58, http://www.federalreserve.gov/monetarypolicy/files/FOMC19971216meeting.pdf.

[27] CNN Money: "Fed cuts Rates a Quarter Point," http://money.cnn.com/2001/12/11/economy/fed/.

[28] Fleckenstein, *Greenspan's Bubbles*, p. 121.

[29] FOMC meeting transcript, September 24, 2002, http://www.federalreserve.gov/monetarypolicy/files/FOMC20020924meeting.pdf.

[30] "Report of the Monetary Commission," p. 16.

[31] Ibid, p. 32.

[32] Albert Jay Nock, *Memoirs of a Superfluous Man* (NY: Harper and Brother, 1943), p. 256.

[33] See http://www.federalreserve.gov/monetarypolicy/taf.htm.

[34] Federal Reserve 2008 Monetary Policy Releases.

[35] "Finance and Economics Discussion Series Divisions of Research & Statistics and Monetary Affairs," Federal Reserve Board, Washington, D.C. p. 4. http://www.federalreserve.gov/econresdata/feds/2015/files/2015005pap.pdf.

[36] Ibid, pp. 110–111.

[37] John Kirton, University of Toronto, "Canada as a Principal Financial Power," 2000, http://www.g7.utoronto.ca/scholar/kirton2000.

[38] See http://www.bankofengland.co.uk/publications/speeches/2009/speech404.pdf.

[39] Ellen Brown, *The Public Bank Solution: From Austerity to Prosperity* (Baton Rouge, LA: Third Millennium Press, 2013), p. 278.

[40] Ibid, pp. 281–282.

[41] Ibid, p. 283.

[42] http://www.bloomberg.com/news/articles/2011-12-21/ecb-will-lend-banks-more-than-forecast-645-billion-to-keep-credit-flowing.

[43] "Central banks can't save the markets from a crash. They shouldn't even try," *Guardian*, August 30, 2015.

44 Johnna Montgomerie, "A Bail-Out for Working Families?" *Renewal Journal for Social Democracy*, Vol. 17 No. 3, 2009.

45 http://www.offshorecompany.com/banking/start-a-bank/your-own/.

46 Doug Henwood, "How to Learn Nothing From Crisis," *Left Business Observer*, 125, February 2010.

47 For more information on the Permaculture Credit Union, see Joel Magnuson, *The Approaching Great Transformation: Toward a Livable Post Carbon Economy* (NY: Seven Stories Press, 2013), pp. 155–165.

48 Ibid, pp. 151–155.

49 Quoted in Christopher Queen, "Introduction: A New Buddhism," in Christopher Queen, ed., *Engaged Buddhism in the West* (Boston: Wisdom Publications, 2000), p. 8.

50 http://www.oregonlive.com/portland/index.ssf/2015/11/former_sunwest_ceo_gets_15_yea.html.

51 https://en.wikipedia.org/wiki/Truth_in_Lending_Act.

52 Mary Gregor, ed., *Foundations of the Metaphysics of Morals* (London: Cambridge University Press, 1991), p. 429.

53 The World Commission on Environment and Development, *Our Common Future* (Oxford University Press, 1987), p. ix.

54 J. Holmberg, K. Robert, and K. Erkisson, "Socio-Ecological Principles for a Sustainable Society," in R. Costanza, O. Segure, and J. Martinez-Alier, eds., *Getting Down To Earth: Practical Applications of Ecological Economics* (Washington, D.C.: Island Press, 1994), p. 17.

55 http://www.buddhistpeacefellowship.org/about-bpf/.

56 Brown, *The Public Bank Solution*, p. 3.

57 All the information that follows here regarding BND can also be found in Magnuson, *The Approaching Great Transformation*, pp. 159–161.

58 "Report of the Monetary Commission," p. 41.

Chapter Six

1 His Holiness the Dalai Lama, *Ethics for the New Millennium* (NY: Riverhead Books, 1999), p. 6.

2 Ibid, p. 5.

3 Ibid, p. 8.

4 Morris Berman, *Why America Failed: The Roots of Imperial Decline* (Hoboken, NJ: Wiley, 2012), p. 38.

5 Richard Heinberg, *Peak Everything: Waking Up to the Century of Declines* (Vancouver, Canada: New Society Publishers, 2010).

6 Mark Sundeen, *The Man Who Quit Money* (NY: Riverhead Books, 2012), pp. 20–21.

7 Ibid, p. 181.

8 See Paul Bahannon, "The Impact of Money on African Subsistence Economy," *The Journal of Economic History*, 1959, pp. 491–503.

[9] Karl Polanyi, *The Great Transformation* (Boston, MA: Beacon Press, 1944), p.44.; see also Karl Marx, *Das Kapital*, Chapter 1, Section 4, p. 76, "The Fetishism of Commodities and the Secrets Thereof."

[10] Ibid.

[11] Paul Rogat Loeb, *Soul of a Citizen: Living With Conviction in Challenging Times*, 2nd ed. (NY: St. Martins, 2010 [1999]), pp. 21–22.

[12] Ken Jones, *The New Social Face of Buddhism: An Alternative Sociopolitical Perspective* (Boston: Wisdom Publications, 2003), p. 212.

[13] David Loy, *Money, Sex, War, Karma: Notes for a Buddhist Revolution* (Boston: Wisdom Publications, 2008), pp. 39–40.

[14] Paramananda, *Change Your Mind: A Practical Guide to Buddhist Meditation* (Birmingham, UK: Windhorse Publications, 1996), p. 5.

[15] Bhante Henepola Gunaratana, *Mindfulness in Plain English* (Boston: Wisdom Publications, 2002), p. 139.

[16] Gregory Kramer, *Insight Dialogue: The Interpersonal Path to Freedom* (Boston: Shambhala, 2007), p. 3.

[17] Loy, *Money, Sex, War, Karma*, p. 81.

[18] Paramananda, *Change Your Mind*, p.5.

[19] Jon Kabat-Zinn, *Full Catastrophe Living: Using the Wisdom of Your Body and Mind to Face Stress, Pain, and Illness* (NY: Bantam, 2013), p. 17.

[20] Ibid, p. xlix.

[21] Sharon Salzberg, *Real Happiness at Work: Meditations for Accomplishment, Achievement, and Peace* (NY: Workman Publishing, 2014), pp. 2–3.

[22] David Gelles, *Mindful Work: How Meditation Is Changing Business from the Inside Out* (NY: Eamon Dolan, 2015), pp. 86–87.

[23] Charles Duhigg, *The Power of Habit: Why We Do What We Do in Life and Business* (NY: Random House, 2014), pp.17–18.

[24] Ibid, p.25.

[25] http://www.salon.com/2015/09/27/corporate_mindfulness_is_bullsht_zen_or_no_zen_youre_working_harder_and_being_paid_less/.

[26] Joe Nocera, "Jeff Bezos and the Amazon Way," *New York Times*, August 21, 2015.

[27] http://www.salon.com/2015/09/27/corporate_mindfulness_is_bullsht.

[28] Gelles, *Mindful Work*, p. 81.

[29] Kabat-Zinn, *Full Catastrophe Living*, p. 473.

[30] http://www.huffingtonpost.com/ron-purser/beyond-mcmindfulness_b_3519289.html.

[31] Thich Nhat Hanh, *The Heart of the Buddha's Teaching: Transforming Suffering into Peace, Joy, and Liberation* (NY: Broadway Books, 1998), p. 64.

[32] Thich Nhat Hanh, *Silence: The Power of Quiet in a World Full of Noise* (NY: Harper Collins, 2015), p. 3.

[33] Ibid, p. 5.

[34] Ibid, pp. 15–17.

Chapter Seven

[1] Roshi Philip Kapleau, *The Three Pillars of Zen* (NY: Doubleday, 1980), p. 308.

[2] Quoted in Ilya Priogine and Isabelle Stengers, *Order Out of Chaos: Man's New Dialogue With Nature* (NY: Bantam, 1984), pp. 22–23.

[3] Pierre Teilhard de Chardin, *The Phenomenon of Man* (NY: Harper Torchbooks, 1959), p. 54.

[4] Priogine and Isabelle Stengers, *Order Out of Chaos: Man's New Dialogue With Nature* (NY: Bantam, 1984), p. 86.

[5] Ibid, pp. 22–23.

[6] Leslie White, *The Evolution of Culture: The Development of Civilization to the Fall of Rome* (NY: McGraw-Hill, 1959), p. 35.

[7] Ibid, p. 39.

[8] Richard Heinberg, *The End of Growth: Adapting to Our New Economic Reality* (Vancouver, Canada: New Society Publishers, 2011), p. 27.

[9] "Why Yellen Blinked on Raising Interest Rates," *New York Times*, September 18, 2015.

[10] Ibid.

[11] Richard Heinberg, *Snake Oil: How Fracking's False Promise of Plenty Imperils Our Future* (Santa Rosa, CA: Post Carbon Institute, p. 52.

[12] Ibid, p. 123.

[13] Lily de Silva, "Early Buddhist Attitudes Toward Nature," in Stephanie Kaza and Kenneth Kraft, eds., *Dharma Rain: Sources of Buddhist Environmentalism* (Boston: Shambala, 2000), pp. 91–92.

[14] Woody Tasch, *Slow Money: Investing as if Food, Farms, and Fertility Mattered* (Vermont: Chelsea Green, 2008) p. 48.

[15] Gunnar Myrdal, *Rich Lands and Poor: The Road to World Prosperity* (NY: Harper, 1958), p. 172.

[16] Morris Berman, *Why America Failed: The Roots of Imperial Decline* (Hoboken, NJ: Wiley, 2012), p. 24.

[17] Randolph Bourne, "Trans-national America," in Olaf Hansen, ed., *The Radical Will: Randolph Borne Selected Writings, 1911–1918* (NY: Urizen Books, 1977), p. 264.

[18] Berman, *Why America Failed*, p.66.

[19] Jones, *The New Social Face of Buddhism*, p. 27.

Glossary

Anicca: A concept found in Buddhism and in other traditions which signifies that things or events are not real in a physical or metaphysical sense. All things are fleeting and impermanent.

Capitalization: The total value of capital raised from a corporation by issuing stocks and bonds.

Central bank: A public institution created to control a nation's money supply and regulate its banking industry.

Chanda: A desire to act in such a way to achieve a result that is not specific to one's self interest or stemming from greed, aggression, or delusion. Chanda is to be distinguished from tanha. (See **Tanha**).

Conspicuous consumption: A term coined by institutionalist economist Thorstein Veblen which refers to spending money on expensive luxuries in order to impress others.

Defilements: Mental states that cloud the mind and result in behavior that is unhealthy or unwholesome.

Dependent origination: A Buddhist concept emphasizing that nothing exists in and of itself and that all things exist in a state of dependence on other things. The existence of things is contingent on the existence of other things. (See also **Holism**).

Deregulation: A process of eliminating or reducing government regulations on markets and other aspects of the economic sector.

Derivative: A financial instrument that has a market value derived from other instruments to which it is contractually tied.

Dharma: In the Buddhist sense, dharma is the way or existence of things as they are in their true, natural, and undefiled state.

Eye of the heart: A termed coined by economist E.F. Schumacher which refers to a profound understanding of things that comes intuitively through spiritual enlightenment, not through scientific investigation.

Four noble truths: Part of the core teachings of the Buddha which emphasizes that true wisdom and liberation extends from an understanding of the following: (1) that suffering exists, (2) the causes of this suffering, (3) that changes need to be made to free ourselves from this suffering, and (4) that there is a practical course for making these changes in order to end this suffering.

Genuine progress indicator (GPI): An alternative metric to gross domestic product (GDP) that attempts to be a more comprehensive measurement of national output by taking into consideration various social and environmental factors in addition to economic production and spending.

Greenspan Put: A monetary policy strategy associated with former Federal Reserve chairman, Alan Greenspan, which involves promoting economic growth through inflating stock prices with low interest rates and available credit. The idea is that as long as people feel wealthier on paper, they will increase their spending, which will cause gross domestic product to rise.

Gross domestic product (GDP): The total market value of all goods and services produced in a country in a year's time. The total market value of all expenditures.

Happy Planet Index (HPI): An alternative metric to gross domestic product that takes into consideration social wellbeing and life expectancy, which are expressed as a ratio to the resource base of the planet.

Hedge fund: An exclusive partnership, or mutual fund, of wealthy investors who invest in a full range of securities, derivatives, bonds, and other financial instruments with the goal of maximizing returns. A highly speculative segment of the financial system.

Holism: A theory of metaphysics that holds that all things exist only as parts of a broader whole and cannot be completely understood: in isolation.

Impermanence: The idea that all things are transient in nature. (See **Anicca**).

Institutionalist economics: A holistic approach to economics that focuses on social institutions and the complex interplay of institutions such as legal systems, government agencies, corporations, financial systems, social norms, media, and households. This approach to economics is generally associated with the work of Thorstein Veblen, John R. Commons, Wesley Mitchell, Simon Kuznets, John K. Galbraith, Karl Polanyi, and other heterodox economists.

Institutionalization: The process of something becoming part of the institutional structure of a society or an organization.

Interbeing: A term coined by Thich Nhat Hanh referring to a state in which one's existence is holistically tied to everyone else's existence. What affects one affects us all.

Invention and diffusion: The concept of cultural evolution developed by Thorstein Veblen. Invention and diffusion occurs when something new enters into the cultural mix such as new technology, a new invention, or an artefact, which renders other things obsolete and subsequently is adopted generally. An explanation for how cultures evolve.

Karma: Cause and effect relationships in which positive action leads to positive outcomes and negative action leads to negative outcomes.

Karmic volition: The thought process in which a person commits to a course of action, which then has either positive or negative outcomes.

Market populism: A term coined by Thomas Frank which stipulates, ironically, that a person's choices made by spending money in the marketplace is an expression of popular democracy.

Materialistic scientism: A term coined by E.F. Schumacher referring to the Western scientific paradigm centered on the notion that all knowledge universally derives from matter and motion. It is science devoid of wisdom, intuition, or insight.

McMindfulness: A term coined by David Loy and Ron Purser referring to the commercial exploitation of mindfulness.

Mindful awareness: A state of awareness developed through mindfulness practice. (See **Mindfulness**).

Mindfulness: A psychological state in which one's attention is occurring fully in the present moment. Mental awareness completely in the here and now without distraction or wandering thoughts.

Monetary policy: Central bank policy regarding the nation's money supply, interest rates, and the availability of credit.

Mutual funds: An investment fund organized by financial management firms in which individual investors pool their money together to invest in a range of financial instruments such as stocks, bonds, commodities, or derivatives.

Neoliberalism: Economic ideology associated with free-market policies such as market deregulation, free trade agreements, low taxes, and limited government involvement in economic affairs. A resurgence of free-market ideology that was most popular in the nineteenth century.

Nirvana A state of complete mental and spiritual liberation. It is a state of liberation from defilements that cause suffering.

Noble eightfold path: Part of the Buddhist's four noble truths suggesting that the path toward freedom from suffering can be made easier using specific approaches to perception, thought, speech, action, livelihood, effort, mindfulness, and concentration.

Non-self: Part of the Buddhist concept of dependent origination that holds that the self is a contingent figment. There is no such permanent thing as a person's "self." (See **dependent origination**).

Nothingness: Pure emptiness. The complete nonexistence of things or thoughts.

Objectivism: A belief system developed by Ayn Rand centered on the notion that societies objectively organize through individualistic self interest and free markets.

Pathology: Disease or other any other conditions that cause suffering.

Quantitative easing: Monetary policy of central banks directed at increasing the money supply, lowering interest rates, and making credit easily available.

Realm of hungry ghosts: A Buddhist parable of a place where all the people are miserably possessed by intense desires that cannot be satisfied. A society in which the population is overtaken by greed.

Shikantaza: (See **Zazen**).

Skillful means: The means by which a person can be a force for good in society by developing oneself with a meditation practice that liberates oneself from egoism.

Sovereign debt securities: Bonds that are sold as a means to financially support governments.

Sovereign wealth funds Investment portfolios that are mainly invested in sovereign debt securities.

Speculation: Buying and selling financial instruments such as stocks, bonds, derivatives, commodities, or real estate for gain.

Tanha: A desire to act in such a way to achieve a result that is specific to one's self interest and also that stems from greed, aggression, or delusion. Tanha is to be distinguished from chanda. (See **Chanda**).

Utilitarian economics: An approach to economics based on utility theory which asserts that all choice making behavior is based on a pursuit of utility (pleasure) and an avoidance of disutility (pain).

Veblenian: Having characteristics that are similar to the ideas of Thorstein Veblen. (See **Institutional economics**).

Zazen: A Zen Buddhist meditation practice in which there is no object of meditation but stillness of the mind. Often said to be "just sitting."

Index